Sustaining Conflict

Sustaining Conflict

APATHY AND DOMINATION IN
ISRAEL-PALESTINE

Katherine Natanel

UNIVERSITY OF CALIFORNIA PRESS

Sustaining Conflict

APATHY AND DOMINATION IN
ISRAEL-PALESTINE

Katherine Natanel

UNIVERSITY OF CALIFORNIA PRESS

*For David Snelling, Gary Johnson,
and Ann Glogau Bibi*

University of California Press, one of the most distinguished university presses in the United States, enriches lives around the world by advancing scholarship in the humanities, social sciences, and natural sciences. Its activities are supported by the UC Press Foundation and by philanthropic contributions from individuals and institutions. For more information, visit www.ucpress.edu.

University of California Press
Oakland, California

© 2016 by The Regents of the University of California

Library of Congress Cataloging-in-Publication Data

Natanel, Katherine, 1979- author.
    Sustaining conflict : apathy and domination in Israel-Palestine / Katherine Natanel.—First edition.
        pages   cm
    Includes bibliographical references and index.
    ISBN 978-0-520-28525-5 (cloth)—ISBN 0-520-28525-5 (cloth)—ISBN 978-0-520-28526-2 (pbk.)—
ISBN 0-520-28526-3 (pbk.)—ISBN 978-0-520-96079-4 (ebook)—
ISBN 0-520-96079-3 (ebook)
    1. Political participation—Israel. 2. Arab-Israeli conflict—Public opinion. 3. Apathy—Political aspects—Israel. 4. Israel—Politics and government. 5. Palestine—Politics and government. I. Title.
JQ1830.A91N37   2016
956.9405′4—dc23

2015025630

CONTENTS

Preface ix

Introduction 1

1 · The Everyday of Occupation 18

2 · Bordered Communities 51

3 · Normalcy, Ruptured and Repaired 88

4 · Embedded (In)action 118

5 · Protesting Politics 152

Conclusion 186

Notes 203
Bibliography 223
Index 243

PREFACE

In the wake of the 2015 elections in Israel, this book is more relevant than ever. A record number of voters—71.8 percent of the eligible public (*Ha'aretz* 2015)—turned out to the polls to re-elect the ruling right-wing party, Likud, and with it acting prime minister Benjamin Netanyahu. Now holding thirty seats in the Knesset, or Israeli Parliament, Likud has chosen to deepen its existing ties to religious and right-wing camps, forming a coalition government with Jewish Home, United Torah Judaism, Shas, and Kulanu.[1] Rather than reaching across political boundaries to form a government with left-of-center blocs and parties, this consolidation of existing political alliances confirms speculation by regional commentators. Indeed, once preliminary election results were announced many predicted the eventual outcome, as Likud's campaign relied upon a familiar discourse of threat and (in)security. Fuelling a sense of fear and antipathy that forecloses—rather than broadens—political horizons, during the lead-up to the elections Netanyahu espoused a transparently divisive rhetoric that named Palestinians, including Israel's "Arab citizens," and leftists as the objects of mistrust. On election day, Netanyahu warned his supporters that Arabs were "voting in droves" as polling stations registered ballots (BBC 2015, *Ha'aretz* 2015), urging Jewish Israeli voters to participate in the political process explicitly on the grounds of fear. While this final effort to prevent a shift in political power sought to increase participation in a particular sector of the electorate, it also underlined the dubious sentiment behind Likud's campaign guarantees, which promised to block the formation of a Palestinian state while supporting and accelerating the expansion of Jewish settlements in the West Bank.[2]

With this election, political leaders and Israeli voters have effectively secured the status quo, here shorthand for conflict, violence, occupation, and domination in Israel-Palestine. At first glance, the democratic process that took place in early 2015 seems to be anything but evidence for a book that concerns political apathy. Here, a record number of voters exemplified how political engagement might be translated to political action, as measured in polling stations across the county. However, critical scholars, activists, and observers should be concerned about these elections not solely for the extent to which they demonstrate democratic political practice but also for their impact on dissent, resistance, and transformation. In granting right-wing, nationalist, and religious parties the opportunity to consolidate their power, the 2015 elections threaten to compound fragmentation and alienation in the already disillusioned political Left. As this book details, these powerful experiences and sensations hold significant implications for political (dis)engagement and (in)action, key forces shaping the future of Israel-Palestine.

Our responsibility is to take apathy seriously, to increase knowledge of the complex—and often surprisingly close—relationship between political action and inaction, and to assess its effects. In doing so, this book paints a rather bleak picture of the political realities in Israel-Palestine; yet this is not to say that the future is already determined. Rather, through providing a diagnostic this analysis offers a critical point of intervention, with the explicit intention of enriching activist agendas as much as academic debates. Then this book affirms the necessity of pairing critique with action, raising the possibility of transformation even as it focuses on the moments and means through which substantive change seems lost.

This engaged mode of scholarship is the product of my time at the SOAS Centre for Gender Studies (University of London), which has underlined the significance of both political commitment and community. While this book adopts a critical stance, my gratitude goes to the individuals who shared with me their perceptions and experiences in Israel-Palestine, generously offering their time and engaging in often intensely personal discussions. For many, the acts of resistance detailed in these pages have come at great personal cost; I am grateful for their openness and trust. I am also thankful to Professor Nadje Al-Ali, whose wisdom and guidance anchored my doctoral research project. This work takes root in her insistence that we must not overlook tension and contradiction as we seek transformation, and that new horizons of possibility may be found even in what seem the darkest of moments. My thanks go as well to Professor Laleh Khalili—this book began as an idea in her classroom, was propelled into existence by her enthusiasm, and finds foundation in her critical thought, particularly her insistence that politics and ethics must not be divided. I also thank Dr. Tsila Ratner, whose encouragement and engagement during my first year of doctoral studies positively shaped this book as it appears today. My thanks additionally go to Professor Clare Hemmings and Dr. Ronit Lentin, whose thorough and thoughtful doctoral examination has helped refine the arguments and analyses within these pages, and whose encouragement has given me confidence.

This book also greatly benefitted from constructive comments by Professor Barbara Einhorn, Dr. Cynthia Cockburn, Dr. Yair Wallach, and Dr. Orna Sasson-Levy—their critical feedback directly resulted in the attention to nuance that I hope the book sustains. I am also grateful to University of California Press and the three reviewers of the original manuscript, who have helped further tighten and extend the arguments presented in this book. My thanks go as well to Ruth Elwell, whose meticulous indexing will aid readers in using this book as a resource. I would also like to thank Dr. Ruba Salih and Dr. Gina Heathcote for sensitive conversations and provocative queries throughout my doctoral studies. I am additionally grateful to the SOAS Centre for Gender Studies—without its critical community this book would not be what it is today. I also thank the SOAS Centre for Palestine Studies for nurturing scholarship among graduate students and providing an important forum for exchange. This book is further indebted to SOAS, University of London, and the University of London Central Research Fund for financial support.

In looking to community, I must thank the two families who sustained this research project, the resulting book, and its author. I am grateful to Tamar and Mark Natanel for their kindness, patience, and wisdom, particularly during my year of field study in Israel-Palestine. I am thankful as well to Michal, Tomer, Omer, Ophir, and Roni Dabby, for moments of levity and grace during a challenging period of research. To my own family I owe tremendous gratitude—Roberta Snelling, Lawrence Krebs, and Joanna L. K. Daggett have shaped my ideas of justice from an early age and their encouragement continues to be a steady source of will.

Finally, my thanks go to Guy Natanel, who has been my partner in every way. The arguments and analyses that appear in this book are a product of our exchanges, sometimes difficult, often clarifying, and always galvanizing.

Introduction

"NOW YOU ARE FREE," HE SAID with a smile.

The workshop has come to a close, and slowly I make my way west, back to Tel Aviv, from Birzeit University in the Occupied West Bank. This time spent in the West Bank feels cathartic, remarkable for the political commitment of those present at the academic workshop, the kindness extended by shopkeepers and strangers in the city, and the intense beauty of the surrounding hills, burned pink and orange at sunrise and sunset. On leaving the university campus at the close of the session, I was apprehensive at the thought of passing through the Qalandia checkpoint on the way to East Jerusalem. Though it would not be the first time I experienced the protocols and practices of Israel's border policies, a feeling of unease still attended the prospect of border crossing. As I readied myself to travel the distance from Birzeit to Qalandia, other workshop participants recounted stories of mobility constrained and denied as Palestinian residents of the West Bank. Restricted to the areas surrounding home and university, limited to travel within the West Bank, allowed entry solely into East Jerusalem—each woman spelled out the different terms of her confinement. In contrast, my trepidation was a privilege.

On the bus I am the only non-Palestinian passenger, staring out the window as images of iconic graffiti come into focus on the looming grey Wall: a young Yassir Arafat; Banksy's girl holding balloons—"Sister, you need more?" asks a creature as it offers another floating globe—declarations in English intended for an international audience and their cameras. The bus stops. Two soldiers board, a man and woman, who look as if they are barely out of high school. The young woman checks the IDs of those still on the bus, while the young man stands behind her with a hulking weapon. They arrive at my seat. I smile. She checks my passport and orders me off the bus to the queue behind the fence.

In the growing heat I stand clustered with my fellow passengers behind the wire fence, not pushing, not shouting, but not pleased—the wait is long and irritating. Many around me are students, with their books and backpacks, and I am struck by the difference from my commute in London, where traveling to university on the Tube at times felt trying. Held like cattle behind the fence, some chat while others look out at the lanes of traffic and auto bays where soldiers and private security agents inspect cars with guns at the ready. They largely seem bored, these agents of the Israeli state, laughing, joking and scuffling between vehicles, inspecting languidly and shouting angrily when needed. We wait for the turnstiles, slowly drawing nearer—these gates allow approximately five people to pass between each click and beep, sometimes more and sometimes less. Seeming to start and stop randomly, they jar those who are passing through when the gate slams to a halt. *Click! Thunk.* The woman ahead gets jammed, looks back at her friends, and carries on chatting from within the cage of metal bars. Around me others talk, text, and wait.

Green light. *Click! Beep!* Go. I am sandwiched between two young men as my turn in the stiles arrives. *Click! Thunk.* The man ahead of me is jammed. He leans against the wall between the bars, waiting. Green light. *Click! Beep!* Go. We are through the turnstile, and I follow what others before me have done: place my bags on the x-ray conveyor belt before walking to a large window with soldiers at the ready. I press my passport to the window, only to be directed to use the scanner—as an American citizen my documents are more "advanced" than the various paper permits issued to different categories of Palestinians.[1] Waved through, I grab my bags and wait again for another turnstile and green light—the inner sanctum is protected on both ends. Green light. *Click! Beep!* Go. We step out into the exit chute, with one more turnstile to negotiate before reaching the line of empty buses. With a sigh of relief I turn to thank the young man behind me, whose subtle guidance made my border crossing less confusing, humiliating, and frightening than it might have been otherwise.

"Now you are free," he says with a smile.[2]

OCCUPATION UNRAVELED

Emerging through the account above is an image of conflict, occupation, and domination in Israel-Palestine, as experienced and understood by a white, middle-class American feminist researcher who possesses the social and economic capital—the privilege—to cross a boundary dividing relative freedom from daily experiences of oppression. Clear within this narrative are relations of power, modes of regulation, technologies of control, and even sites of contestation, as a bus is emptied of its human cargo, demarcating zones of "here" and "there" along with categories of "us" and "them." As individuals animate the material terrain of a military checkpoint, identities are suspected and confirmed, threat is assessed and dispelled, and belonging is produced and denied. Whether they are citizen-soldiers, subjects of military occupation, or doctoral researchers, this movement of bodies across and within a constructed border reveals a familiar picture to those who would see it: guns, walls, and fences; youth, aggression, and barely checked power; humiliation, frustration, and steadfastness.

Yet remaining hidden in relation to this image of control and domination is the other side of the checkpoint—what lies beyond the turnstiles once the final green light is granted. Certainly, the Israeli state commands a robust tourism industry whose campaigns and advertisements usher visitors into the dusty antiquity of Jerusalem's Old City lanes and the European modernity of Tel Aviv's cafes and beaches. So, too, scholarship critical of Israel's practices and policies of occupying, annexing, and colonizing Palestinian lands makes visible the political and economic relations that continue to connect Israel with Palestine. Then academics, activists, observers, and visitors indeed "see" Israel through the circulation of discourses and images, sometimes modern, liberal, and democratic, other times repressive, colonialist, and despotic. However, rarely do we travel the road from Qalandia through Jerusalem to Tel Aviv in order to ask how its end might sustain its beginning—how lives made livable on the shores of the Mediterranean Sea might depend on lives constrained and cut short in the hills of Birzeit and Ramallah.

Green light. *Click! Beep!* Go.

In a journey beyond the checkpoint and into the urban centers of Israel, this book makes visible the micropolitical logics that produce and maintain the realities, practices, and experiences conveyed through the account above.[3] Beyond the turnstiles and soldiers of Qalandia, a coach travels to the East Jerusalem bus station, and a researcher walks toward the city's west to board a *monit sherut,* or minibus, bound for Tel Aviv. This vehicle winds westward along the highway leading toward the White City, where restaurants bustle and hum as the sun sets blazing orange behind the beachfront boardwalk. At the road's end lies a kind of normalcy that appears entirely disparate from everyday life in the West Bank, where even in relatively affluent Ramallah an elderly man turns the earth of a tiny plot with a donkey and plough. Yet normalcy at the (Jewish Israeli) end of the road relies on and arises through the relations of power that necessitate agricultural subsistence within cityscapes, that lock academics at Birzeit University in metaphorical and material prison cells, and that fashion understandings of "freedom" through experiences of oppression at the border. Read thus, continuity replaces contrast as practices of occupation, colonization, and domination bind Israel with Palestine and Jewish Israelis with Palestinians.

In the interest of better understanding how this continuity shapes material conditions and political realities, this book appraises how the everyday attitudes and actions of Jewish Israelis impact Israel's control of Palestinian territories and populations. Through feminist ethnography and gender analysis, this book explores how political stasis is produced and maintained at the levels of subject, community, and society, with dire implications for the broader region of Israel-Palestine and its peoples. Contributing to a growing body of critical research that regards Israel-Palestine through lenses including history (Shlaim 2000, 2010; Abu El-Haj 2001; Masalha 2003; Khalidi 2006; Pappe 2006; Pappe and Hilal 2010; Dallasheh 2013), politics (Piterberg 2008; Ghanem 2010; Allen 2013; Sa'di 2013), sociology (Lentin 2000; Shafir and Peled 2002; Ron 2003; Allen 2013), political economy (Gordon 2008; Hever 2010; Abdo 2011), critical geography (Yiftachel 2006; Weizman 2007), and activism (Dallasheh 2010; De Jong 2011; Richter-Devroe 2011, 2012; Weizman 2013; Plonski 2014), the following chapters highlight how the status quo of occupation, colonization, and domination emerges not only through social sanction and popular consent but also through disengagement and inaction—the production of political apathy. However, here apathy does not constitute a lack or absence of care but emerges as underwritten by modes of awareness and investment that elide, erase, or make palatable the discomfiting reality of violence and control. Shifting focus from violent or extraordinary events to the seeming banality of everyday life, the analysis in the following pages uncovers degrees of division and entanglement, modes of avoidance and activism, sites of investment and withdrawal, and moments of normalcy and rupture which directly sustain conflict in penetrating and enduring ways.[4] Guided by the belief that new routes to transformation emerge through understanding *how things stay the same,* this book asks what the relationship between conflict, apathy, and domination means for visions of the future in Israel-Palestine.

Troubling Normalcy, or Ma la'asot?

Perhaps due to the value judgment often openly attached to apathy as a concept that circulates in public and political discourses, academic inquiries have largely shied from this topic, focusing instead on the desire for and pursuit of normalcy. As this book reveals, in the context of Israel-Palestine the question of political apathy is directly connected to the pursuit of normalcy in conditions of protracted violent conflict. This said, the terms *apathy* and *normalization* should not used interchangeably or treated synonymously—as narratives and experiences reveal, while processes of normalization are central to the production of political apathy, alone they cannot account for the depth and durability of disengagement and inaction. Rather, apathy takes shape through the intersection of multiple social processes, emerging through acts of resistance as much as complicity, interruption as much as accord.

Shifting focus from rupturing events to "the monotony of an unresolved conflict," scholars of Israel-Palestine highlight how the mundane acts as a site wherein "aborted events and frustrated expectations" might accumulate with significant effect (Allen 2013, 27). Primarily undertaken by anthropologists working with Palestinian communities in the West Bank, existing studies of the will to normality depict practices of "getting by" Israel's occupation or adapting to its disruption of daily life, violence visited upon bodies, and dislocation from homes and histories. Lori Allen's (2005, 2008) work in the West Bank highlights the particular kind of agency that accompanies "getting used to it" (Arabic: *ta'wwudna*) in practices of managing and adapting to the dynamism of occupation during the second *intifada*. Here, as individuals and communities "tame violence," they reincorporate the extreme into the ordinary and contest its ability to determine life. Depicting the same period in the West Bank, Tobias Kelly's (2008) scholarship looks at the ways in which the desire for "ordinary life" in a context of sustained political violence may take on political and ethical charges, revealing a gap between what "is" and what "ought to be." Sophie Richter-Devroe's (2011) post-*intifadas* work also regards the production of normality among Palestinians, highlighting how the pursuit of normalcy and joy among women in the West Bank, East Jerusalem, and Israel might constitute a significant act of resistance. Here, practices and experiences of pleasure challenge not only the Israeli occupation but also internal power structures within Palestinian communities that entrench patriarchal and social forms of control.

Collectively, this scholarship reveals critical aspects of conflict previously elided by a focus on violent events and macro-level politics, insisting that survival, *sumud* (Arabic: steadfastness), and everyday life can tell us something new about power in Israel-Palestine. Then what is fundamentally different about these practices, processes, ideals, and aspirations among Jewish Israelis, who share a frame of conflict with Palestinians? While methods of "getting by" practiced by Palestinian populations—from travel patterns (Allen 2008; Richter-Devroe 2011) to modes of commemoration (Khalili 2007; Allen 2008), narration (Sayigh 1998; Allen 2008; Ghanim 2009a; Kassem 2011), marriage (Johnson, Abu Nahleh, and Moors 2009; Jad 2009), and desire (Kelly 2008)—might be mirrored in mechanisms developed by Jewish Israelis, the practices of this latter group unfold not as subject to domination but rather as productive of it. Here, longing for a normal life assumes a function and value apart from the normalization of uncertainty, fear, violence, and despair. As this book details, normalcy among Jewish Israelis not only elides power or renders it tolerable but also produces and maintains the sociopolitical relations that underwrite conflict.[5]

Emerging in tandem with violence, normality among Jewish Israelis serves to gloss, streamline, and consolidate, promising a sense of stability and certainty within the felt precarity of everyday life. Yet, paradoxically, this condition of seeming dependability relies on the very practices, processes, and relations that it purports to overcome or erase—occupation, colonization, and domination—becoming a way of life and state of mind among those whose relative power and privilege require maintenance of the status quo. Thus, a state of flourishing appears to exist despite conflict while taking root in its very perpetuation, an apparent contradiction that makes possible "the good life" for some (Mendel 2009, 2013; Vick 2010; Ochs 2011; Simon 2012; Deger 2012; Natanel 2013) while reducing existence to "bare life" (Ghanim 2008) for others.

Short of claiming that all Jewish Israelis pursue a single vision of "the good life" or disavow what its production and maintenance entail, this book engages with a category of social and political actors whose expressions of opposition indicate a critical awareness of the surrounding world. Based on research conducted in Tel Aviv and West Jerusalem with Jewish Israelis who self-define as politically "leftist,"[6] this analysis considers how individuals and communities knowingly grapple with their implication in power. At its root, this book is motivated by the seemingly passive will to surrender, as expressed in the phrase *Ma la'asot?* (What to do?) More than purely rhetorical, this ambivalent sentiment concluded many political discussions with self-described leftists during my early visits to the region. Relaying a sense of shared fatalism, hopelessness, and disenchantment, this question effectively erases "I" and "we" as culpable actors; yet at the same time it points toward a sense of shared responsibility and the knowledge that action *should* be taken.

This very tension—when knowledge of what occurs is met with inaction or effacement[7]—lies at the core of *political apathy,* a sociopolitical process and practice examined to a limited extent in contexts beyond the borders of Israel-Palestine. As undertaken by political scientists and sociologists, existing studies of apathy are framed primarily in terms of detachment from politics and declining formal political participation (Rosenberg 1954; Sevy 1983; Boyer 1984; Herzfeld 1992; Eliasoph 1997, 1998; Dolan and Holbrook 2001; Hay 2007; Greenberg 2010), while psychological and anthropological approaches connect these practices to interpersonal and intimate dimensions (Cohen 2001; Allen 2005, 2008, 2013; Auyero 2007; Kelly 2008; Johnson, Abu Nahleh, and Moors 2009; al-Werfalli 2011; Richter-Devroe 2011). However, apathy itself remains largely undefined within this collective body of work, emerging as a shifting cluster of perceptions and practices that somehow defies rigid categorization. Entangled with wider global trends, at once individual and relational, bound to attitude and belief, and rooted in emotion and desire, apathy evades definition in academic inquiries even as it gains conceptual thickness.

Through a case study of Jewish Israeli society, this book begins to fill the gap in existing scholarship, laying the foundation for further critique and investigation. Among Jewish Israelis political apathy presents a particularly complex and sometimes contradictory puzzle—indeed, the participation of 71.8 percent of the Israeli voting public in recent national elections (*Ha'aretz* 2015) seemingly points to anything but apathy. At the same time, the resulting consolidation of existing political power has compounded the sense of despair and fatigue articulated by many of those who feel that they *should* and *would* take action against government policies and practices, if only they *could*. Through engaging with these tensions and nuances, this book challenges accounts of apathy that focus solely on a "lack" or "absence" of engagement as evident in formal political participation. Instead, apathy takes shape among leftist Jewish Israelis as *active disengagement*: a socially produced form of political passivity underwritten by acts of knowing, caring, seeing, feeling, and doing.[8]

Apathy as Active Disengagement

To a limited extent, existing scholarship on political non-participation raises this very possibility: that apparent apathy might be anything by passive. In his work on the "social production of indifference" in Western contexts, Michael Herzfeld (1992) argues that state bureaucracies explicitly cultivate political apathy as an instrument of domination. Here, indifference, or "the rejection of common humanity" (1), is produced through government-led bureaucratic structures as a means of securing consent for systems of exclusion. By providing subjects with a "means of conceptualizing their own disappointments and humiliations," bureaucracies might generate assent to the humiliation of others (13). For Herzfeld, the danger of social indifference lies in its potential to become habitual, a possibility that arises through the pervasiveness of bureaucracy and its reach into everyday lives. Focusing on post-socialist Serbia, Jessica Greenberg (2010, 41) raises a different possibility in relation to political non-participation: that apathy might constitute a significant "citizen response" to changing sociopolitical contexts, rather than reflecting a lack of political and social progress. Here, withdrawal from the realm of politics becomes a powerful lens with which to analyze how citizens understand and experience democratization on local, national, and international levels (46). In approaching apathy thus, Greenberg highlights individual agency and asks what individuals are withdrawing *from* when they choose not to participate in politics (63). Among politically disillusioned Serbians, the moral frame that underpins political disengagement and inaction is incredibly significant. In this case, apathy constitutes a kind of moral anti-politics actively practiced by those who understand political participation as entailing untenable compromises, and who experience politics as an ineffective form of democratic engagement or a failed route to moral-cultural regeneration (56–58, 63).[9]

Together, this work on "non-participation" foregrounds both the sociality and activity inherent in political apathy, while at the same time differently drawing attention to how disengagement and inaction intersect with wider relations of power. In the case of Western bureaucracies, the social production of political indifference yields important insights into how state power is produced and maintained through individual experiences of institutional structures (Herzfeld 1992). In the case of Serbia, political apathy sheds critical light on democratization as an inherently social and moral process, challenging the connections assumed to bind democratic participation with social, political, and moral transformation (Greenberg 2010). Through the lens of political non-participation, studies of indifference and withdrawal helpfully situate women and men firmly "within the mass" (Gramsci 1971), whether reflecting on top-down state power or on the macropolitical ideal of democracy. However, the case of political apathy among leftist Jewish Israelis cannot be understood solely through the mechanisms, structures, and ideals made visible by the scholarship above. As noted earlier, Jewish Israelis outwardly display an impressive commitment to democratic participation, with well over 60 percent of the eligible public consistently voting in national elections. In addition to their active participation in formal politics, "indifference" (Herzfeld 1992) does not characterize the attitude of most Jewish Israelis who self-define as "leftist"; rather, these individuals continue to care deeply about "common humanity" and grapple with questions of morality (Greenberg 2010). Yet here the moral frame undergirding apathy reflects back not on democracy as a political practice or process but on what *can, does,* and *should* bind a community together in conditions of protracted conflict.

This investigation into apathy among leftist Jewish Israelis addresses the social worlds and political realities sustained by disengagement and inaction, while at the same time detailing the intimate mechanisms through which they take shape and root. To an extent, the expression and practice of apathy is a privilege in the context of Israel-Palestine, as individuals are differently able to disconnect or disengage from the realm of politics based on their location within hierarchies of power. As this book reveals, the extent to which an individual or community can subscribe to apathy reflects the degree to which they are served in some way—economically, socially, politically, or personally—by the status quo, whether knowingly or not. Relatively "free from the touch of the occupation"[10] in comparison to Palestinians living within or beyond Israel's recognized state borders, Jewish Israelis as a category may overwhelmingly experience conflict as a kind of "ambience"[11] or tension at the margins of everyday life. However, differences based on gender, class, ethnicity, generation, geopolitical location, sexuality, and degree of religiosity complicate any claim to a near-universal experience or understanding of conflict and violence: the ability to defer, displace, or disavow the wider reality is in part determined by social position. For example, when asked how she experiences the occupation in everyday life, thirty-year-old leftist activist Tali remarked: "We have the privilege to feel it when we want to—at demonstrations and even in Jerusalem, we don't have to. During wartime you can feel it, but even then I asked my girlfriend what she wants to do if war comes again ... and she said that she'll buy a ticket and go away. Leaving is an option when you have enough money. You can live somewhere else.... I'm working on getting Bulgarian citizenship and my girlfriend has residency in Germany."[12] As a secular, middle-class Ashkenazi citizen of Israel who lives in Tel Aviv, Tali possesses the kinds of capital that allow her to selectively engage or escape the occupation—a privilege afforded to those Jewish Israelis whose European passports and economic resources provide the promise of a new life "somewhere else" if violence flares.

In drawing attention to how power and privilege inform apathy as a political practice among Jewish Israelis, this book considers how lives, communities, and realities are differently imagined and constructed—and with what political effects. By highlighting the action, intimacy, and sociality inherent in political apathy in Israel-Palestine, the narratives and experiences in these pages challenge readers to rethink their basic assumptions around the term. What is the *substance* of political apathy? What are its mechanisms and logics? Can apathy involve investment, action, and care? Through questioning prevailing assumptions, apathy emerges not as a measure of polls and statistics but as a tension between conflict and normalcy, politics and intimacy, and action and inaction that takes shape at the level of everyday life.

THE POLITICS OF EVERYDAY LIFE

In posing the questions above, this investigation necessitates a fine-tuned lens of analysis that draws attention to how macropolitical power is produced and maintained at micro and meso levels. Underlining sentiments that power may circulate and operate most effectively where it is least obvious (Gramsci 1971; Foucault 1998 [1978]; Mitchell 1990), everyday life increasingly commands attention as a significant site for academic enquiries that aim to analyze politics across multiple sites and levels (see e.g. de Certeau 1984; Scott 1985; Singerman 1995; Bayat 1997, 2010).

In using this prism of the everyday or ordinary, scholars of Israel-Palestine have produced critical ethnographies that indeed link subjects and social relations with Israel's continuing occupation of the Palestinian Territories. Whether centering on (Jewish) Israeli or Palestinian narratives, experiences, or practices, these accounts provide glimpses into the textures of daily life while revealing individual strategies and structural frameworks for negotiating sustained political violence. From Julie Peteet's (1994) first-*intifada* account of beatings and imprisonment turned masculine rites of passage among Palestinian men in the West Bank, to Juliana Ochs's (2011) second-*intifada* ethnography of security and suspicion as embodied practices linking Jewish Israeli subjects with the state, these insights into daily actions and perceptions shed light on macropolitical trends and processes. By tracing terms of connection, this shift to the everyday facilitates the meeting of scholarship located on either "side" of the presumed divide between Jewish Israelis and Palestinians—here, narratives of suspicion and the politics of security among Jewish Israelis (Konopinski 2009; Ochs 2011) might share a frame with accounts of *sumud*, or steadfastness, practiced by Palestinian residents of the West Bank, Gaza Strip, and East Jerusalem (Allen 2008; Kelly 2008; Johnson, Abu Nahleh, and Moors 2009; Shalhoub-Kevorkian 2009; Richter-Devroe 2011).

Whether in Israel-Palestine or in contexts beyond, investigations into everyday life pivot around a central methodological belief: that the seemingly ordinary and inconspicuous are key to understanding politics and power. Through varying means, scholars of the everyday work to "defamiliarize" or "make strange" the sites, actors, and dynamics often taken for granted in academic analyses (Highmore 2002, 22).[13] Gender analysis presents one such "interruptive strategy" (Brecht 1964, cited in Highmore 2002, 23) that is particularly suited to the work of estranging the ordinary. Framed by a historical legacy and continuing commitment to "telling stories differently" (Hemmings 2011), gender analysis raises critical questions of norms and normality, of divisions assumed to be static, and of how space, place, and politics are valued. Simultaneously an aspect of subjectivity, a relation of power, and a structure of states and societies, gender is integral to the practices and politics of everyday life, though often elided. As illustrated by feminist scholars including Cynthia Enloe (1989, 2010) and Diane Singerman (1995), the apparently depoliticized or apolitical spaces of the everyday and domestic act as forums for political thought, expression, and action. Maligned as "low politics" vis-à-vis the "high politics" of states and elites, the too-neat division of private realms—associated with women and family—from those deemed "public" is always an already political act (Singerman 1995, 5–9; Yuval-Davis 1997, 80). In contexts of war, conflict, and violence, which are often characterized as particularly masculinized enterprises (Cohn 1987; Enloe 1989; Cockburn 2007; Segal 2008), this imposed distinction impacts access to political voice and available registers for action. As this book reveals, political space, voice, and action are central to understanding political apathy.

The capacity of feminist gender analysis to estrange the ordinary is particularly significant to studies of conflict and domination, whose histories of gender-blindness limit the scope of both understanding and transformation. However, the lens adopted must be finely tuned, not just capable of "interrupting" academic discourses and assumptions but also vigilant in accounting for contradiction, complexity, and interrelation. In the context of Israel-Palestine, this vigilance means consistently problematizing obvious dualisms, such as here/there and us/them, which obscure what lies at stake in the maintenance of power. Then, rather than appraising broad categories of "women" and "men," this analysis employs an *intersectional* lens that draws attention to "the complex, irreducible, varied, and variable effects which ensue when multiple axes of differentiation—economic, political, cultural, psychic, subjective and experiential—intersect in historically specific contexts" (Brah and Phoenix 2004, 76). Approaching political apathy through an intersectional understanding of gender allows this book to maintain focus on power and privilege, foregrounding how constructions of femininity and masculinity, relations between women and men, and meanings of "male" and "female" intersect with race, class, sexuality, religion, generation, and geopolitical location. Rather than considering intersectional disempowerment—how axes of difference serve to constrain, subordinate, and oppress (Crenshaw 1989)—this book shifts focus to *intersectional power,* engaging with those actors ordinarily assumed to constitute the standard or norm.[14] Thus, the analysis that unfolds within the following pages operationalizes intersectionality in new ways, enriching not only understandings of conflict and domination in Israel-Palestine but also feminist approaches to power.

Engaging Apathy in the Field

In its focus on power, this book engages with a body of "would-be" and "should-be" actors whose (dis)engagement and (in)action hold significant implications for the future of Israel-Palestine: Jewish Israelis who express opposition to the occupation and annexation of Palestinian territories, yet feel unable or unwilling to act. Admittedly, this group does not constitute a critical mass that, once mobilized, might change the existing policies and practices of the Israeli state. To the contrary, recent analyses and statistics reflect wide public support for the political status quo,[15] along with the growing marginality of opposition (Levy 2012; Sherwood 2012; Verter 2014). Given these trends, some commentators express a wish for *greater* apathy among Jewish Israelis, as a lack of care might enable substantive change.[16] Even so, this book argues that scholars, activists, and observers must take the prevailing political despair among the leftist minority seriously, as this phenomenon matters deeply to the trajectory of Israel-Palestine—for its very embeddedness in power and for the mechanisms made visible in an age of increasing political alienation.

From October 2010 through September 2011, interpersonal exchanges and direct experiences of political action yielded the ethnographic data that supports this book's central claim: that political despair among self-defined leftist Jewish Israelis must be understood as a kind of apathy that maintains conflict and domination, not through denial or passivity but through action. Drawing attention to power and privilege, the analysis in the following pages primarily engages with the experiences, attitudes, beliefs, practices, and aspirations of secular middle-class heterosexual Ashkenazi[17] Jewish Israelis living in Israel's two main urban centers. Experienced differently based on gender, race, class, ethnicity, sexuality, generation, religion, and geopolitical location, "Jewish Israeliness" cannot be understood as monolithic. As a result of historical dominance, Israel's Ashkenazi citizens continue to enjoy privilege and largely define the norms within Jewish Israeli society, even as the face of the elected government changes over time to include Mizrahi,[18] Russian, Ethiopian, Druze,[19] and Palestinian representatives (Shafir and Peled 2002, 88; Sasson-Levy 2013, 28, 33). Indeed, while Mizrahi Jews now constitute the majority of Israel's Jewish population (Lavie 2011, 57, 2014, 1–2; Abdo 2011, 89; Sasson-Levy 2013, 32), "Ashkenaziness can be viewed as a resource, a form of symbolic capital that in turn grants access to additional resources" (Sasson-Levy 2013, 33). In its focus on power, this book is concerned with the (in)action and influence of this minority.

With contacts made through "snowball sampling," largely enabled by the support of Jewish Israeli family and friends,[20] I conducted fifty-eight semi-structured interviews with political leftists, first in Tel Aviv and later in West Jerusalem. Active research centered on these two urban sites, chosen for their differing proximities to the Occupied Palestinian Territories and histories of political violence, which provided both contrast and continuity within Israel's internationally recognized 1949 Armistice Agreements borders (Shlaim 2000, 41–47, 2010, 31).[21] Though everyday life in Jerusalem is commonly juxtaposed with Tel Aviv (see e.g. Ram 2008), these cities importantly share relative political, economic, social, and historical privilege vis-à-vis rural towns, villages, *kibbutzim*, and *moshavim* (Yiftachel 2006, 223).[22]

Snowball sampling enlarged the effective area of these urban sites, as a small number of individuals living in Jaffa took part in the Tel Aviv interviews, while participants living on the outskirts of Jerusalem in locales such as Mevasseret-Zion and Har Adar contributed to the data collected from this second city.

In the interest of understanding how gender and generation impact political engagement and action, interviews were evenly split between women and men, with the youngest participant twenty-two years old and the oldest nearly ninety. While participants were selected according to their membership in the (dominant) Ashkenazi minority, I additionally interviewed a small number of individuals who identified as Mizrahi or "Arab Jew." The narratives and experiences contributed by these participants simultaneously clarify and complicate how ethnicity, race, and social class intersect with domination in Jewish Israeli society. Among the participants in both locations, sexuality and martial status constituted further significant social markers, as a range of experiences and attractions shapes individual beliefs and practices. So too within the category of "leftist," participants' self-professed degree of political engagement emerged as critical to their narratives and the subsequent analysis. At the outset of research, I intended to interview two broad categories of Jewish Israelis, "activists" and "non-activists," as defined by their direct involvement (or not) in initiatives that challenge Israel's occupation of Palestinian territories and populations, as well as discrimination and inequality within state borders. However, research participants quickly complicated this easy distinction, presenting a rich continuum of action ranging from "former activists" to "should-be activists," "passive activists," "couch activists," "sometimes activists," "radical activists," and "recovering activists." Importantly, this diverse group of individuals is bound together through their collective relationship to politics in Israel-Palestine, a kind of melancholic attachment of despair or disillusionment that seemingly precludes action.[23]

In addition to conducting interviews in Tel Aviv and West Jerusalem, throughout the duration of research I undertook an ethnography of everyday life, recording varying experiences of the mundane, from casual conversations and personal travels to participation in community events, large-scale political demonstrations, and international solidarity actions. Beginning with three months of *ulpan*—the state-sponsored Hebrew language program—I became immersed in everyday life even as I remained an outsider, a position that provided me with a unique lens through which to experience the discourses, processes, and practices of community. My location "inside" Jewish Israeli society was secured through marriage to a Jewish Israeli man whose parents had emigrated to Israel from Poland—educated, Ashkenazi, urban, and middle-class, their relatively privileged social location impacted my own, opening doors to the community I wished to study. Yet at the same time my location also remained outside—neither Jewish nor Israeli, I could not overcome a certain distance from the community at the heart of my research. However, this "outsiderness" served to enrich the exchanges and experiences of fieldwork, as I gained access and earned trust, yet remained in need of explanation. This dynamic meant that research participants often related precisely how they viewed the world around them, narrating attitudes and experiences in an effort to clarify and aid understanding.

Then, perhaps inevitably, this book takes shape in part as a mode of autoethnographic writing (Ellis and Bochner 2000), which implicates the researcher in the dynamics and analysis at hand. Admittedly, as an "outsider" to Jewish Israeli society, there is a limited extent to which my analysis and writing can be autoethnographic in the sense of researching and writing about oneself as the subject of study or a member of the community in question (see e.g. Throsby 2013). However, by reflecting on my own impressions and experiences during fieldwork in Israel-Palestine, this book bridges the personal and political—and illustrates more precisely how conflict shapes everyday lives, binding individuals to the collective.

A TAPESTRY OF THE ORDINARY

Weaving the personal with the political throughout, this book unmasks power at the level of everyday life to reveal the logics and mechanisms that sustain apathy, conflict, and domination in Israel-Palestine. Here, normalcy takes active work to produce; it cannot be understood as a neutral state of passivity or a "default" setting but only as a practice of living, politically charged by aspiration and action. In this context, apathy is conceptualized as active disengagement—a kind of hoping, trying, building, believing, knowing, relating, engaging, and acting oriented toward self-preservation. Through feminist gender analysis, apathy emerges as the product of intimate relations and social patterns that give substance, depth, and durability to macropolitical power.

By engaging with a cluster of sensations, practices, and processes including despair, disillusionment, disenchantment, ambivalence, disengagement, avoidance, and inaction, the analysis in the following pages grants texture and complexity to apathy as a political phenomenon. While tension and sometimes contradiction consequently frame the accounts that emerge within the following chapters, this book is driven by the certainty that as prevailing structures, narratives, and practices produce political effects, so too do our analyses (Mohanty 1988, 69)—thus complexity must be engaged, rather than elided. In tracing the everyday production and maintenance of apathy, each chapter reveals how patterns of gender are understood, experienced, and mobilized in ways that often sustain conflict, and with it, domination. Chapter 1 explores the ways in which gender structures and normalizes hegemonic narratives, institutions, and politics in Jewish Israeli society. Here, cynicism and alienation emerge as the prevailing terms through which many leftist Jewish Israelis relate to politics, producing an inward-facing "politics of living" that aligns with the central narrative of Zionism. Chapter 2 examines how principles of spatial separation—"us here" and "them there"—remain underwritten by entanglement, contact, and dependency. Because communities and geography are produced and experienced as incompletely divided, apathy takes shape as willing disengagement from the social, political, and economic conditions that make everyday life possible. Chapter 3 focuses explicitly on the production of normalcy, appraising how mechanisms of repair and maintenance are activated by the intrusion of politics, violence, and conflict on family and community. In these intimate sites, relations of care and investment reveal how transformative action is not entirely rejected but is taken selectively, in manners and arenas deemed meaningful and effective. Chapter 4 further complicates the apparent division between action and inaction, exploring various sites and forms of political activism that reveal how resistance may become caught up in power. Here, apathy emerges as not the opposite of activism but sometimes paradoxically the very product of political engagement and participation. Drawing together the mechanisms outlined in preceding chapters, Chapter 5 analyzes the social protests that swept across Israel during summer 2011, considering how political participation might be "world-making" rather than "world-changing" on massive scales. By fashioning a space between action and inaction, the protests succeeded in mobilizing and cohering a formerly quiescent public without challenging the key political condition that underlies economic and social life in Israel.

Through the frame of political apathy, this book depicts how leftist Jewish Israelis in Tel Aviv and West Jerusalem actively weave a tapestry of the ordinary in Israel-Palestine, threaded through with power, privilege, and politics. In doing so, the analysis within these pages ultimately challenges the conceptualization of apathy as an absence or lack, instead revealing how politically significant worlds and relations take shape in the tension between action and passivity. However, diagnosis and critique are not the sole tasks at hand—rather, this book aims to enrich activist strategies through indexing the logics, mechanisms, and structures that presently limit political engagement and action. By uncovering how social relations underwrite systems of macropolitical power, my intention is to open a new conversation about Israel-Palestine, one in which political apathy is taken seriously and regarded as significant to the future of the region.

ONE

The Everyday of Occupation

TWO CITIES, TWO TALES.

Tel Aviv—at once "the bubble" and the crown jewel. Each summer day as hot and humid as the next, every morning a sun burning bright against a clear blue sky. On an ordinary Friday morning the wooden deck of the affluent seaside port in the city's northern district is heaving under the weight of relaxation: cafe patrons reclining with the financial paper; cyclists and joggers weaving their way through crowds and restaurant tables; families strolling languidly with toddlers and prams; photography clubs capturing images of fishermen testing their luck along the breakwater; and beaches filling with colorful umbrellas, tanned bodies, and the day's first swimmers. We make our way past the balloon seller with his cluster of brightly colored floating Mylar in shapes of unicorns and fighter jets, and avoid the growing audience awaiting the variety act about to begin. En route to our favorite brunch restaurant, Gilly's, I think back on our first late-morning breakfast, at the start of my fieldwork in October, when the nearby daily farmers' market was a weekend-only affair and showcased producers instead of boutique vendors.

On that October day my partner, Guy, and I had settled into an afternoon brunch with appetites sharpened by a morning spent shopping at IKEA. We found an empty table near the water. I made note of the peculiar surroundings, whose juxtaposition of leisure and industry would eventually become "normal": Reading Power Station, with its towering smokestack; low-flying planes passing overhead to land at Sde Dov Airport; and the occasional military helicopter, almost invariably flying south. Amid this mix of luxury, industry, and military we tucked into mimosas, brioches, olives, omelets, salads, and cappuccinos, seeking respite from the exhaustion of furnishing our flat. However, when I was midway through my omelet a rather extraordinary object appeared on the sea's horizon: a small gunship, just off the coast, near enough to see the silhouette of a gun turret mounted on the front deck. Yet no one seemed to notice. As I sat watching, the boat moved south and finally curved back northward and out to sea. "Oddly normal, I guess," I wrote in my field notes that night, curious as to why this type of ship should appear on that day and not others during visits in years past, and perplexed as to why I should find it strange while my companions did not.[1] Later that night, I would learn that the Israel Air Force had bombed a car carrying three suspected militants in the Gaza Strip (*Ha'aretz* 2010b) as I contented myself with lunch beside the sea. Over time, I understood this tension to be a kind of normalcy specific to Tel Aviv: an act of violence miles away unfolding unknown, unseen, and unheard.

Jerusalem—the holy city and a sectarian labyrinth. A complex network of enclaves bisected by a charged and shifting seam. I arrive early for my interview in Baka, a neighborhood in Jerusalem's southeast identified as one of the city's remaining secular Jewish areas. My regular walking route takes me from Jaffa Street—near the boundary between (Palestinian) East and (Jewish Israeli) West—skirting the Old City's Christian Quarter, down through the gardens and studios of Gan Shmu'el, and finally up to Bloomfield Garden, with its windmill and panorama of the ancient city and looming wall beyond. By this date in June the journey and view have become routine, ordinary. As I make my way past shuttered shops waiting to sell religious memorabilia to the throngs of tourists congregating at Jaffa Gate, the dry heat and dust of Jerusalem offer a welcome reprieve from the humidity of Tel Aviv. Arriving at the Old City, I note the regular presence of Magav (border police) at the New Gate, my preferred entrance to the city's winding streets and Christian Quarter. Rather than entering, I pass along the exterior walls toward the valley below. Quickly I descend and then ascend, climbing limestone steps past planters and window boxes lush with the pink, purple, yellow, and orange of flowers bidding entrance to the artist studios nearby.

Across the valley I pass the windmill and overlook, arriving at the junction of the affluent German Colony and its humble neighbor, Baka. Down Emek Refayim await cafes, restaurants, shops, and boutiques with an energy similar to Tel Aviv's, but on a street where English is as common as Hebrew and modern religious dress mingles with European fashion. For the first time I continue straight, walking along Derech Beit Lechem (Bethlehem Road) and turning into a small park to wait for the scheduled hour of my interview. I feel unusually tired this day, experiencing the strain of field study compounded by the weight of the calendar date—today is Naksa Day, the anniversary of the 1967 War.² Bored and fatigued, I call Guy in Tel Aviv to pass the time. His news comes as a shock: accounts are emerging from Israel's northern borders with Lebanon and Syria that Palestinians are attempting to break through the fences into Israel, and succeeding. Majdal Shams, a Druze village in the northern Golan Heights, has become a site of intense violence, with live ammunition being shot into crowds of protesters by the Israel Defense Force (IDF). Crowds and violence are also growing near the Qalandia checkpoint outside Jerusalem, but somehow I am certain that this danger cannot touch me. Minutes later, I climb the steps of a nondescript apartment building, passing identical doors with personalized nameplates that lead to the intended flat. While beyond the door a radio broadcast blares news of the north, the interview unfolds as a pleasant conversation in the space of a home, without any mention of the day's violence.³

Through these personal tales of Tel Aviv and West Jerusalem, ordinary experiences and interactions reveal how a tension between absence and presence, violence and calm, frames everyday life for many Jewish Israelis living in Israel-Palestine. Rather than the destruction, devastation, and displacement that accompany episodes of spectacular violence—and characterize the prevailing material conditions for many Palestinians—the day-to-day reality of conflict is often experienced as a kind of ambivalence, an underlying sense of unease, or an incident or object that might willingly go unseen. Here normalcy takes shape as a perpetual state of "becoming," an ability to enact and experience the steady regularity of ordinary life seemingly despite the continuing presence of extraordinary violence. While the mutuality between violence and normalcy will be explored at length in chapter 3, this chapter explores the substance and patterns of Jewish Israeli "everyday life" in Tel Aviv and West Jerusalem, or what makes particular lives livable therein. Here, gender emerges as a principal structural thread lacing together dominant values, institutions, meanings, and practices, revealing how "the political" runs just beneath the surface of everyday life (Navaro-Yashin 2003). In making visible the social, political, and economic baseline underwriting Jewish Israeli society, gender analysis exposes how central social pillars of fraternity, security, and modernity are actively bolstered by military, family, education, and media institutions. Together, these constructs reveal that patterns of gender are key to the assumed stability of everyday life among Jewish Israelis, providing a sense of constancy and dependability through hegemonic roles, relations, codes, and norms. Yet this stability remains framed by the normative precarity of Zionism, a prevailing ideology and practice whose narrative of threat, persecution, and transcendence shapes collective politics in profoundly negative and avoidant terms.

FRATERNITY, SECURITY, MODERNITY

Central to the varying visions and practices of everyday life within Jewish Israeli society are three core social values: fraternity, security, and modernity. Simultaneously distinct and relational, each construct takes shape through the others and joins with the overarching frame of modern-day Zionism. While often narrowly cast as the dominant form of Jewish nationalism, focused on achieving and securing statehood, contemporary Zionism encompasses economic policies, social practices, and political agendas, suffusing and binding together interests once regarded as disparate. Importantly, each social pillar relies on the presence of its seeming opposite or "other," as all combine to form the prevailing ethos of state and society. Following Ferdinand de Saussure's linguistic assertion that "meaning is made through implicit or explicit contrast" (as paraphrased by Scott 1988, 36–37), among Jewish Israelis fraternity requires division and exclusion, security necessitates threat and instability, and modernity rests on the persistence of tradition. As these core values produce accord between seeming contradictions they create the foundation for a stable social structure, intersecting on subjective, social, and state levels through hegemonic patterns of gender.

In broader Jewish Israeli society, military service provides the clearest illustration of the ways in which stabilizing patterns of gender bind together fraternity, security, and modernity in the ethos of modern-day Zionism. As argued by Ronit Lentin (2000, 188, 217), the explicitly gendered construction of Jewish Israeli society results in the primacy of "military-masculine hegemony," a form of domination and vision of normality that privileges "national security," generates discourses of "no choice" engagement in conflict, and produces specific categories of "others" which affirm the substance of "self." Here, "normal" Jewish Israeli subjectivities are constructed in keeping with the framing of Israel as overtly masculine. As noted by numerous scholars of Israel-Palestine, the perception of collective Jewish weakness and emasculation in diaspora was historically repudiated through the figure of the Israeli-born *tsabar* or Sabra, who effectively redeemed Jewish manhood—and the nation—through his health and courage (Sharoni 1995, 41; Lentin 2000,

198–201; Katz 2003, 21). Significantly, this figure is depicted as a particular kind of male: "The *Sabra* was born into a vacuum in which the ideal figure was not the father, but the son ... portrayed in 'Aryan' terms as healthy, tanned, often with blond hair and blue eyes, confident, proud and brave, presumably cleansed of all 'Jewish' inferiority complexes" (Lentin 2000, 198). While this construction of the new Israeli generates clear terms of inclusion and exclusion based on gender, race, and physical ability, the pairing of masculinity with pervasive militarization in Israel extends Sabra ideals throughout society.

On completion of high school, all Jewish Israeli women and men are required to undertake national duty in the form of mandatory military service, for periods of two and three years, respectively (Shafir and Peled 2002, 143). Though various forms of conscientious objection and limited terms of legal exemption exist (Helman 1999b; Kidron 2004; Lentin 2004; Rimalt 2007; Lerner 2010; Natanel 2012; Weiss 2014), military service remains highly normative in Jewish Israeli society, shaping individual subjectivities, social relations, and political realities. This normativity prevails regardless of whether young women and men actively fulfill national "duty," ushering Jews—citizens and noncitizens[4]—into a specific constellation of fraternity constructed around narratives of threat and protection. As related by Shoshana, a sixty-eight-year-old Jerusalemite born in the United States, Jewish immigrants to Israel are often acutely aware of the relationship between military service and social belonging. "I didn't do military service. I wanted to—the army builds and protects. We all wanted to do that. From a social point of view, to be in the army is to be Israeli, to be a 'real Israeli,' to be 'in.'" Shoshana had expressly hoped to contribute to the Israeli state's military efforts as an eager volunteer, yet arrived in Israel two weeks after the end of the 1967 War and expressed regret that "They started the war without me!" Unable to enlist in the IDF due to her advanced age—she was twenty-five at the time—Shoshana participated in postwar fraternity by cleaning the Mt. Scopus university campus. "I was sent to clean up," she recounted, "but I read Israeli newspapers so I knew that the volunteers were there to take over the jobs of the men in the army." In gendered terms, this narrative illustrates how the sexual division of labor between women and men appears to collapse as the result of active conflict. However, Shoshana later described the ways in which militarized gender norms and hierarchies persist in structuring social roles and relations: "My husband was a noncombatant, so he wasn't called up [in the 1973 War]—he was in a way 'like a woman.' There's a difference between who has to stay at home and who gets to go out and be part of it."⁵ Oded, a thirty-three-year-old filmmaker now living in Tel Aviv, confirmed this claim as he reflected on his experience of military service after immigrating to Israel from Eastern Europe at age sixteen: "I came to stay [in Israel] and it was important to me to 'be Israeli.' First I learned that to be Israeli you have to go to the army—and do full combat. Otherwise you won't be considered a man. It was important to me to be a 'real Israeli man,' to play the tough guy."⁶

Creating fraternity through participation in security, mandatory military service institutes a "brotherhood" of (Israeli) Jews, while the same time fulfillment of national duty produces "real men" and women. In correspondence with the construction of militarized masculinities across diverse contexts, here ideal men assume the characteristics of machismo that often accompany tasks of protection and control. Indeed, Oded described the links between conflict, military service, and social normativity specifically through the language of pervasive (masculinized) "macho" cultures: "The cultures in both societies—Palestinians, Middle Eastern societies, Israeli society—are very macho. It's about power. Here [in Israel] it's all mixed up with an insane military thing. . . . The army is seen as producing the best characteristics of society."⁷ Once absorbed and adopted by individuals, this brand of masculinity circulates at the level of society, reproducing and maintaining the prevailing norm. Despite the historical construction of the ideal Jewish Israeli man in clearly exclusive terms, the normativity of militarized masculinity in Israel creates a mode of belonging that seemingly cuts across hierarchies of race, class, and sexuality. Yoni, a twenty-eight-year-old Jerusalemite activist of Yemeni origin, again invoked militarism and "macho" social norms in describing his reaction to everyday experiences as a gay Mizrahi man:

> I embarrass people, not really to embarrass them but as a tool to make them think about what they said a few seconds ago. Like at a *Shabbat* [Sabbath] dinner, there was a guy there who I didn't know and some straight guy asked me, "Do you think he's hot?" I said, "Sure, he's hot." Then the guy said, "So, do you want to suck his dick?" I turned to him and said, "Baby, if anyone is going to be sucking someone's dick it's *you*!"
>
> I don't want to be violent like this, but you have to. It's this macho thing that comes through the military and society. You can't be polite. If you don't know how to argue here . . . it's very violent, but this is how you establish your presence. You have to say "Fuck you! I'm going to *show* you." I'm softer with my Sephardic identity because I'm still trying to figure it out—I'm stronger in being gay.⁸

Despite his non-normative sexuality, Yoni's ability to speak the violent language of hegemonic masculinity grants him belonging in Jewish Israeli society; learned in part through military service, the performance of security indeed begets membership in fraternity.

However, while Yoni might experience social belonging through his subscription to militarized masculinity, the racialized otherness of his body and identity remain points of unease. Self-identified as an "Arab Jew," Yoni's racial "Arabness" constitutes a threat to both security and fraternity, a tension that remains unresolved. Though portrayed as a "melting pot" in which diverse social locations are forged into the unity of national community, military service produces exclusion as much as inclusion. Like their Jewish counterparts, Palestinian, Bedouin, and Druze citizens of Israel are obligated by law to fulfill national duty, and each year members of these communities indeed enlist to fill the ranks of the IDF (Kanaaneh 2008; Cohen 2014).[9] Yet the military's promise of integration proves false, as these individuals and their communities continue to face discrimination at the hands of the Israeli state; likewise, their constructions of masculinity are not "valued" in the same way as the hegemonic Jewish ideal.

As the relationship between security and fraternity makes visible how tension and accord coexist within Jewish Israeli society, this seemingly contradictory dynamic extends to a third social pillar: modernity. Entangled with security and fraternity through narratives of (Western) "progress," "civilization," and "liberalism," modernity is central to Israel's militarized and masculinized brand of nationalism. In correspondence with other patriarchal nationalisms, the construction and prestige afforded to militarized masculinity is accompanied by contestation around the category of "women." Within Jewish Israeli society, women are broadly situated at the nexus of tense polarities: at once inside and outside the nation, in need of protection and posing a threat, a symbol of both progress and custom (Yuval-Davis 1997; Kandiyoti 1991; Lentin 2004; Jacoby 2005). As Israel claims status as a modern, liberal state at the forefront of institutionalized gender equity, women as a broad category have enjoyed various "advances," including admission into combat positions in the military (Lentin 2004; Jacoby 2005; Sasson-Levy, Levy and Lomsky-Feder 2011, 743; Hopkins 2012). However, the participation of women in military service, including combat, does not serve to "soften" or "feminize" Israeli military structures, policies, or practices but often entangles women in pursuit of masculinized attributes of strength, aggression, and power (Sasson-Levy 2005 [2001])—normative qualities associated with both fraternity and security in this context.[10] During her military service, thirty-year-old feminist activist Meital worked as an artillery guide stationed on base, (re)training reservists for service in combat. As we spoke in Tel Aviv, she described her position and experience positively: "When people in the *miluim* [reserves] come back for service they need to refresh their memory about the process and practice in the field for a week, so I did that with them. It was fun! I really enjoyed this." Yet toward the end of our exchange, Meital reflected on how this pleasurable experience of military service impacted her attitudes and behaviors later in life, generating increasing tension with her feminist ideals:

> Two years ago I came to a psychology treatment and I came with a strong feminism. It took me time to realize that although I was feminist, I was militant about it—I was telling women what they should do, what they should think. I was practically doing what I was trying to stop! It took me a long time to see what I was doing through feminist *mishkafaim* [glasses]—a feminist lens. Now I try to bring this to my friends and myself, but I judge myself cruelly. The psychologist helped me to see that there are more options than just "right" and "wrong."[11]

Like Meital, the majority of women interviewed in Tel Aviv and West Jerusalem related experiences of military deployment in an educational or training capacity, reflecting the codes that associate women with "home front" and reproduction in this context (Sharoni 1995, 2005 [1994]; Herzog 2005 [1998]; Jacoby 2005).

However, the terms of Meital's service also correspond to the rise of a new "modern" Jewish Israeli woman, defined by her willingness to participate in combat, actively fighting and sacrificing for security and fraternity. Underwritten by a shift to neoliberalism in Israel beginning in the mid-1980s, these new constructions of femininity reflect the "equal to if not better than" mantra of liberal feminism in the United States, a major proponent of neoliberal policies (Mohanty 2003; Mohanty, Pratt, and Riley 2008; Hemmings 2011). Meirav, a twenty-five-year-old feminist activist, gave voice to how the overlayering of modernity, fraternity, and security are evident in figure of the female combat soldier. "Israel is a militaristic society—either you're in combat or you have babies for them," she claimed early in our interview, outlining the familiar gender roles associated with high levels of militarization. She later followed this assertion with a story about her younger sister:

> My sister did the most "combat" thing you can do and she changed some procedures—she's actually leftist. She was on the border with Gaza, in the lookouts in charge of the war room. She's also an animal rights activist and she refused to shoot at herds of sheep to deter the herds and Palestinians from going next to the wall. She directed the forces and saved a lot of lives on both sides. She's very hands-on. Three times she was next to suicide bombings. I asked her once, "How are they?" She said that they aren't as frightening as seeing rockets flying above. She's my baby sister, so I'm protective, but she's tough. She's going to Africa to volunteer.[12]

Coupled with future heroism on the final "frontier" of Africa, Meirav's younger sister embodies the contradictory symbolism of the female combat soldier and the ways in which modernity, fraternity, and security operate in tandem through military service. Here "combat" entails not only hand-to-hand fighting but also saving and caring, moral practices ostensibly suited to women, according to the logic of gendered roles and binaries. While this young woman's participation in combat clearly bolsters security in material and ideological terms, it simultaneously reinforces a significant constellation of fraternity: militarism and leftist politics align in the interest of the nation. This very ease of accord positions Israel and Jewish Israelis among those states and societies deemed "modern" and "liberal," as ultimately a young woman's courage on the battlefield translates into humanitarian bravery and benevolence.

The "Usual Life" of Zionism

Thus, through the prevailing security paradigm, militarism binds together a nation in fraternity, while laying the foundation for claims of belonging in a larger collective of "liberal" and "modern" Western states.[13] Yet, as argued earlier, the construction of these core social pillars relies on the continued presence of seeming opposites—fraternity needs division, modernity requires tradition, and security arises through conditions of instability and threat. In this way, new norms remain bound with old, "progressing" while carrying forward the roles, codes, and relations of the past.

Gender is again instructive here, as "modern" women remain subject to the "traditional" pressures of reproduction, though now allowed, through the successes of feminism, to participate in combat as pilots and infantry troops. So, too, emergent constructions of Jewish Israeli masculinity demonstrate this dynamic. Previously deployed in military intelligence, the new "high-tech" man working in the latest start-up company continues to fulfill the masculinized role of protection, ensuring collective safety in ways perhaps now more expedient than hand-to-hand combat. Like modernity, fraternity also takes root in its seeming antithesis—division and fragmentation. While the individualism of neoliberal ideologies and economic policies might seem poised to shatter the collective base of nationalism and early socialist ideals in Israel (Shafir and Peled 2000; Ram 2008), in effect this stratification reproduces familiar bonds. As Yonathan, a Tel Aviv filmmaker in his mid-thirties, claimed, "With capitalism came this idea of the individual, self-survival, and also trauma. New developments are fuelling old ideas."[14] In (re)creating experiences of collective trauma, social splintering underlines the lingering normativity of fraternity as an aspiration and ideal. Importantly, this accord between seeming contradictions takes shape within the frame of security, compounding a prevailing sense of threat and ensuring readiness for violence.

In these ways, the pillars of security, fraternity, and modernity entrench and resuscitate Zionism as an ideology and practice, from the cafes and boutiques of Tel Aviv to the dusty streets and markets of Jerusalem. This updated vision of Zionism, a belief draped in drones and rainbow flags, does not aim at the goals of its origin—a sovereign state and guaranteed safety for the Jewish people (Herzl 1988 [1896]; Goldberg 1996; Lentin 2000; Ram 2003; Piterberg 2008)—but rather becomes an endless iteration of its founding narrative: persecution, trauma, perseverance, and triumph. Taking root in the negation of historical exile (Piterberg 2008, 93–96), the narrative of Zionism positions victimhood and powerlessness at the core of the Jewish nation-building project. As historian Idith Zertal (1998, 2005) and sociologist Ronit Lentin (2000) convincingly argue, this narrative has been transformed into a myth that promises transcendence and triumph, completing the modern-day cycle. Following Martin Jaffee, Zertal (2005, 2) contends that Zionist mythology permits the victim to simultaneously understand himself as victor, "always destroyed but always reborn in a form that overcomes the victimizer." For both Zertal and Jaffee, "The chief beneficiary of that empowerment . . . is the community, which perceives itself as the historical witness to the degradation of the victim and his subsequent transcendence, as the historical body whose very existence preserves and relives the moment of degradation and transfiguration" (Zertal 2005, 2). Presently, this dynamic of preservation and reliving is made possible through active memorialization of the Holocaust and a popular understanding of the Israeli state as existing in "a world defined repeatedly as anti-Semitic and forever hostile" (4). Indeed, the lyrics of Israel's national anthem—*HaTikva*, or "The Hope"—attest to this ethos of constant struggle and striving:

> As long as deep in the heart,
> The soul of a Jew yearns,
> And forward to the East
> To Zion, an eye looks
> Our hope will not be lost,
> The hope of two thousand years,
> To be a free nation in our land,
> The land of Zion and Jerusalem.

Thus ideology and practice, narrative and materiality, become entwined through acts of repetition, producing and maintaining a world particular to Zionism. Importantly, this iteration not only constructs a version of reality but also structures and potentially incorporates resistance and subversion. Matan, a thirty-five-year-old Jerusalemite artist, spoke candidly of this tension:

> The rebellion I told you about in my twenties, with not knowing against what, but something strong came up. Probably you don't know about Holocaust families, that you can find common issues. You see many times that the Holocaust generation doesn't talk with the second [generation], but they talk to the third [generation].[15] That's what happened exactly in my family. My grandfather talked to me.... All my childhood, every Saturday almost, I listened to my grandfather. My grandmother didn't talk, she never did. He would talk every time, this loop of Holocaust stories—it was six years, the Holocaust, so there were a lot of stories! And before [the Holocaust]: the Communist Party, the Soviet Union—it was ten years of life. It was very important, it was injected into me from my early childhood to when my grandfather died. I was in the army [when he died]. *Then* was my rebellion. It was very unconscious. I'm not sure that I'm right about it now either, but now I have a bit more maturity. My internal structure is like this: animals, Sheikh Jarrah, the occupation comes in—whatever makes you cry comes in.[16]

Though "third generation," Matan identifies as a "survivor of the Holocaust" despite his clear recognition of the work done by this narrative as it is carried from past into present and future. While Matan would later describe himself as "post-Zionist" during our interview, the trauma of his grandfather's generation and Zionism's central narrative of vulnerability, persecution, and striving pervade his vegan and anti-occupation activism. Again, apparent contradictions sit easily within a single frame, where the presence of polarities helps Matan make sense of the surrounding world as a place where "whatever makes you cry comes in." In this way resistance enacted by Jewish Israelis in Palestinian Sheikh Jarrah—a site geographically distant from the Poland of Matan's grandfather—becomes integrated with the wider frame of Zionism, fuelling the cycle of repetition and trauma.[17] As Zertal (2005, 2) writes of Israel's relationship to the Holocaust:

> Through the constitution of a martyrology specific to that community, namely, the community becoming a remembering collective that recollects and recounts itself through the unifying memory of catastrophes, suffering, and victimization, binding its members together by instilling in them a sense of common mission and destiny, a shared sense of nationhood is created and the nation crystallized. These ordeals can yield an embracing sense of redemption and transcendence, when the shared moments of destruction are recounted and replicated through rituals of testimony and identification until those moments *lose their historical substance,* are enshrouded in sanctity, and become a model of heroic endeavor, a myth of rebirth.[18]

Extending beyond the historical past, remembrance and (re)narration are actively renewed at contemporary sites of trauma that give rise to fraternity, security, and modernity on scales at once micro and macro. Describing this ability to influence and pervade, Lentin (2000, 178) writes: "Zionism is 'nationalism as narrative,' in that it claims a privileged narrative of the nation and thus justifies its own capacity to narrate its story and construct its history in an assertion of legitimacy and precedent for present as well as future."

Thus the narrative of Zionism transcends its original intentions, as it creates a self-sustaining contemporary world characterized by the repetition of instability. In doing so, Zionism fashions a society based on trauma and processes of redemption and healing, which can be only ever be partially complete. Yet what gives this world solid grounding? As depicted above in the tale of two cities, everyday life in Tel Aviv and West Jerusalem often unfolds seemingly in the material absence of violence and conflict—in these sites "normal" assumes a distinct form. Gil, a thirty-five-year-old musician, artist, and social worker in Jerusalem, described this experience of normalcy:

> [The occupation is] an ambient thing. It's like, you know you can live [as if] not noticing it, but it is an ambience here. I just talked with a friend who returned from Spain a few months ago. We talked about Israel, the different feeling here. It starts with the feeling of security. In so many places, if you go

> to sleep outside you don't feel safe—either because you're afraid of Arab ... terror attacks or you're afraid of the army, the police.... We hear about [the occupation] all the time: there's an attack, a fight, a conflict ... we absorb the feeling. You think that this is a usual life, but it is different from life in other places.[19]

Beyond the material conditions of a prospering economy, this "usual life" of conflict-as-ambient is made possible through social structures and relations that provide the sense of constancy assumed to underwrite "normal life" in model contexts, primarily American and European. Analyzing the social dynamics through which Israeli society has become actively masculinized vis-à-vis the perceived feminization of the Holocaust, its survivors, and the Jewish diaspora, Lentin (2000, 200) writes, "The Israeli aspiration to an elusive 'normality,' to being just like all other (preferably Western) nations, required adhering to strong social norms, which define that 'normality.'" Here, gender emerges as key to the conduct of everyday life, shaping subjectivities and interpersonal relations, demarcating the realms of public and private, structuring the political and domestic spheres, and providing a sense of belonging to a wider (patriarchal) world. As detailed above, patterns of gender directly enable the coexistence of polarities, permitting old and new, traditional and modern, collective and individual, security and instability to remain in tension and accord. Thus, while multiple social relations clearly contribute to the production and maintenance of power, gender uniquely lends stability to the construction of normality. As pervasive roles, norms, codes, and relations create a dependable social structure, at once familiar and continually in process (Connell 1987, 2002), gender underwrites the construction of a "usual life" and enables its cohesion with Zionism.

INSTITUTIONAL IMBRICATIONS

By embedding everyday life within the frame of Zionism, gender facilitates the conversion of the normative narrative of threat, persecution, and transcendence into a collective emotion, a sensibility, and a manner of engaging with a larger world. Here, Lauren Berlant's work on American culture is instructive, as she argues that political meaning may become attached to the sensations of particular groups, describing how specific emotions come to be experienced as "the national" (1993, 556, 560). So too Berlant (1998b, 640) posits that the affective regimes of nation-states—those institutionally supported emotions deemed politically meaningful and "national"—might justify domination. Importantly, this overlap of sensation with institution resonates in Jewish Israeli society. Less a matter of which individuals are excluded from the production of national emotion and whose sensations remain beyond the boundaries of political meaning, in the context of Israel-Palestine the question becomes exactly *how* a particular narrative gains and holds traction.

Military, Family, Education

As Connell (1987, 120) writes, "We cannot understand the place of gender in social process by drawing a line around a set of 'gender institutions.' Gender relations are present in *all* types of institutions. They may not be the most important structure in a particular case, but they are certainly a major structure of most." With these guiding and cautionary words in mind, an investigation into the role of gender regimes, or "the state of play in gender relations in a given institution" (120), reveals the extent to which normative narratives are reinforced in Jewish Israeli society through the blurring of boundaries among three key institutions: the military, family, and education.

To borrow the language of feminist intersectional theory, in Jewish Israeli society the institutions of military, family, and education cannot be separated into "discrete and pure strands" (Brah and Phoenix 2004, 76), in a manner similar to the overlayering of security, fraternity, and modernity discussed earlier. As indicated in extensive research conducted by feminist scholars in Israel (Sharoni 1995; Lentin 2000; Abdo and Lentin 2002; Jacoby 2005; Gor 2007; Gor and Mazali 2007; Abdo 2011; Peled-Elhanan 2012), each institution produces and reflects the others, becoming entangled through patterns of gender that become manifest in distinct regimes. Ana, a university lecturer in her mid-thirties who now lives in Tel Aviv, recounted the complex relationship thus: "Related to the occupation is the big role of the army—it's in everyone's lives. In order for an eighteen-year-old to go to the army he must be brainwashed from the day he is born. And part is the gendered military discourse. I remember in high school the girls with the soldier boyfriends were 'so cool.' The discourse is very gendered. Now women can be fighting [combat] soldiers and the position is very high-status because it's a *male* position."[20]

Ana's narrative is not unique in highlighting "brainwashing" as the reason for participation in mandatory military service, nor is she alone in noting the links between education and militarization. Many interview participants cited indoctrination as the conduit through which they took part in national duty, just as they reflected on how their experiences of schooling were shot through with narratives and practices aimed at preparing students for participation in mandatory service. Yet Ana extends the period of "convincing" and "learning"—here "brainwashing" occurs from the time of birth, signaling a site of instruction beyond the formal national education system: the family. Interestingly, Ana remembers the education system less for nationalistic or militarized lessons and field trips than for popularity contests won by those girls with (older) soldier-boyfriends, revealing a novel type of militarized hierarchy present in many Israeli schools.[21] So too this narrative points to the centrality of heterosexuality to Jewish Israeli society. As contemporary Zionism exists as a nation-building project rooted in patriarchal nationalism, biological reproduction remains a top social imperative, propelled in part by the construction of an imagined "demographic race" between the Jewish and Palestinian residents of Israel-Palestine (Yuval-Davis 1989; Kanaaneh 2002; Halperin-Kaddari 2004; Steinfeld 2012). Underwritten by the founding narrative of threat, persecution, and transcendence and bolstered by the corresponding historical experiences of European Jews, heterosexuality retains primacy within Jewish Israeli society. Yet Ana's account also echoes the "exceptional" standards of gender equality promoted by state and society, complicating those narratives which would relegate Jewish Israeli women to private domains and reproduction while locating men in the public sphere—in her concluding sentence Ana attests to the achievements of liberal feminism in Israel, highlighting the recent admission of women to combat positions formerly open solely to men.

This brief account then demonstrates the ways in which the national education system becomes bound with the Israeli military through patterns of gender, experienced as social relations. While the role of the heterosexual family is implicit in this passage, Ana's further remarks during our conversation reflect on this institution directly:

> I have a son, he's half black and half white—he's four years old now. In the summer we moved to Tel Aviv and he started a new *gan* [kindergarten], which isn't easy. I was reading a big ad in the paper about "supporting Arabic gas"—this was when there was a huge fight about gas over the summer. For now most of our gas is from Egypt and it's referred to in the paper as *gaz Aravi* [Arabic gas]. Anyway, I was talking about it with my husband and my son asked me, "Is that my gas?" I asked him what he means and kids in the

new *gan* say that he is an Arab.... They're three and a half—how do they know what an Arab is?! I answered him and said *A*, no, you are not an Arab, and *B*, it's not a bad thing to be an Arab. Later I had an argument with my husband—he told me that by telling our son that he wasn't an Arab I already gave him the feeling that it *was* a bad thing. I don't know.... At three and a half how does the conflict influence their lives when they learn this?[22]

In a sense, Ana answers her first question—"How do they know what an Arab is?"—moments later when she links the occupation with the "big role of the army in everyone's lives." Here values of "us" and "them" are translated from the language used in familiar and formal education systems to the terms of national security, only to recirculate within families and schools once more. As Ana reassures her son that he is not an Arab, her husband intimates that her insistence on the distinction bestows meaning and value on the category—Arab becomes "a bad thing" despite her belief to the contrary. Aware of conflict at three and a half, Ana's son brings militarism home in his kindergarten backpack, setting on the family table the harsh lessons learned in school.

As the thread binding regimes of military, family, and education within a given order, gender appears largely absent in Ana's account above, save what might be read intertextually with existing scholarship. However, the role of women as biological and cultural reproducers of the nation (Yuval-Davis and Anthias 1989; Kandiyoti 1991; Yuval-Davis 1997) seems only partially applicable here, again demonstrating how patterns of gender remain dynamic even while providing structure. Immediately following her memory of high school social hierarchies, Ana changed tack to speak once more of her son:

> You know, on Holocaust Day they tell my son at two and a half, three and a half, about the Holocaust. It's this intense string of holidays: Passover, Holocaust Remembrance Day, then Memorial Day. So first it's "the Egyptians are trying to kill us," then it's "the Germans are trying to kill us."... My son heard me say the word *German* and he said, "These are bad people." What?! And it wasn't even near Holocaust Day. Next Holocaust Day I won't send him there. But what if I have to work? I'm seeing my son being brainwashed.[23]

In combination with the previous account, Ana's quandary over Holocaust Remembrance Day reveals a division of labor based on and productive of the prevailing gender relations in Jewish Israeli society. Despite her work as a university lecturer and co-parenting with a male partner, Ana asks what will happen the following year if she is unable to look after her son; and it is Ana who answers the question of whether or not "Arabic gas" belongs to him. Though subscribing to the tenets and critiques of feminism, Ana retains primary responsibility for her son's care and development—yet with this provision of care comes the desire to safeguard, challenging those norms that link men with defense and protection. However, the duty of protection is shifted within the remit of motherhood through her husband's non-Jewishness and non-whiteness, as ethnicity and race intersect with gender roles, relations, and norms.

Clearly, gender indeed remains in process as a site of contestation and accord. Mothers like Ana provide both care and protection, as they answer difficult questions and engage with lessons learned at the nexus of military, family, and education. Then "home" becomes a site of stability within a sea of uncertainty, a place where repeated norms, values, and narratives might be laid to rest at the same time as they gain new purchase. Yet while Ana's accounts attest to the cycles that sustain Zionist narratives, her investment in their repetition is not guaranteed—rather, Ana describes the means of her embeddedness in an attempt to disentangle herself and her family from dominant narratives and values. Then how does she become part of the hegemonic system, expressing a sense of "depression" at her own political inaction and an inability to transcend the subsequent feelings of guilt? Not solely produced through the intersection of military with family and education, Ana's entanglement with power points to alternative sites of norm production and maintenance, no less central to a sense of collectivity.

The News-Holiday Cycle

As apparent in Ana's account of her son's early exposure to Holocaust narratives, the annual holiday cycle in Israel not only (re)produces prevailing norms but also fashions national subjects. Building on and complicating the foundational work of Michel Foucault and Marxian post-structuralist scholars, queer theorists such as Lauren Berlant (2008, 2011) and Judith Butler (1993, 1997b, 2004) study the production of norms and subjects closely, uncovering potential sites of interruption and transformation even as their scholarship details the pervasive and constitutive qualities of normativity. Indeed, Butler (1993, 1–3) describes the ways in which matter gains "boundary, fixity, and surface" through processes of (re)materialization, yet posits that these cycles of repetition necessarily remain unfinished: "That . . . reiteration is necessary is a sign that materialization is never quite complete, that bodies never quite comply with the norms by which their materialization is impelled." While raising the possibility that strategies of "threat and disruption" might offer a critical resource in efforts to transform the standards of "legitimacy and intelligibility" that frame and constrain subjects (3), in the context of Jewish Israeli society these very ruptures and interruptions resonate with the precarity central to Zionist narratives. Then even as iteration yields "abject beings" (3) whose nonconformity and agitation promise transformation, cycles of repetition and their unruly subjects may become implicated in the maintenance of power, reinforcing normative narratives, values, practices, and relations.

It is no coincidence that the holiday period foregrounded by Ana above, as she expressed trepidation at her son's "hailing" (Althusser 1971, 48–50; Brah 2012 [1999], 12) into the national fold, reappeared as a key time frame in numerous interviews. Preceded by Pesach (Passover), a week-long holiday whose narrative centers on persecution and escape,[24] Yom HaShoah (Holocaust Remembrance Day) prepares the ground for Yom HaZikaron (Memorial Day), which the next day yields to Yom Ha'Atzmaut (Independence Day), all within the time of one month.[25] It is a period of "high nationalism" similar to American Independence Day with its flags, parades, and expressions of patriotism, but during this time the narrative of persecution and redemption particular to Zionism suffuses everyday life to an extreme. Compounded by media coverage in the form of films depicting personal stories of loss, television broadcasts of official commemorations attended by government officials, and dedicated radio playlists of songs whose lyrics evoke those emotions considered "national," the cycle of holidays produces specific selves, subjects, and collectivities.

Sitting on the airy balcony of a Jerusalem cafe tucked into the winding narrow streets behind Kikar Zion (Zion Square), Matan touched on the holiday-media cycle as he related his process of coming to political action:

> In the '90s, I was twenty, after the army. After [the army] I didn't know what it was against, but [an energy] was coming up. It didn't have specific content, it was through art, music, raves—rethinking, rebuilding community. I was twenty or twenty-one. It wasn't conscious, it happened through nature. Art, music, freedom—this is what we were building community through. We had some very serious people there, a lot of fantasies of what we could do. We were very young. I don't know the cause and effect, but then the terror attacks started in Jerusalem. The ideal community—art, music, freedom, etc.—broke apart during the bomb attacks. It was very hurtful, every two to three days

there was an attack in Jerusalem. I would cry every night. I would hear a bomb—I was living in the center—and turn on the TV to see how many were killed. I would cry every night, every other. I had a period of three to four years of emotional breakdown, again and again and again and again and again. This is a very special culture in Israel.

KN: That the culture is so emotional?

Matan: We are born, raised, educated with holidays—not as Jewish but as *Israeli* culture, new Israeli culture. There are some big holidays like Holocaust Memorial Day and Memorial Day for soldiers, and from [age] four, five, six, seven, every year we are crying, feeling ecstatic feelings. You are born and raised that way, it's a feeling of being picked up as a child. It's in the music. I would become addicted to the music after a bomb attack, the music played on the radio. The music is so sad. It's special, with an artistic touch and talent, not *kitsch*. After every attack there were days of songs. In a way it was like a party.[26]

The same man who earlier recounted his grandfather's "loop of Holocaust stories" and their impact on his political identity and activism, Matan during our interview explicitly invoked the cycles of holidays, violence, and media discourse, relating their repetition to the production of "new Israeli culture" as separate from Jewish culture. In keeping with Butler's (1993) optimism that space for transformation exists within repetition, this wider national cycle indeed produces its own resistance, as Matan sought the formation of an "ideal" community as an alternative to the mainstream that he rebelled against after military service. Described in terms of "art, music and freedom"—for Matan, what the mainstream community could not offer—this collective engendered a space of action, for "rethinking, rebuilding," even if now explicitly associated with fantasy. Yet Matan's account draws attention to the very pervasiveness of national narratives and emotions, a quality that lures him back to the fold even in his noncompliance. Catalyzed by violent events, Matan's ideal community dissolves as media images and discourses (re)produce the culture unique to Israeli society; here, tears induced by bombings meld with the tears of holidays past. With his microcommunity disintegrating, Matan feels himself rejoin wider society as experiences of violence mirror childhood memories and produce a sense of identification through emotional extremes. This relation of new-old trauma then points to the ways in which feelings of sadness and ecstasy can "pick up" an adult as if a child once more. Through the intimacy of trauma, Matan is effectively reinterpellated or "hailed" back into the national community—his escape from narrative and collective was never quite complete.

Structures of Fear and Fatigue

Though Matan's narrative concludes in his seeming reintegration with Jewish Israeli society, as we spoke in the cafe near the "seam" with East Jerusalem our exchange remained framed by his impending departure from Israel—Matan would soon be leaving, for the first time in ten years. "Now I'm starting a political immigration," he told me when we began our interview. "It's something inside and outside—I'm not that famous that it will be a *real* 'political immigration,' but inside, yes. I'm searching for a place. I'm going to Amsterdam for options."[27] Not only producing resistance, which might later be reabsorbed into national narratives, overlapping holiday and media cycles also create "structures of feeling" (Williams 1977), or socially constructed patterns of intimacy that bind together a collectivity.[28] While (re)producing "Israeli culture" in keeping with the extremes of emotion, so too these structures generate terms of inclusion and exclusion, engagement and disengagement. Not recognizing himself—or perhaps seeing his reflection too clearly—in the structures of feeling that order Jewish Israeli society, Matan now seeks escape. Then by entrenching the precarity of experience and emotion at the core of Zionist narratives, the repetition of holidays and media discourses fuels cycles that result in the desire to detach, displacing resistance and maintaining domination. Here discourse indeed yields subjects, social structures, and material realities with significant political effects (Foucault 1988; Butler 1993, 1997a, 1997b; Lentin 2000; Berlant 2011; Hemmings 2011).

For Dalia, a filmmaker and journalist in her mid-thirties living in Tel Aviv, the discursive repetition of trauma is mediated not only through television and radio but also through her partner and her young daughter. As the only interview conducted with a couple, my exchange with Dalia and Avi emphasized the extent to which intimacy becomes bound up in institutional frameworks and cycles. In response to my query about their individual activism, Dalia and Avi negotiated their relationship not only to hegemonic discourse but also to each other as partners within the wider collective:

> Dalia: There is so much to suppress here—if you don't, you go crazy. If you read all the news, be an activist on all the things, there is no time to breathe between demonstrations and legal actions. There is so much wrong you must suppress in order to live. *But* when something is broken in the suppression it's overwhelming because you recognize how much you have to suppress to live

your little life. It makes me think, what is the collective cost? If you just live your life the big circle gets smaller—there are less people who think like you. And when less people care, there is more corruption.

Avi: Dalia was reading the paper three hours a day at one point, she would get really angry. We both work at home—we fold our bed up and it becomes our office. I couldn't take it, so I cancelled our subscription to the newspaper, the newspaper she writes for! If you read all the headlines in the morning... maybe it's better to read them at night.

Dalia: But through Twitter I know the news before it reaches the paper. I go through cycles or waves of rage and suppression—now I'm on a wave of suppression. I can't even read all the blogs. I think the last straw in the last cycle was a document about the military trial of two Palestinian minors. It was so awful, I felt helpless about it. People a hundred times more activist than me were crying about it. But if *they're* crying about it, what can I do? Join them and cry? And in the meantime neglect my own kid? I just can't take it anymore—let this place blow up. I don't care.[29]

Dalia's narrative, that of a self-professed "couch activist," makes visible how the extremes produced through national holidays and media discourses produce disengagement, bolstering existing political and material realities. Bound to Matan's earlier account through acts of crying, feelings of helplessness, and simultaneous expressions of antipathy and connection to "this place," the exchange between Dalia and Avi reveals how normative national cycles compound more personal ones, here intervals of "rage and suppression." As Avi resists the intrusion of discourse and politics, to the extent of cancelling a subscription to the newspaper that employs his partner, both he and Dalia adhere to a broader public, one invested in the pursuit of "little lives" amid necessary uncertainty. Thus through actions both taken and withheld Dalia and Avi reaffirm stasis, despite distinguishing their leftist politics from those of the dominant mainstream and right-wing factions in Israel.

Though notable for its illustration of how resistance becomes reabsorbed into power at the level of everyday life, Dalia and Avi's account additionally highlights a key component of the structure of feeling specific to Jewish Israeli society: *fatigue*. Problematizing popular arguments that "fear" constitutes the pervasive political sensation among Jewish Israelis, lived experience reveals other sensory and affective products of the national narratives that circulate through holiday cycles and media discourses. Even as participants in nearly every interview indeed articulated sensations and experiences of fear, this emotion masks the extent to which investment in trauma engenders fatigue and with it political disengagement. Meirav, a twenty-five-year-old activist from Jerusalem, made the link between fear, fatigue and disengagement explicit:

> People are tired, fear is wired so deeply. For years I can't watch more than ten minutes of the news without getting mad ... just the way they tell it. ... The way the story is told becomes *myth*. Once you understand that life isn't a story, that myth is and can be something else, you are setting your own goals for yourself. I'm frustrated ... I care so much. One month ago I was given the option to go to Montreal for next year—it was fun and depressing because I realized how much I feel tired, I want to escape. I want to gain perspective from a place where I don't have to put so much effort into living.[30]

As Sara Ahmed (2004, 68) argues, fear may produce collectivities through impelling movement away from one object and toward another, fostering attachment to the chosen loved object. Yet within Jewish Israeli society fear additionally coalesces community through generating fatigue. In this context disengagement is part of the privileged position held by Israel's Jewish citizens; they can afford to allow themselves distance from conflict and violence while Palestinians, both inside Israel and in the Occupied Territories, cannot. Here, fraternity emerges through security and modernity in new ways, as the cyclical perception of threat creates a community caught up in (post)modern paralysis—as described earlier, "apathy" is a condition not unique to Israel but relevant to a range of contexts, including the United States and United Kingdom. Awareness of entanglement ("I am part of it, whether I like it or not") then severs the ties that make transformation seem a possibility rather than a momentary fantasy, while at the same time yielding new terms of connection. As trauma is relived through cyclical emotions of fear, aspiration, and fatigue, the admission of implication in this repetition erodes will to the extent that Amsterdam, Montreal, and "little lives" promise a new object of desire: effortless living.

COLLECTIVE POLITICS

As these imbrications result in disenchantment and disengagement, pervasive institutionalization further enmeshes the normative Zionist narrative with patterns of gender in Israel. Indeed, as political fatigue emerges through the repetition of trauma, these cycles reinforce prevailing gender norms, codes, roles, and relations. As Connell (1987, 141) writes, "gender is institutionalized to the extent that the network of links to the reproduction system is formed by cyclical practices. It is stabilized to the extent that the groups constituted in the network have interests in the conditions for cyclical rather than divergent practice." Yet as collective investment in the performance and repetition of trauma stabilizes gender, these cycles also bear critical implications for meanings and practices of politics.

Alienation and Cynicism

In Jewish Israeli society, Zionist narratives of threat, persecution, and redemption have shaped "politics" as an interest and practice, tying this construction to the privileging of men and masculinity. Popularly associated with conflict and violence, here politics emerges as a bastion of security and defense, interests with which most Jewish Israeli women were deemed to have little "formal" familiarity until the recent inclusion of female conscripts in combat positions (Lentin 2004; Jacoby 2005; Sasson-Levy, Levy, and Lomsky-Feder 2011). With scant experience as actors of (state) violence, Jewish Israeli "women" as a category were effectively granted little political voice and few positions of governance, despite the Israeli state's passage of a Women's Equal Rights Law in 1951 and its revision in 2000 (Raday 1991, 18–20; Yuval-Davis 2005 [1980], 122; Yishai 2005 [1997], 203; Halperin-Kaddari 2004, 17, 20). While recent intersectional analyses undertaken by feminist scholars such as Nahla Abdo (2011) complicate any claims made around "women" as a homogeneous category in Israel-Palestine, the prevailing meaning and arbiters of national politics remain masculine. In keeping with intersectionality, understandings of politics, access to voice, and positions of leadership are informed not only by gender but also by ethnicity, race, class, sexuality, and religion. From the state's naissance and the dominance of Labor Zionism, to the rise of Likud in the 1970s and the exclusive nationalist political parties currently gaining influence, primarily white, middle- and upper-class heterosexual Jewish men have populated successive governments and exercised audible political speech (Shafir and Peled 2002, 88–94; Sasson-Levy 2013, 28; see also Swirski and Safir 1991; Yishai 2005 [1997]). While recent reorganization and demographic shifts in the military have opened roles formerly closed to women and reflect a rise in rates of religious conscription, for many citizens political practice and interests remain exclusive. Though "politics" may be theorized as conduct and exchange in the public "realm of human affairs" open to all citizen-subjects (Arendt 1998 [1958]), lived experiences and popular perceptions in Israel-Palestine yield an image of alienation.

Yet even as the figures of Jewish Israeli politicians remain relatively unchanged, the content of their politics has shifted, from the liberal Labor platforms dominant until the 1977 elections to agendas and policies increasingly centered on ethno-nationalist concerns (Shafir and Peled 2002, 213–30). Along with the waning influence of historically strong left-of-center parties in Israel, the consolidation of political power among right-wing factions as a consequence of the 2015 elections attests to the intensification of these trends and processes. As the growing influence and appeal of the Right draws new actors into the political realm, the scope of alienation consequently spreads to encompass those who once enjoyed considerable political power. Among many Jewish Israelis, "corruption" becomes a way of talking about estrangement from politics and the political elite—not only are we "not like them," but also their policies and practices are seen to benefit a select few gathered in the upper echelons of political office. "I see Bibi [Prime Minister Benjamin Netanyahu] on the television and it's embarrassing to see his body language—he's sitting on a chair and there is a row of gangsters behind him," Yael, an Israeli citizen originally from Australia, recounted as we spoke in her home in Jerusalem's German Colony. She continued, "It's about money and religion—they hide behind the cloak of religion, religion which is so full of righteousness. What can I do with all of that? Except for run away if it gets too bad."[31] Likewise, Dalia explicitly linked politicians with corruption during our exchange in Tel Aviv: "I'm pessimistic about Israeli politics, it's corrupted in a neglecting manner. It's not evil, or fat cats, but detached. They can't think of creative things. Everyone is *old* and they look to the way things used to work."[32] So too Dana, a self-professed "politically avoidant" interview participant in Tel Aviv, spoke of the political elite in terms of estrangement as we conversed in a Tel Aviv cafe: "There is no one to go to.... Now that all the generals have died, like [Ariel] Sharon[33] and [Yitzhak] Rabin, the new generation is all white-collar crooks. It's a cynical notion, but these pictures of the ministers now look like the pre-Holocaust caricatures of Jews: hooked noses, fat bodies, beady eyes."[34] With politicians characterized as gangsters or crooks, righteous, detached, and archaic, feelings of alienation circulate among citizen-subjects as they increasingly fail to see their interests reflected in state policies or their values mirrored by those who lead the country.

Through these declarations of alienation Yael, Dalia, and Dana attempt to differentiate themselves from Jewish Israeli politicians and politics, yet their actions and sensations do not escape the wider structures of power in the region. Yael expresses a willingness to flee as she feels herself increasingly powerless against the money and religion of politicians; Dalia invests in her child and professes scant concern if Israel "blows up," as related above; Dana stopped reading newspapers when she was twenty, and now at thirty-two sees no one she can vote *for* rather than against. Through articulating estrangement from politics, the speakers seek to distance themselves in claim and practice. However, the phrasing of alienation-as-corruption points to a relation of attachment, an inescapable entanglement that again implicates dissent, resistance, and "bad subjects" in power. Yonathan, Dana's former partner and the Tel Aviv filmmaker who earlier related how "new developments fuel old ideas," described this connection in response to a question about politics:

> I see [politics] as the expression of the currents in societies. You can collect political influence when you have a central movement to collect it in. Now all the corruption in movements is an expression of what is happening in society. It is a mirror. They are corrupt because we are. We are corrupted, and people don't see that. Corruption is everywhere: in relationships, in work, in renting an apartment—it is expressed everywhere. Many times people aim their energy to change politics without looking at how society is taking part in it.[35]

Implicating himself and his society in the corruption that produces sensations and experiences of alienation, Yonathan challenges the distinction imposed between "them" and "us," the political realm and its subjects.

When read for gender, this discussion of political alienation appears to reaffirm the problematic normative relations that position Jewish Israeli men as political knowers/actors and women as outside the political sphere. Yet within everyday life sensations of alienation are often accompanied by expressions of cynicism, a combination that complicates prevailing gender norms. Though invoked by Dana as she paired contemporary politicians' images with pre-Holocaust anti-Semitic propaganda, cynicism conveys a tense relationship to the politics professed by both women and men, stressing connectivity, overlap, and enmeshment. Like alienation, the subtext of cynicism reveals attachment to the object from which a speaker feels distanced, divided, or excluded. Among Palestinians living in the Occupied Territories, Lori Allen (2013, 16, 27) observes that cynicism constitutes "a stance, attitude, mode of expression, and value judgment" that "can be not only a way that power is reproduced and political stasis maintained, but also part of how people continue to critique and search, or at least hope, for something better." While cynicism may indeed produce a situation in which "the possibilities of thinking and freedom open up precisely when one cynically gives up on such values of ideals" (Asberg 2008, 2), during interviews in Tel Aviv and West Jerusalem this sentiment expressed a felt inability to institute change in conditions of knowing entanglement. Oded, the Tel Aviv filmmaker who earlier related the construction of "real men" via military service, spoke directly of the links between corruption, cynicism, and (in)action:

> Politics here is a great way to shift attention away from real issues. Like how we're being robbed by people who squeeze money from the country, who own it, who have their way with the country. Now we have the highest fuel prices in the world! In the world! And no one knows why. There is no substantial public transport here. In France everyone would go on strike and paralyze everything, they would bring the country down. Here it won't happen because it's a "social issue"—"How can you compare this to the suffering of people in Sderot with missiles every day?" And when something happens politically, people stay home . . . because they have such cynicism. "What can we do? People are corrupt, and if we get rid of them, more corrupt people will come! What can we do? I'm going to watch *Big Brother*."[36]

A self-professed "former cynic," Oded embeds the helplessness of *Ma la'asot?* (What can we do?) in a wider frame of politics and alienation, demonstrating how the absence of reflected interests and values still manages to bind individuals with the collective. Unable to locate "social issues"—community matters in need of attention and transformation, such as the cost of fuel or dearth of public transportation—within the discourses and policies of "corrupt" government officials, concerned citizens remain in their homes feeling the situation in need of redress, effectively joining those unconcerned about or supportive of the status quo. Then beneath cynicism lies a sense of responsibility, piqued by acknowledgement of implication in a situation that should be transformed, yet dulled by the conviction that action is futile.

Political Emotions

Together, alienation and cynicism defy restriction to a single category of "men" or "women," complicating the prevailing gender norms that largely position Jewish Israeli men within the political and women without; regardless of gender, the realm of politics encompasses those whose interests and values it reflects. Varyingly excluded are men as well as women, Ashkenazi as well as Mizrahi, Jewish as well as non-Jewish, each on the basis of subscription to hegemonic national narratives and ideals.[37] Shaul, a twenty-year-old student of religion and philosophy active in the leadership of Jerusalem-based Sheikh Jarrah Solidarity,[38] described what he saw as new terms of political division: "Politics has changed drastically in the last twenty years—the 'two states versus larger Israel' debate is gone, although Parliament still speaks in this language. But if you look at the political platforms, they are quite similar—Kadima, Likud, [Ehud] Barak's Atzmaut, and even [Avigdor] Lieberman, too! We have one large right wing narrowly interpreting Zionism and then smaller ideological parties on both sides of it. The political discussion has shifted to an ethno-nationalistic majority versus a civil society/democratic minority—these are the new fault lines."[39]

Pragmatically delineating the shifting boundaries of politics in Israel, Shaul's account resonates with the increasingly conservative political atmosphere apparent in recent elections and public discourse. Yet the intensity with which he articulated this view was just as striking as the accuracy of his depiction—in response to my queries Shaul almost spat the words, largely expressing irritation and anger, and at times answering with obvious derision. In contrast to the frustration and despair that characterized many interviews in spoken word and bodily comportment, those who still felt able to politically act came alive in their seats before me. "It took me a while and a lot of anger," Jerusalemite activist Meirav admitted as she recounted her path to feminism, which now forms the basis of her political action. "I credit my anger.... I can be angry for ten minutes and say what I want, OK, but people won't let me do that—I'm not cute and harmless. So I got cynical.... People get cynical, they get tired." When I asked how she manages to avoid the cynicism in which she once felt included, Meirav answered, "I don't! I go to the places that allow anger."[40] While Meirav remains subject to the feelings of relative inefficacy and fatigue that produce cynicism and alienation among Jewish Israelis, she actively works through her relationship to politics by allowing space for an emotion commonly understood as a driver for conflict.

Like Shaul's disposition, Meirav's account attests to how for many anger and action do not constitute default positions, a surprising revelation within a society where militarization pervades everyday life and interpersonal relations. In contrast to those sensations and practices often associated with active conflict, the majority of research participants expressed despair, disillusionment, shame, and guilt as primary political emotions—sentiments that reflect and reproduce aspects of the normative Zionist narrative. Importantly, interview participants did not situate political depression opposite anger, but rather drew connections between these extremes, completing and reaffirming the cycle of trauma.[41] Similarly to Meirav, who does not escape cynicism even as she takes action, contradictions suffuse understandings and experiences, and again complicate prevailing gender patterns. Shoshana, who arrived "late" from the United States to Mt. Scopus on the heels of the 1967 War, personified these tensions as we sat together in the cafeteria of Hebrew University in Jerusalem:

> [After the Oslo years] I grew more and more disillusioned. I probably became extremely pessimistic, *extremely*. I think probably the attacks from Aza [Gaza] after we pulled out ... the attacks from Lebanon ... From Aza it was pretty bad, but the thing from Lebanon—I know people from Beirut, and my first reaction was "Flatten that country!" It took twenty years to get the army out, starting with the Four Mothers [Arba Emahot]. Then I said, "Wait, it's Zaher and Salim, [friends] in Beirut...." It gives you an idea of how angry I was. A lot of it is what happened to the Israeli Left.... But my son is much worse: he went from being an activist. It's true, he was a student at the time, there's some life-cycle influence. But he was at a meeting every week, then a meeting in Tel Aviv, every Saturday he'd go out. "To Hebron?! You'll get arrested!"—you don't know whether to be proud or worried! Now he's disillusioned. He's worse than me. He feels they're all liars! The Left, the Palestinians—everyone is liars.
>
> It's very interesting. I went through a period of tremendous, tremendous pessimism. I began to think that there was no way of stopping [the occupation]—this is not why I settled in Israel, to have a binational state. Now I say that I am saving my strength for "right to vote" demonstrations. After the right wing grew stronger, there are more things to make a two-state solution impossible—then there will be one state and we need to fight for the rights of Palestinians to vote. "What can we do? Isn't this ridiculous?" I said to a woman at the store. "You *do*!" she told me. "Why don't you come to Sheikh Jarrah? There are a lot of people from the university there." But I don't like that—it's like a performative social club.... Whoever plans the demonstrations on Fridays doesn't have to make *Shabbat* dinner, that's for sure![42]

Appearing within a single narrative, alienation, anger, and disillusionment clearly coexist, compounding one another as they culminate in a form of cynicism that legitimizes inaction. Pervading the political subjectivities of both Shoshana and her adult son, disenchantment transcends categories of gender as Jewish Israeli society is again divided, although the moral boundary between the politically dominant right wing and that minority of "performative" leftists appears uncertain. Vacillating between the solemnity of depression and the righteousness of anger, Shoshana and her son settle somewhere between in the moral safe space of an ideological, if inactive, Left.

Thus disillusionment, despair, shame, and guilt complicate the streamlined image of an order that associates "active" emotions with militarized masculinity and ostensibly "passive" positions and sensations with femininity. Expressed by women and men alike, political depression pervades and gives shape to that group situated opposite "the ethno-nationalistic majority" by Shaul. Yet while the following chapters work to complicate such an easy distinction, this collective relationship to politics—alienation, cynicism, and disengagement—indeed entrenches and reproduces particular norms and relations on larger levels. In gendered terms, even as political depression transcends categories of "men" and "women," the embeddedness of this sensation within existing relations of power effectively reaffirms "politics" as masculine. Unable to effect change in the realm of those "crooks" and "gangsters" of formal politics, who appear almost invariably male, white, and upper class, those subscribing to political despair are collectively feminized through their very distancing from politics, even as gender codes become complicated. That is, while both women and men experience despair, disillusionment, shame, and guilt in relation to politics, the ways in which these emotions cross category boundaries serve not to revalue political sensations but rather to devalue those who express them.

The Politics of Living

As prevailing gender patterns are simultaneously complicated and reified by the expression of political emotions, everyday life becomes further entangled with the desire for stasis and stability. As illustrated above, the depth and contradictions of sensation, experience, and belief overwhelmingly produce disenchantment and disengagement among women and men, generating investment in realms more immediate and intimate. In her work on optimism, Lauren Berlant (2011, 259) describes how the transference of action and attachment may take shape expressly through a condition of depression:

> The depressive position ... is taken up by a subject who acknowledges the broken circuit of reciprocity between herself and her world but who, refusing

to see that cleavage as an end as such, takes it as an opportunity to repair both herself and the world. But ... such an arc and rhythm can also amount to attempts to sustain optimism for irreparable objects. The compulsion to repeat a toxic optimism can suture someone or a world to a cramped and unimaginative space of committed replication, *just in case* it will be different.

In the narratives of research participants recounted above, the realm of politics often does not become the object of reparative action; rather, as explored in chapter 3, "small worlds" emerge as a locus of action and site of investment. Yet this breakdown of reciprocity between self and world indeed catalyzes a form of suturing—here, the combination of relations, emotions, and actions generates a politics of living.

Oriented toward a state of normalcy and dependent on replication and repetition, the worlds created through political depression again take shape through stabilizing structures of gender, (re)suturing "bad subjects" to the national fold. Bound tightly with Holocaust narratives and invoked in contemporary accounts of everyday life, survival remains central to the politics of living in Tel Aviv and West Jerusalem. Yet this mode of existence also constitutes the very practice against which visions of normalcy are desired and constructed. Yael, the fifty-six-year-old Jerusalemite who earlier characterized politicians as "gangsters," detailed her perception of the extent to which survival pervades daily life among Jewish Israelis:

> I do think it's an amazing accomplishment, this state—it's a miracle, a miracle. I heard a sentence recently from a friend, an actress, who made a wonderful play about the Holocaust: "The truth is more important than the facts." Here, what is the fight over? Land and entitlement to it. "It's mine. No it's mine! No it's mine!" I don't know how it's ever going to ...
>
> It's quite amazing that life goes on, on so many levels here. It's like a frog in water and more gets added so he swims up to keep his head above water. Then more is added, and more ... Life is going on! I think that the ultimate act of optimism is to continue having children, creating families. There are a lot of people in the West who don't have the urge [to have families], they think "What's it worth?" But here we are, in a more complex situation, more disheartening, and we continue on. You know, demographics are a very important issue here. Who is having babies?—the religious and the Arabs. This will be important![43]

In this short statement, the Holocaust becomes a subtextual grid for appraising successes of the state, contemporary practices of living, gendered imperatives for reproduction, and visions of a better tomorrow just beyond reach.

Survival, then, encompasses past, present, and future, a practice and ethos that must be continually—and incompletely—transcended through acts of repetition as it makes the world intelligible.[44] This mode of living directly produces the values of security, fraternity, and modernity, as here a "fight" creates families and categories of "us" within a frame shared with the West. Cyclically repeated as water is added again and again to nearly cover the swimming frog's head, survival melds with Zionist narratives of trauma instilled through the military, family, education, media, and commemoration. So too survival draws on and activates relations of political alienation, if not cynicism, as Yael leaves unfinished her thoughts about a resolution to the (political) argument over land and entitlement. Culminating in an expression of "optimism," this account of everyday survival momentarily resists dominant political emotions and yet implies those very "disheartening" sensations.

Thus, Yael's account is instructive in the ways that it gathers together the many threads of Jewish Israeli everyday life, enmeshing dominant values with overlapping institutions and popular appraisals of politics. Yet the precise content of her optimism is striking as here Yael foregrounds reproduction, showing how complexity engenders simplification and entrenches those norms that render life most stable. As Yael deems the (collective) act of "having children, creating families" the ultimate expression of optimism, the contradictions, subversions, and potential transformations detailed in this chapter are streamlined and reduced, entrenching the normative narratives that position Jewish Israeli women as reproducers and men as protectors. Providing constancy amid political, demographic, and moral uncertainty, hegemonic gender norms become the backbone of a new normalcy and constitute that which makes immediate survival possible. Again, this structure links directly to narratives, experiences, and values rooted in the Holocaust. "You have to make life in the hard places," Matan told me as he crushed another cigarette in the dish between us. "This life is going and building a community—other actions can be built on it because it's fun. Fun is part of life. Even in the Holocaust I'm sure they had fun. My grandparents made my mother inside the Holocaust, so they had *some* fun!"[45] Extending beyond metaphor or discourse and into the physicality of everyday life, survival-born drives to "make life," "build community," and even "have fun" possess material and normative dimensions—at its most triumphal, survival implies the biological continuation of life. Bound with cycles of trauma, narratives of survival, and visions of normalcy, patterns of gender become central to the creation of a community that is paradoxically stable in its precarity, with new generations invested in its reproduction.

CONCLUSION

As individuals become entangled with relations of power, institutional structures, and normative narratives, a range of bonds links everyday life in Tel Aviv and West Jerusalem with wider political realities. Here domination takes on particular qualities and sensations, producing material and emotional conditions that resonate with Zionism as an ideology and practice. While creating a sense of constancy and stability in conditions of protracted conflict, the very durability of "ordinary life" paradoxically remains dependent on the continuation of conflict. Knowledge of the depth of these ties, the strength of the prevailing narrative, and implication in the status quo then fosters political disengagement among those Jewish Israelis opposed to Israel's occupation and annexation of Palestinian territories.

Yet this is not to say that self-defined leftist women and men are passive sites for the inscription of power (McNay 1992, 12), victims of the "brainwashing" feared and described by many. Rather, this account of everyday life reveals a dialectical relationship between structure and agency, which begins to destabilize the seeming opposition between passivity and action. In this context, Michel Foucault's (1997) concept of "biopower" rings true, in the sense that "massifying" relations of power function on the level of population to maintain control. However, the actions and perceptions of politically depressed Jewish Israelis redirect attention to the role of the agential subject and social relations. Notes Timothy Mitchell (1991, 90), "The power to regulate and control is not simply a capacity stored within the state, from where it extends out into society. The apparent boundary of the state does not mark the limit of the processes of regulation. It is itself a product of those processes." The state, then, does not solely drive mass-oriented modes of power—rather, here a population normalizes and regularizes through its own design.

As subjects good and bad are hailed and subjectified by Zionist ideology, discourse, and material practices, an eye must be kept on the active role of individuals in producing and maintaining the very structures of power in which they remain embedded. As Louis Althusser (1971, 55) writes, "the individual *is interpellated as a (free) subject in order that he shall submit freely to the commandments of the Subject, i.e. in order that he shall (freely) accept his subjection,* i.e. in order that he shall make the gestures and actions of his subjection 'all by himself.'"[46] In Althusser's work on ideology, free subjects continue to exercise choice, as "good" subjects regulate themselves while "bad" subjects incur the weight of the repressive state apparatus—one chooses a subject position.[47] Thus, the individual retains the capacity to act. She may be constituted and constrained by power, but she remains agential. Indeed, as Judith Butler (1995, cited in Davies 2006, 426) asserts, "To claim that the subject is constituted is not to claim that it is determined; on the contrary, the constituted character of the subject is the very precondition of its agency."

Then the prevailing sense of despair, disillusionment, shame, and guilt among Jewish Israelis cannot be understood solely as the product of macropolitical power; rather, these sensations also generate the very conditions in question. While cynicism and alienation differently imply a relationship of victimization on the part of the subject, this chapter has illustrated the ways in which individual women and men actively take part in constructing their relationships to politics. Here, subscribing to prevailing political narratives and emotions directly sustains domination by laying the foundation for a collective sense of melancholia (Lentin 2010), which validates hopelessness as an acceptable state of mind and being. Prompting reinvestment in a "politics of living," the ties between Zionism, gender, and social structures do not eclipse the realities of conflict, violence, and occupation, but rather distance them from knowledge and action. As powerful affective associations generate political disengagement among those Jewish Israelis who resist state practices and practices, these ties implicate even those who resist in the project of Zionism. Thus to insist on agency in the everyday of occupation is to call into question the effects of ordinary life envisioned, desired, and pursued and to begin unraveling the social bonds that promise belonging and constancy, however precarious.

TWO

Bordered Communities

AN EARLY START ON A CLEAR WEEKEND DAY. We drive north on Kvish HaHof, the coastal road, away from Tel Aviv into the warm light of morning and the promise of open space. Guy and I arrive at the parking lot at Naha'l Taninim (Crocodile Stream), a nature preserve and bird sanctuary whose trails are popular among bird watchers and families seeking fresh air and adventure. Having been told that the preserve is "near Caesaria," one of the wealthiest towns in Israel, I am surprised when in truth we enter the site via a gravel road beneath Jisr az-Zarka, an "Arab town" so impoverished that it stood in for the Gaza Strip in the filming of a recent British television serial.[1] Passing a van parked alongside the dirt path, we turn into the preserve as the security guard languidly sets out his lawn chair for the day's work. He glances quickly in our direction and does nothing to "securitize" the situation, save perhaps mentally check our car against his assumptions of who and what constitute a threat—in a shiny silver Volkswagen, we pull into the lot without question or inspection.

Minutes later we take to the trail, exchanging smiles with a Palestinian woman and her three children seated in the empty picnic area. Buoyed by the thought of new avian and human encounters, we set about finding birds and flowers in the cultivated "wilderness" before us, shuttering our ears against the soundscape of excited children arriving and emptying into the parking lot by the carload. It strikes me that tiny Naha'l Taninim exists as a presumably safe space for experiencing nature—someone has gone before us, investigated the area, built trails and infrastructure, opened the recreation site, stationed a guard, and requested payment. Unlike in the deserts, mountains, canyons, and forests of Israel-Palestine, here families and bird watchers alike can experience wilderness with the promise of security.

As Guy and I debate this point, we attempt to avoid the increasing stream of fellow recreationists, whose presence strips our surroundings of their wild façade, by bounding off into the tall grasses and short trees. On emerging from the bush we immediately meet a group identifying a *pashosh* (a diminutive graceful prinia) and arrive at the stream, where pied kingfishers dive and dance. Now alone, we continue on the path toward Jisr az-Zarka, feeling relative solitude return, as it seems that the others have turned back. Increasingly, the humanscape becomes Palestinian. We meet a man and his children fishing "for fun, no luck"; nearby we pass a woman and child, presumably the fisherman's family, grilling meat; we come upon another group seated around a picnic table, their sheep and goats grazing on the grass; yet another family picnics in the tall grasses around a bend, and the young children wave excitedly, calling "*Shalom!*" over and over. Eventually, we reach a clearing and Jisr az-Zarka stands before us, a visible and audible presence.

The call to prayer sounds from the mosque's minarets as we walk past horses, crossing the preserve's official border, where the open field stops at a berm and the manicured paths resume. Inside the preserve once more, the arches of ancient ruins loom large, their round stone forms rising against the grasses and blue sky. We stop and face only this direction. From this vantage point our view covers the ruins and Israel's ancient history, with Jewish Israeli families exploring between and amid the layers. Here visitors consider "other inhabitants" of Israel—Romans—former residents now devoid of connection to everyday life. However, current "others" are alive and embodied: Palestinians, who reside in the town behind us and fish the stream, grill meat, and graze livestock, living on the preserve's margins, should we choose to see.

Continuing toward the parking lot, we pass through a small creaky gate that is likely an entrance for the local Palestinians who populate the preserve's periphery. Beyond the gate we arrive at the security van, and to the right of the parked vehicle an impromptu Palestinian parking lot has taken shape, marked by families with women wearing *hijab* and cars of an older, less shiny caliber. There are clearly different points of access and relationships to the land we "share" on that warm March day—we pay and tour with Jewish Israeli visitors, following official guides and marked paths; they enter through secondary gates free of charge and use the land, yet remain suspect in its interior. Though cars are parked in close proximity and human encounters inevitably take pace, there is no deliberate mixing in the area of the sanctuary. Rather, Palestinians keep largely to the south, while Jewish Israelis explore the north, maintaining two very different worlds within a single small space.²

That morning in Naha'l Taninim, the divisions and unease pervading wider Israeli society became newly visible and palpable, suddenly somehow more alive in their concentration. Here, the spatial distinction between Israel's Jewish and Palestinian citizens reveals not only how macropolitics permeates everyday leisure and recreational pursuits, but also how the segregation of space and communities remains incomplete. Through narratives of separation and entanglement, this chapter considers how Jewish Israeli and Palestinian lives remain actively woven together despite the conditions of protracted conflict which seemingly divide "us" from "them" and "here" from "there." While subscribing to a principle of separation advanced by the Israeli state (Weizman 2007, 161–84; Gordon 2008, 197–222), Jewish Israeli society remains dependent on Palestinian "others" for the material production of normalcy. Here, relations of contact, attachment, and dependency reveal that the divisions of conflict are often poorly bounded—understood and experienced as real on one level, but collapsed on another.

In exploring diverse modes and sites of entanglement, this chapter challenges the claim that Jewish Israelis have become increasingly separated from Palestinians in their everyday lives. Yet at the same time, the following narratives detail how spatial and social processes produce "othering" and estrangement, as evident in the space of Naha'l Taninim.³ As communities and geography are produced and experienced as incompletely divided, apathy emerges as necessarily *active,* entailing willing disengagement from the social, political, and economic conditions that make everyday life livable.

THE SOCIAL RELATIONS OF SPACE

As the construction of borders and boundaries shapes lived experience in Israel-Palestine, micropolitics likewise impacts the production and maintenance of power across economic, social, political, and spatial scales. Attending to the relationship between geography and society in Israel-Palestine, scholars such as Juval Portugali (1993), Oren Yiftachel (2006), and Eyal Weizman (2007) reveal how the prevailing "principle of separation" (Gordon 2008) relies on continuing socio-spatial entanglement. Collectively, this critical scholarship draws attention to the varying ways in which spatial division—as manifest in political, social, juridical, and material boundaries—effectively obscures and facilitates expansionist colonial logics. Yet while technologies of control may be evident or obvious in their appearance as physical borders and political policies, the resulting geographies additionally sustain conflict through more subtle means.

In work on topographic space in the context of Israel-Palestine, Portugali identifies "implicate relations" as the explicitly social means through which space is produced as divided, yet at the same time remains entangled. Following David Bohm (1980, cited in Portugali 1993, 57), Portugali posits that the "explicate" realm of separate things—those "entities and parts, independent of, and external to, each other"—exists through the "unfolding" of the "implicate" order, where "everything is enfolded into everything." As Portugali writes:

> Implicate relations as a conceptual notion implies that space and society are indeed independent entities, but only within the limits of the explicate domain. At a subtler level they enfold each other, exist inside each other, and in this respect coexist in implicate relations. From this point of view space is not a passive entity, but an active actor in the theatre of social reality. (xiii)

This active dimension of space is made possible through its very embeddedness in society—as divisions unfold and totality enfolds among social actors, neither process is fixed, nor finished.

This emphasis on process and relation overlaps with critical scholarship by Doreen Massey (1994), a feminist geographer whose work emphasizes the role of gender in the sociality of space. While Portugali (1993, 57) asserts that unfolding or distinction at the explicate level occurs through the articulation of hierarchically arranged "generative social orders"—or "code(s) according to which people socio-spatially order their lives"—Massey clarifies their contours and contents. For Massey, space is infused with and shaped by specifically gendered and classed relations of power, while at the same time producing these very social hierarchies. In her work in the UK context, Massey offers a critical intervention in prevailing conceptualizations that separate space from time, valuate time more highly than space, and strip space of political potential. Like Portugali, Massey (1994, 2) draws the social and spatial together, conceptualizing space as social relations "stretched out." According to Massey, the relationship between social relations and space is not unidirectional or linear, wherein social relations produce or constitute space; rather, she points to the ways in which space "is integral to the production of the social, and not merely its result" (4). Importantly, Massey locates both politics and gender within this fluid, multidimensional space. Here, Massey considers how a series of dualisms in classical thought have fused the realm of time with politics and action—through ideas of History (with a capital H) and "progress"—leaving space behind as a realm of stasis, absence, and passivity (6). Subsequently, space has been coded as feminine, and time as masculine, in hegemonic Western thought. Yet despite the depth and durability of these exclusive dualisms, Massey contends that "if spatial organization makes a difference to how society works and how it changes, then, far from being the realm of stasis, space and the spatial are also implicated . . . in the production of history—and thus, potentially, in politics" (254).

Through Portugali's foundational work in Israel-Palestine and Massey's ground-breaking gender analysis, space emerges as a product of social relations—a site of action, process, and power. Yet at the same time, space continues to shape society in highly normative ways; as Massey (1994, 179) argues in relation to gender, "From the symbolic meaning of spaces/places and the clearly gendered messages which they transmit . . . spaces and places are not only themselves gendered but, in their being so, they reflect and affect the ways in which gender is constructed and understood." Enfolding and unfolding, blurring and dividing, as space emerges and operates through seemingly contradictory dynamics it gives texture and substance to experiences of everyday life, becoming central to conflict and domination in Israel-Palestine.

DEGREES OF SEPARATION

At the level of the explicate domain—or the "realm of separate things" (Portugali 1993, 57)—various mechanisms of distinction arise from and circulate within Jewish Israeli society, concealing deeper relations of contact and exchange. Here, gender emerges as central to the processes and practices of mapping, "telling," racialization, and moral coding that ostensibly divide "us" from "them," constructing a reality in which "an average Jewish Israeli can live an entire life without personally knowing, let alone befriending, a single Palestinian citizen of the same country" (Mendel 2009, 29).

Mapping

As Portugali (1993, 156) details, in order to make sense of the environments in which ordinary life unfolds, individuals create "cognitive maps" that facilitate interaction among particular constellations of community. Mutually inscribing the social and spatial, in Tel Aviv and West Jerusalem these maps take shape through gendered and racialized valuations of safety, revealing specific terms of exclusion and belonging.

Sitting at a popular cafe in Jerusalem's Machane Yehuda market, twenty-five-year-old Meirav recounted her experience of the city's spatial "zones" or internal boundaries, describing the seams along which its topography and social fabric become enfolded and unfolded. A blogger and online activist who created a popular campaign against street harassment, Meirav understands and navigates her adopted city according to a sense of security:

> Personally, there are three neighborhoods that I feel safe on a good day to walk in. For the average Palestinian man there are five....
>
> You feel the neighborhood boundaries when you crash into them—I can't walk on the East side alone. People know who is Palestinian or Jewish, it's more than history. Palestinian guys stare at your eyes directly and Mizrahi Israelis won't. I feel more threatened by the Palestinian guys. Someone from the university, an activist, came to the AIC [Alternative Information Centre][4] cafe in the east of the city. This guy suggested that two girls walk to the cafe in the east! I didn't go. He probably thinks I'm racist, but he doesn't realize. I used to live in French Hill for three years—I've been called "Jewish whore" enough. I was stalked, the group made my life hell. But I can't tell, because what would people say? Even the police.... The police won't help French Hill students and also on the lines between. They won't help on the borderline. So the liberal leftist male activist won't believe me, the police I can't tell—I was forced into silence because it's not okay to say what Arabs do to me.

For Meirav, encountering Palestinians in the space of annexed East Jerusalem activates experiences and memories of gendered and sexualized subjectivity, which now inform her understanding of the cityscape. Having lived on the "borderline" in the French Hill (Giv'at Shapira) neighborhood, technically built over the Green Line in occupied territory, Meirav's subjection to gendered harassment as a student shapes her appraisal of personal safety, clearly illustrating the reciprocity between space and social relations. Significantly, Meirav's feeling of precarity is distinctly racialized, as she relates feeling "more threatened by the Palestinian guys" as an Ashkenazi Jewish Israeli woman. Yet this felt insecurity emerges as the product of multiple social relations as she expresses subsequent feelings of abandonment, misunderstood by the Jewish Israeli leftists with whom she shares common politics and the police charged with her physical protection. Together, these patterns and dynamics intersect within the shared space of the city to compound Meirav's sense of vulnerability, producing a specifically gendered mode of insecurity. Later in our exchange, Meirav recounted a recent initiative on the Mount Scopus campus that explicitly spatialized these experiences of social relations:

> The campus safety discussion is zero in Israel. I was angry about campus safety at French Hill and the college suggested that Im Tirtzu[5] was organizing to escort women back to their rooms. That's how bad it was. I wasn't frightened enough to ask them for help, but I was close. Campus safety is known all over the world, but not in Israel. There was a "[prevention of] violence against women day" and the Left shut our mouths when we tried to do the most vanilla activist thing: we wanted to draw a map with areas that women shouldn't walk in. In the organization we're all left if not radical left—we won't draw something racist, just what to expect [in the neighborhoods]. There are different types of harassment in different places. But the Left on campus shut our mouth about it because they were afraid that it might hurt the Palestinians on campus—they weren't worried about [offending] the religious [students]. It was just a photocopied map![6]

This second narrative is immediately notable for the extent to which the extreme political Right presents itself as the protector of women while the Left sits paralyzed by propriety, resulting in the preservation of insecurity and existing social relations. The proposed physical manifestation of cognitive maps catalyzes and clarifies seemingly latent tensions between race, gender, politics, and security. While declaring herself and her colleagues "not racist," Meirav alludes to how these maps align with the city's many racialized zones as they purport to ensure (Jewish Israeli) women's safety—"Palestinians on campus" are the group ostensibly protected by leftists at the cost of female students' security. In a move to perhaps illustrate her own sensitivity to prejudice, Meirav notes the absence of concern among leftists vis-à-vis the impact of the safety map on the university's religious students; in this instance "political correctness" highlights further lines of division predicated on social relations. However, for Meirav, the young women targeted by street harassment ultimately remain vulnerable without safety maps to guide them through the city, entrenching the prevailing gender norms that deem women in need of protection. Mapped plainly here, the sociality of space indeed affects experiences and understandings of gender.

Yet those men deemed "threatening" in Meirav's account also experience the gendered construction of city spaces, though differently so. For many

Palestinian men who traverse the same Jerusalem streets, the spatialized entanglement of gender, race, and fear also yields experiences of vulnerability rather than a sense of power (Smith 2011). However, Jerusalem offers a surprising degree of security for Yoni, a twenty-eight-year-old Mizrahi gay activist, despite the frequency with which he is mistakenly identified as Palestinian:

> My Ashkenazi friends have been harassed or beaten, but I'm a big, Sephardic[7] man. When I go down the street I feel very safe. These Ashkenazi friends are white, a bit scrawny . . . it goes through the whole macho, manly thing. . . . I have an advantage that way—if you're a dark man and big, you feel safe in the city.
>
> KN: But what about when they check your ID?
>
> Yoni: I feel safe then because I know it will be okay. The inspection operates through the idea that the person blowing up is an Arab—and he looks like me. I understand the holistic experience of going through it all the time. When they realize I'm a Jew it's all right, but for Palestinians there's more.[8]

Safety in Jerusalem appears a forgone conclusion for Yoni, even as his appearance identifies him as "threatening" and "other" to Meirav's white female body and clear Jewish Israeliness. Paradoxically, Yoni's very security rests in his physiognomy, as physical size and racialized perceptions of violence converge to insulate him from the homophobic attacks experienced by friends. Though Yoni lacks the social capital of whiteness and heterosexuality, his physique and attitude correspond to the values produced and prized through military-masculine hegemony among Jewish Israelis (Lentin 2000), here labeled as "the macho manly thing." While appraised against and within safety maps as dangerous, Yoni's brown male Arab body ensures his security when paired with the performance of hegemonic masculinity, as on inspection he provides proof of national belonging. Here social relations again clearly shape space in explicitly gendered terms, while at the same experiences and understandings of space reflect back on gender (Massey 1994, 179), entrenching the dominance of militarized masculinity.

Through these two accounts, explicate and implicate domains unfold and enfold through social relations embedded in space, place, and time. While illustrating the drive for separation, Meirav's narrative makes visible the ways in which individuals and communities necessarily come into contact despite neighborhood boundaries. So too Yoni's account highlights degrees of simultaneous enmeshment and distinction, this time locating encounter within the subjectivity of one person, a self-identified "Arab-Jew" often outwardly (mis)recognized as Palestinian. Here, space is understood in terms of (in)security, juxtaposing gendered and racialized understandings of safety within a shared cityscape. Seemingly left vulnerable is the (white) Jewish Israeli woman; left intact is the hyper-masculinized (ostensibly heterosexual) Jewish Israeli man.

Yet, as Meirav and Yoni attest to the construction of "us" and "them" through valuations of safety and danger, their accounts also shed light on how gendered experiences and understandings of social space simultaneously divide and entangle "here" and "there." Meirav's narrative underlines the existence of a "borderline" between Israel and Palestine, where (Jewish) inhabitants seemingly lie beyond the reach of police and social protection. Carried into later life, these experiences of liminality and vulnerability as a female student inform her reading of bodies in space, now moved from the top of French Hill to the valley of Jerusalem proper. The borderline folds into the city from above, demarcating neighborhood boundaries which one "crashes into" as eyes meet—for Meirav, the safety and belonging of (Jewish Israeli) "here" is felt viscerally as separate from the danger and otherness of (Palestinian) "there," even while remaining in close contact. With belonging and otherness read together on Yoni's male Mizrahi body as he moves through this shared cityscape, racialized experiences of inspection indeed serve to reify spaces as separate; at the same time, however, the frequency of requests for identification indicates continuing proximity. As the process of inspection confirms Yoni as "one of us," he is able to move safely through the securitized space of "here" in his embodiment of hegemonic masculinity even as he expresses non-normative sexuality—a privilege not shared by friends whose bodies fail to convey this mode of belonging. Common to both Meirav and Yoni's narratives, then, is the maintenance of stasis, as the negotiation of gendered space differentially affirms categories of "us" as separate from "them" and "here" as divided from "there," in keeping with relations of conflict and domination.

Telling

As the separation of "us" from "them" and "here" from "there" emerges through spatialized narratives of safety, distinction clearly remains incomplete. Due to the persistence of entanglement and proximity, individuals and communities adopt further strategies of identification on smaller scales, assessing social and national belonging in moments of interpersonal encounter. Meirav highlights these mechanisms above, when she claims that Mizrahi men act qualitatively differently from Palestinian men in the shared streets and alleyways of Jerusalem—here eye contact becomes the telling sign of threat. In the interest of preserving individual security and maintaining community cohesion, gendered bodies are read and decoded for sameness and "strangeness" within space (Yuval-Davis 1997, 47–48; Ahmed 2000, 7–9, 21–37; Lentin 2000, 182–83); at the same time, the "self" requires the continued presence of the "other." Through routine encounter and practices of identification, separation is again problematized by entanglement. As Sara Ahmed (2000, 7) writes: "Identity itself is constituted in the 'more than one' of the encounter: the designation of an 'I' or 'we' requires and encounter with other. These others cannot be simply relegated to the outside: given that the subject comes into existence as an entity only through encounters with others, then the subject's existence cannot be separated from the others who are encountered."

Admittedly, these dynamics and mechanisms are not unique to Israel-Palestine, nor are they solely characteristic of Jewish Israeli society. In his study of the relationship between bodies and violence in Northern Ireland, Allen Feldman (1991) explores a practice of corporeal identification first theorized by Frank Burton (1979) in the same context. For Feldman and Burton in their particular site of conflict, the human body is subject to "telling" or "the sensory identification of the ethnic Other through the reception of the body as an ideological text" (Feldman 1991, 56). Yet, rather than exclusively serving to identify and compartmentalize the "other," acts of decoding actually encode the self, as belonging and cohesion arise through and against the presence of "strange" bodies in a manner similar to Ahmed's claim above. Reminiscent of the ways in which social relations take shape in space (Portugali 1993; Massey 1994), here physical bodies are read within place, with particular attention paid to matches and mismatches. As Feldman (1991, 58) writes of Northern Ireland, "The proper reading of the various signs of embodiment, including dress, insignia, and speech, creates a circuit that indicates the residential affiliation of the subject and thus his precise relationship or nonrelationship to the social space in which the subject is encountered." In this circuit, bodies are either "in place" or "out of place," with potentially violent encounters resulting from the somatic and symbolic reading of (non)belonging.

Within the incompletely segregated spaces of Israel-Palestine, "telling" becomes a practice indeed often explicitly bound with violence, as related by

Yoni in his narrative above: "The inspection operates through the idea that the person blowing up is an Arab—and he looks like me." Here, clothing, posture, and language are read alongside gender and race within highly charged spaces, and readings of belonging and strangeness carry palpable implications. Yet telling also orders and regulates the everyday, irrespective of bodily threat and harm, generating boundaries of geographic space and the moral codes of communities therein. Through the assessment of gendered and racialized human bodies in topographic space, "Palestinians" emerge as separate from "Israeli Arabs," religious Jews are detached from their secular counterparts, and *Yerushalmim* (Jerusalemites) are judged against *Tel Avivim* (Tel Avivians). However, on the broadest political level, in the context of Israel-Palestine, telling attempts to differentiate categories of "us" from "them," or "Jewish Israelis" from their many "others." In the Jerusalem suburb of Mevasseret Zion, Ronit, a fifty-seven-year-old Ashkenazi academic, made clear the difficulties and tensions that accompany these practices of telling in her everyday life:

> I can't tell the difference between an Arab and a Jew from Morocco. My hairdresser is Arab—he has fifteen kids and six brothers who are all working together. They are very nice! Every day they go to work. They pass the checkpoint and come to work—their shop is completely full with Jewish women and Arab women. I go every two months to dye my hair.... I always take my work with me, some readings, but I don't work because I like to watch people. On the promenade, in the coffee shop, I watch people—I like to figure out the relationships between them. When I sit there are many Arab women who come to the shop, but they are very modern. Eighty percent of them I can't say they are Arab, I can't distinguish. It's only when they start talking and I hear the accent that I know. I don't want to think like this![9]

In the gendered homosocial space of her (Palestinian) hairdresser, Ronit is unable to distinguish national belonging based on the "modern" bodies of the women entering the shop. These women presumably share her relative social class—just as they share Israeli citizenship—and appear recognizably Jewish in phenotype, dress, and comportment; here language and accent ultimately become the markers of strangeness in what appears to be a shared secularized semi-private space. Telling produces a broad category of "Arabs," which encompasses both Palestinian citizens of Israel and Palestinian subjects living in the occupied territories, flattening internal distinctions to create a sense of looming threat. While concluding with a declared desire to cease in the practice of telling, during our exchange Ronit prefaced her account of the beauty shop with the statement "They [Arabs] are everywhere!" and followed with the admission, "I don't pity them—we all have hatred." Though seemingly contradictory, this cluster of sentiments possesses internal logic for Ronit as fear drives her to identify strangeness and threat in the bodies and language of the women around her. As she decodes her fellow citizen-customers in the space of the salon, Ronit determines the meaning of their skin color—Arab or Jewish—against their modern, secular dress, with curiosity disguising anxiety.

This ambiguity is key to the work done by telling, as through repetition identities and communities of commonality are continually reaffirmed. As Ahmed (2000, 7) writes, "In daily meetings with others, subjects are perpetually reconstituted: the work of identity formation is never over, but can be understood as the sliding across of subjects in their meetings with others." Thus, just as "we" depend on the presence of "them," clarity requires a degree of murkiness and telling necessitates moments of misidentification. While Ronit's narrative above makes clear the prevalence of ambiguity, my own experience of learning to "tell" is additionally instructive. Admittedly, the account that follows is laced with problematic assumptions about Arabs and Palestinians, demonstrating how over time I too absorbed stereotypical notions and their othering language of description, even as a researcher and scholar.

In early May 2011, I began the West Jerusalem interview sessions and shifted from the familiarity of Tel Aviv to the unknown of Israel's capital city. As night fell, I sat on a bus, traveling from the Jerusalem central bus station to Tel Aviv, exhausted and ready to be home. At the highway bus stop just east of Abu Gosh, a Palestinian town near Jerusalem, our vehicle began to slow and pulled to a halt. As was customary on this route, the driver opened the doors and allowed two passengers to board the bus, both young men, who sat down in empty seats, and we entered the main road, resuming our travel. While I had been nearly asleep when we stopped to collect the passengers, now I was wide awake. One young man, no older than his early twenties, had chosen the seat in front of me, and he was searching through his pockets as he settled in for the ride in the darkened bus. I had not scrutinized this man as he boarded the bus, but now my heart raced, my eyes widened, and my palms began to sweat—what was he looking for? I made a snap judgment on seeing the back of his head, recognizing his darker skin and hair as ethnically and racially "other" to the majority of passengers on the bus; that he boarded near Abu Gosh increased the likelihood that he was

Palestinian. Had he been dressed in the dull greens of an IDF uniform, I would have quickly judged him Mizrahi, but this young man wore a thin grey coat and fashionable jeans, common attire for Palestinian men of his age. I studied him as best I could from behind, attempting to determine whether he was Jewish Israeli or Palestinian, as he extracted a smartphone from his pocket and began listening to music.

Feeling guilty, I berated myself for the extent to which I had absorbed prevailing fears, along with the techniques of their reproduction. Gradually calmed by the seeming misplacement of my suspicion, I settled back in my seat. "Anyhow, if he was going to blow up the bus, he would have done it by now," I told myself. The location of his aged, gendered, and racialized body within distinctly layered space both frightened and reassured me—a young Palestinian man on a bus became less threatening as that vehicle passed locales imagined to be strategically or symbolically significant.

I had sunk slowly into something close to sleep when suddenly the young man in front of me stood up. Instantly my heart began pounding. Had I been right in my earlier suspicion? What was he doing? Looking only at the floor, the young man removed his coat and sat down, more comfortable now wearing a T-shirt in the warmth of the bus. In that moment of racing pulse, I realized that *how I experience the occupation*—a question I posed to interview participants—was in part through guessing ethnicity, learning to care about national belonging and religious affiliation, starting to fear otherness and ambiguity, and reading "political transcription[s] of the human body" (Feldman 1991, 57). In Tel Aviv, we disembarked at the Arlozorov bus station and I descended the steps behind the "suspicious" young man as he dialed a friend—and spoke in perfect Hebrew, far better than my own, walking into the night seemingly sure of the city and his belonging within it.[10]

Blackness and Racialization

As clearly illustrated above in the accounts of mapping and telling, race is central to the identification of "others" or "strangeness" in relation to and within the Jewish Israeli community. Complicating Oren Yiftachel's claim that ethnicity structures rights and governance in Israel-Palestine, David Theo Goldberg (2008, 42) argues, "Palestinians are treated not *as if* a racial group, not simply *in the manner* of a racial group, but *as* a despised and demonic racial group."[11] In developing and substantiating this argument, Goldberg makes visible how prevailing theories predicated on ethnicity and nationality offer explanatory frameworks which elide the status of Palestinians as a "subjugated race" vis-à-vis Jewish Israelis (43). From "Palestinianizing the racial" to "racializing the Palestinian," Goldberg convincingly argues that race, rather than ethnicity, underwrites the production and maintenance of power in Israel-Palestine. As in my bus ride to Tel Aviv, gender directly informs these racialized practices of differentiation: "The figure of the Palestinian, of the threatening suicide bomber, of a refugee rabble reducible to rubble, is overwhelmingly male, supported by women considered, unlike their military-serving Israeli counterparts, too weak and too late to do anything about it" (31). As seen in the above narratives, it is the color of skin—the ostensibly phenotypical *race*—that sets processes of mapping and telling into motion.[12] Here, categories of Mizrahi, Palestinian, and indeed "Israeli Arab" collapse into each other, leaving "tellers" to grasp at further readable signs and symbols of belonging.

Again, Yoni's experiences as a self-defined "Arab Jew"[13] shed important light on these tensions and complexities, this time with respect to active processes of racialization:

> KN: So I'm curious about something. As someone who identifies as an Arab Jew, do you get stopped or mistaken for a Palestinian ever?
>
> Yoni: All the time. I'm stopped all the time for my ID, all the time. At the Central Bus Station in Tel Aviv they stop me and I've finally asked them to stop it, but I understand why they're doing this. And it's one one-thousandth of what . . . [Palestinians experience]. During the time when I was a soldier, on leave I'd wear my uniform really sloppy and of course that looks suspicious, an Arab dressed this way, so they'd stop me. Once in Tel Aviv two guys jumped me, they said, *"Ma hamatsav, ahi? Ma shlomcha?"* [What's up, brother? How are you?] *"Ahi"* [brother]—but they said it harshly—they didn't want to know how I was, they wanted to hear my accent to see if I was Arab. Sometimes I'm tempted to do the accent—but it's not worth sitting fifteen hours in jail. . . . One time at the Rishon LeZion train station there were two guards—one was really hot so I was checking him out. But it looked to them like something else; they were afraid that I would blow up! How do I explain this to them? "It's not what you think! I'm not going to explode *that* way, but maybe another way!" What would they rather?

Here Yoni recounts the experience of telling from the position of one "told," highlighting his relative privilege while conveying the sensations that accompany being read as Palestinian. For Yoni, racial and national (mis)identification are read through his gendered male body, a suspicious form presumed to be heterosexual in its threat to Jewish Israeli lives. As we spoke in his Jerusalem apartment, Yoni continued to reflect on perceptions of his racial identity. "If I sit on a bus of Palestinians here, you can't tell, and I *like* this. This is who I am. At the university, everyone is white—or maybe I should say that I'm one of the only 'colored' people there. And I can feel this. People say to me, 'But Yoni, you're just dark,' as if this means I'm not Arab."[14]

Drawing distinctions between "darkness" and "Arabness," Yoni's (white) university colleagues make clear how popular conceptions of race underwrite valuations of threat and belonging, as his specifically colored male body undergoes differentiation. At his university, Yoni founded an organization of Mizrahi Jews that openly uses the term "Arab Jew" rather than ostensibly less political labels. While those who know him more intimately assure him of his Jewish "darkness" rather than Palestinian "Arabness," Yoni actually embraces the latter label, understanding precisely the work done by his Palestinianized "blackness" and exploring how it might offer an alternative space of belonging or site of resistance.

Similarly to mapping and telling, racialisation and qualities of blackness serve not only to divide the broader categories of "us" from "them" but also to distinguish degrees of inclusion within the Jewish Israeli community. As Ronit Lentin (2000) demonstrates through her gendered analysis of Israeli society and the Holocaust, or *Shoah*,[15] stigma operates within a given society "as a way of categorizing and socially grading individuals and groups.... Society establishes the means of categorizing, and grading is measured by ideal standards completely beyond attainment for almost every member of society" (Goffman 1968, cited in Lentin 2000, 170–80). Importantly, Lentin argues that "stigmas ... tell normals not only about their normality, but also about their own weaknesses" (181). While for Yoni, Jewish "darkness" rescues him from Palestinian abjection, this lighter reading of race must be understood in conjunction with other criteria of social belonging—Yoni is young, fit, handsome, and confident, describes himself as macho when needed, completed mandatory military service, and at the time of our interview was soon to begin master's-level studies in Paris. In this, Yoni may indeed be marked as "normal." Even Yoni's non-normative sexuality—potentially read as a sign of "weakness" in a context characterized by "military-masculine hegemony" (Lentin 2000, 178)—might be seen as a reason for social inclusion, as "homonationalism" increasingly binds particular gay and queer subjects to Israeli state and society.[16] Yet for other Jewish Israelis, there are far fewer opportunities for rescue from blackness and racialization.

Often referred to as "black hats" in popular (secular) Israeli discourse, Orthodox Jews face a similar contempt to the aggregate category of "Arabs" with whom they share the spaces and places of Israel-Palestine. Both communities are denounced for living off the "welfare state," contributing little labor or taxes, and "exemption" from mandatory military service (Shafir and Peled 2002, 126–27, 143–45, 324–28).[17] As *Ha'aretz* journalist Gideon Levy (2011b) wrote of the uproar regarding increasingly public practices of gender segregation among the Israeli Haredi community: "This struggle is also characterized by generalizations about Haredim, every one of whom is a parasite and an exploiter, a black and benighted community, without any shadings of color—just like the Palestinians, who are all bloodthirsty people who want only to destroy Israel. That's how it is with racism." Neta, an Ashkenazi woman in her mid-sixties living in West Jerusalem's Katamon neighborhood, relayed a similar understanding of religious "blackness" and stigmatization:

> I accept most people, religious too—I have no problem with religious people. I heard from the *kibbutz* people, "How can you live in Jerusalem? There are black people"—in Mea She'arim [an ultra-Orthodox neighbourhood], in dress, not skin color—"How do you live with them?" To me, you know, people with black clothes have different faces, different characters. I see the person first, then whether they are religious, Arab, or whatever. . . . I have a friend in Eli, she went from being on the *kibbutz* to religious to a *mitnachelet* [settler]. Her name is Danielle. We're still friends! When I worked at the television station, they were looking for more researchers so I offered my friend—she had no experience, but she was very nice and intelligent. I didn't say she was religious because it wasn't important, it had no connection to the work. My boss, also a woman, said, "OK, invite her! Where does she live?" "Eli." "What, she's from a settlement?" I said yes. "Does she dress like a settler?" "Yes—what's the problem?" My boss was open enough to meet Danielle and loved her. The dress question—they don't ask me about how *I* dress. I don't think it's a big issue. Many people look at Danielle when she comes—she said that she feels like a Negro who comes to the wrong bus. But because she's so charming, a genius with relationships, many people love her in the end. They see behind the dress.[18]

In this instance a female body is symbolically inscribed and decoded, not only marking a woman as religious but even gleaning her particular mode or degree of observance. If she is dressed in long flowing skirts and with her hair covered in a knotted scarf, vestment becomes the discernable marker of belonging, as "settler" status is read on Danielle's gendered body. A shade of black apart from those living within Jerusalem's municipal borders in

Orthodox Mea She'arim, Danielle becomes further darkened by her visible identification with the religiosity of the "ideological" settlement movement.[19] However, she rescues herself from this double blackness by charming her co-workers, though qualifying this inclusion by relating how she still "feels like a Negro who comes to the wrong bus" as she enters the workplace. While both Yoni and Neta again substantiate the significance of space and sociality to practices of telling, racialization additionally draws attention to the shifting contours of belonging. Here exclusion might be navigated and inclusion differentially extended, as Jewish Israeli society not only attempts separation from Palestinian "others" but also internally categorizes and divides itself.

"What They Do to Their Women"

As mapping, telling, and racialization actively unfold space while at the same time attesting to the enfolding of individuals and communities, these acts of differentiation also make visible the construction of moral codes believed to further separate "us" from "them." In this, specific individuals and groups become the markers of collectivity, guarding the boundaries of community. As feminist scholars have convincingly demonstrated, in addition to biologically, culturally, and even ideologically reproducing the nation, women are often ascribed this symbolic position (Yuval-Davis and Anthias 1989; Kandiyoti 1991; Yuval-Davis 1997, 23; Yuval-Davis and Stoetzler 2002, 334). Nira Yuval-Davis (1997, 46) makes this connection explicit, arguing that in their fraught position at the limits "women, in their 'proper' behavior, their 'proper' clothing, embody the line which signifies the collectivity's boundaries."[20] Yet at the same time as they become symbols of the national collective, women simultaneously embody its external "other(s)," existing both within and without the polity (Kandiyoti 1991, 433–35; Yuval-Davis 1997, 47; Yuval-Davis and Stoetzler 2002, 335). Familiar yet somehow foreign, gendered and sexualized bodies come to symbolically, discursively, and materially represent that which makes us who we are, just as they suggest who we are not.

With regard to Jewish Israeli society, particular women are positioned as boundary markers or border guards, indeed serving to identify, maintain, and reproduce "us" in accordance with existing social hierarchies. Importantly, not all women represent the collectivity equally; rather, these figures have been constructed as largely secular, Ashkenazi, middle-class, heterosexual women who represent both tradition and modernity, custom and progress. However, even as this boundary work appears largely internally focused, "their" women are also read as symbolic texts, whether through corporeal semiotics or cultural practices, differently reflecting the moral orders of both communities. As with processes of mapping, telling, and racialization, the "othered" collective may be internal or external to Jewish Israeli society, with seemingly stark lines separating categories of religious from secular and "Israeli" from "Arab." In keeping with the work of Yuval-Davis (1997, 42), though irreducible to one another, culture and religion often constitute the basis for judgments read on the bodies and comportment of "other" women. Popular perceptions of "what they do to their women" thus identify ostensibly irreconcilable cultural and moral difference, as particular gendered bodies are read as "victim" in their symbolism as markers of the community.

Significantly, the construction of morality and depravity through the bodies and treatment of women bolsters wider political arguments, particularly those regarding the protracted peace process and the impossibility of political change. Hila, a sixty-eight-year-old artist and former archivist at the Knesset[21] who lives in Jerusalem's Arnona neighborhood, collapsed perceptions of Bedouin and Palestinian women as she described the intractability of conflict:

> What if there is peace for us? Is it possible? I'm pessimistic. Two nations want the same country—there can't be peace. I think there can be if there wasn't the extreme political Right in Israel and not the Hamas extreme on the other side. Also if they [Palestinians] give their women equal rights. It's culture, it will take time for them to want to be a democratic country and give human rights to their people. The Bedouin in Israel, if a woman wants to go to visit places in Israel, they prepare her journey. In the morning the woman goes to the bus and all the men came with rifles and shoot her—they don't allow her to go on the journey! Or if a Bedouin woman wants to work, they make a place for [selling] carpets and the men burn it. Why? The women earn money, they help the family—why burn it? They don't want her to earn money, they don't want an independent woman in any way. With a mentality like that how can there be peace between us and them?

Projecting her understanding of the gendered power relations specific to Bedouin communities inside Israel onto the aggregate category of "them" (read: Palestinians, whether citizens or subjects of the Israeli state), what Hila identifies as the typical treatment of any Arab woman suffices to legitimate the status quo of conflict and political stasis.[22] Through gendered terms Hila situates the ideals of democracy, human rights, independence, and the capacity to accumulate capital opposite "their mentality," as the treatment of women comes to constitute a major political obstacle alongside claims to land and growing extremism. Later in our exchange Hila raised the issue of honor killings, linking this phenomenon to both her parents' experiences in nascent Israel and Palestinian statelessness:

> My parents made a revolution, against their own parents they came to build a country. The Palestinians were asleep, very primitive. There wasn't a nation or country of Palestine, there were people who sat here under the Turkish and the English. Then they wake up and want to be a nation? I understand, but it was too late. The state of Israel already was. You can see until today that they work in the field with very primitive [instruments]. It will take time until they are more educated, liberal, and democratic—they still murder their daughters. So many murders. Because they think she looks at another man, because she doesn't listen to her brother or father, they kill her. For "honor." It's not honor, it's murder—it's awful to kill your daughter. When they change the mentality there will be peace. Until then, I don't think so.[23]

Raising the specter of a "mentality," Hila ascribes moralistic labels of civilized and primitive, active and passive to the parties historically present in Israel-Palestine, assessing the prevalence of justice and murder through the figures of women. Peace remains at a great distance as "we" wait for "them" to become *more like us,* while simultaneously initiating the very policies and practices that pre-empt the possibility of greater similarity. While the use of "primitive" tools in the field is often not a choice but a necessity, due to the imposition of immense social, political, and economic constraints (Roy 1995, 1999; Hever 2010, 2012), more readily invoked are the female border guards, whose seemingly rampant violent deaths limit difference to the more comfortable realms of culture and morality.

In this narrative the space populated by Palestinians, granted neither country nor nation, exists as "backward" and "primitive" in both historical and contemporary times, infused with gender relations that serve to illustrate the extent to which Israel remains distant and progressively "other." Possessing education, liberalism, democracy, and the "mentality" that ostensibly eludes Palestinians and precludes the possibility of peace, Israel as a space and Jewish Israelis in their social relations gain positive substance through *what they are not.* Again, this process of differentiation reflects not only outward but also inward, as related by Rachel, a twenty-eight-year-old secular Ashkenazi filmmaker in Tel Aviv: "In terms of women, I think of the other side and what they have to live with—they have no rights, they have to have children, their husbands treat them badly.... Really, Palestinian women and Hasidic women are in similar situations."[24] In collapsing the experiences of Palestinian and Jewish religious women, Rachel's community takes shape through two "others" marked as aberrant by the treatment of "their women," providing narrower categories of "us" and "them" while validating a sense of superior morality.

Collectively, the gendered techniques and processes of identification recounted here—mapping, telling, racialization, and "what they do to their women"—constitute a "common-sense" system of classification through which strangers are individually and collectively "othered" as they are separated in spatial and social terms. Then the reciprocal relation between space and society advanced by Massey and Portugali extends beyond the confines of a given location and the limits of its internal relations. Rather, here the overlayering of multiple spaces and social relations grants discursive shape and material substance to wider configurations of community and place. The movement and presence of Palestinian citizens of Israel, Palestinian subjects living in the West Bank, Bedouin communities, Jewish settlers, and the Orthodox religious combine to produce a very particular sense of "who we are" and "what makes us belong." Drawing on topographic space, race, culture, sexuality, and religion, gendered bodies are decoded for various degrees of belonging within the frames of conflict and domination, with women coming to signify the perceived irreconcilability of moral orders that maintain "us" against the tide of "them."

THE TANGLED WEBS WE WEAVE

Across the geographies of seemingly divided space traverse identifiably raced and gendered subjects, generating zones of safety and harm, spaces of "here" and "there," and categories of "us" and "them," as detailed above. However, separation necessarily remains incomplete as the production of space and social relations relies on the continuing presence of the ostensibly inverse or obverse; here, borders and boundaries emerge through processes of inclusion made possible by active exclusion. Then despite spatial and social divisions instated by the Israeli state and Jewish Israeli society, everyday life remains contingent on relations of contact, exchange, and dependency. Here, the meanings and material conditions of normalcy emerge explicitly through the presence of "othered" populations and territories; built neither "around" nor "in spite of" occupation, conflict, and domination, everyday life takes shape *because of* these very processes, policies, and practices. Marked by a history of permeability, the boundaries between "here" and "there" remain porous in order to sustain the conditions of normality as imagined, pursued, and constructed by Jewish Israelis. Much like the role of "strangers" as explored by Ronit Lentin (2000, 182–83) with respect to Holocaust survivors in Israel, here "a union of closeness and remoteness" defines an "inside" through its outside, "normal" through interaction with "strange." Again taking shape through experiences and understandings of gender, encounter and entanglement make Jewish Israeli everyday life possible while at the same time granting structure, texture, and content to "Israel" as if distinct from "Palestine."

According to Lorenzo Veracini (2011a, 2011b, 5–6), "non-encounter" describes the infrequent moments of contact that characterize social relations between settlers and "others" in contexts of settler colonialism. In conditions of non-encounter, instances of social or interpersonal exchange are rendered nearly nonexistent as a given settler colonial project attempts "to supersede its own systems of operation . . . to cover its own tracks, to erase" (Veracini 2011a). Disavowing both founding violence and indigenous presence (Veracini 2010, 84), colonial "contact" is imagined to occur solely between "man and land," effectively erasing the history and presence of those "others" sharing in space and residing in place (see also Wolfe 1991). As a settler colonial project proceeds apace in Israel-Palestine (Rodinson 1973; Abdo and Yuval-Davis 1995; Shafir 1999; Lentin 2000, 2008; Abu El-Haj 2001; Veracini 2011a; Pappe 2012; Wolfe 2012), the logics and practices of non-encounter at first appear to resonate—from social segregation to material walls, fences, and checkpoints, on the explicate level, contact between Jewish Israelis and Palestinians can be understood as limited at best. It is almost nonexistent with Palestinians living in occupied territories of the West Bank and Gaza Strip, and contact with even those Palestinians who live within the borders of the Israeli state is minimal for many, if not most, Jewish Israelis. Yet narratives of encounter with both populations highlight how the principle of separation (Weizman 2007; Gordon 2008) remains underwritten by particular modes of exchange, which entangle space and communities while at the same time reproducing difference.

As David Theo Goldberg (2008, 31) asserts, "Israel cannot live with the Palestinians, purging them persistently from green-line Israel, but cannot live without them, conceptually as much as materially, existentially as much as emotionally." Through building, maintaining, and feeding (Jewish) Israel, Palestinian citizens and subjects are sewn into the fabric of everyday Jewish Israeli life, producing the material conditions for normalcy, the space of Israel-Palestine, and the social relations of domination.

Who Builds Us? Raising Israel

Dating to the first formalized waves of Jewish settlement in Palestine,[25] Palestinian labor has in part realized the task of building Israel with construction trades filled by men from within and without Israel's internationally recognized borders (Shafir 1999; see also Shafir and Peled 2002, 325; Gordon 2008, 65; Hever 2012, 15, 127). In the years following the economic restructuring and violence of the 1980s and early '90s, the number of permits issued to laborers seeking entry from the occupied Palestinian Territories drastically declined, ceasing entirely for those living in the Gaza Strip (Shafir and Peled 2002, 324–28; Hever 2012, 125–26).[26] Yet construction-based narratives of encounter between Jewish Israelis and Palestinians in Israel extend from historical memories through present-day practices, as "they" cross the border from "there" to help raise "us," "here." Neta, the Jerusalemite whose settler friend illuminated dynamics of racialization among Jewish Israelis, contextualized and recounted an early experience of Palestinian labor:

> I have two memories from my childhood about Arabs—they really affected me. The first was when I was between three and five years old. The village where I lived, before '48 it was an Arab village and for some reason some of the houses were left. When the Arabs ran away the soldiers occupied [the houses], but sometimes people didn't run away or they came back. It went to the court to see which they did—if it's proven that they ran away, they lost the house. In the village one Arab family stayed forever, the court found that they didn't run. Another [family] was waiting for the court, so they lived in the middle of the village, in two or three houses, until the court decided that they had to leave because they left and returned. I was there at the time when the soldiers or police took them from the house. The women cried. On one side they took them out, and on one side the bulldozer.... I think the whole village came to see. This really affected me.
>
> The second time I was older, between eight and nine years old—it was in the '50s during *mimshal tsvai* [military government].[27] During that time the Arabs in Israel couldn't move.... Before, they could move, but they needed a permit—like now. My parents were putting more rooms in the house and there were Arabs working for us. Suddenly the police came to check if they have permission—some ran or some had permission. One of them hid in the

bathroom of our house, it wasn't being used. He was hiding and the police didn't find him, and my parents didn't tell. I remember when the police left he was shaking, he was so frightened. My parents had to explain why this old man—he wasn't old, but I was young—why he has to hide.[28]

Recalled here at length, Neta's account is significant not only for highlighting the presence of Palestinian laborers in a Jewish Israeli home during the 1950s but also for the arc from dispossession and destruction to active construction. Her narrative is suffused with tension, as the police, courts, and military appear in memory as entities that act against the interests of Palestinians and Jewish Israelis alike; yet Neta's experience additionally demonstrates the extent to which gender is integral to understanding encounter. In what was formerly a Palestinian village, Neta clearly remembers the tears of the Palestinian women as families were pulled from their homes, with bulldozers simultaneously beginning demolition. The gender of soldiers, police, and demolition crew—those deconstructing Palestinian homes and presence—can be assumed to be (Jewish Israeli) male, yet it is the (Palestinian) women and their emotionality which enters the weave of Neta's memory. She recounts a similarly feminized vulnerability in the subsequent narrative, though this time embodied by a Palestinian man in the face of near-certain persecution. He enters Neta's home with other (male) Palestinian builders, helping to raise the space of the family in a role that corresponds to gendered and racialized norms in the context of Jewish Israeli society: building is cast as a man's job, in practice now often associated with "other" race, ethnicity, and class. Importantly, Neta recalls the physicality of the builder's fear, which requires explanation to a child unaware of the power relations that could produce in a man—an older man—the need to flee and quake.

In building the spaces of Jewish Israeli families, the coupling of security concerns with the entry of male Palestinian laborers is not unique to Neta's childhood memories, nor is it specific to the era of 1950s Israel. During the same exchange, Neta recalled more recent instances in which encounter occurred through gendered and racialized relations of construction:

> One of the times we built this house some of the workers were Arab. My daughter asked me, "You aren't afraid alone with the Arab workers?" I'm not, but my daughter is. Maybe for her, if you're born into an *intifada,* the first thing you know about Arabs is something bad. I lived in the Galilee, I knew a lot of Arabs, Israeli Arabs, when I was young. It wasn't a war and I didn't think about them as enemies—so I stayed inside the house even when the Arab workers were there with me. At the time of the *intifada* people were

telling me, "Don't put them [Palestinians] in your house!" Now I think that maybe I was stupid, but I don't think that Arab people are more dangerous than others. But my daughter is scared.[29]

A capable woman, Neta has rebuilt her Jerusalem home by hand a number of times—sometimes alone, often with her husband, and occasionally relying upon outside assistance. In this second narrative, she recounts her continuing willingness to employ Palestinian builders and her ease in their presence, juxtaposing this with the palpable fear expressed by her daughter; in both cases, the laborers likely shared the family's Israeli citizenship. Though bound by close relation as mother and daughter, these women matured in different locations during specific historico-political moments, and these contexts then shape their experiences of encounter. Beneath Neta's daughter's anxiety lies a recurring theme, that of (en)gendered danger. Drawing on themes familiar from narratives of threat and protection in other colonial contexts (McClintock 1995; Stoler 2002), race and sexuality again inform the terms of encounter in Israel-Palestine.[30] Here, sexualized male Palestinians present a danger to the young (Ashkenazi) Jewish Israeli woman, as gendered bodies symbolically replace nations.

Yet in the space of a Jewish Israeli settlement near Palestinian villages, gendered, sexualized, and racialized fear becomes supplanted by "knowledge" gleaned from more frequent interaction and exchange; again encounter arises through labor practices, with the male Palestinian worker central as catalyst. Just above Abu Gosh, a Palestinian town inside Israel's 1949 Armistice Agreement borders, the village of Har Adar sits on a hilltop east of the Green Line. "It's technically over the Green Line—I guess we're 'settlers'!" forty-five-year-old Keren said laughingly during our interview at her workplace in Jerusalem. She continued, "But the fence goes around us and keeps us on the Israeli side; it cuts across the [Green] Line and encircles us." During our interview, Keren narrated this liminality as a preface to her experiences of Palestinian labor:

> In this country you're always "in" or "next to"! This isn't really freedom, you're not really "out there." You have to watch your kids all the time, even when they're watching television. I see a lot of new couples with kids living in either small apartments in the city or in a bigger place between villages. There is a lot of fear ... but also there is no fear because people need to live, they want something better—so they go [to live in the settlements].
>
> I should tell you that I know a lot of the Arab side of all this. We built our Har Adar house ourselves.... In Har Adar you sign up on a list and they

bring [Palestinian] workers from the next village with permits to work only for you—they can't be anywhere else.

Keren paused to laugh, continuing:

> By law, [Palestinian] workers aren't allowed into Israel, but they are allowed into Har Adar! You can end up being friends, like we were friends with the electrical man. If he wasn't living in Qatane I'm sure he would be an artist, he's soft and gentle. But he needs work, so he's an electrician. He has five kids, which is little for them—most of them have ten kids and more than one wife! It's so different where we live and where they live. I don't know any Arab women because only the men are allowed in [to Har Adar]. The roof guy became a friend of my husband—when my husband was in Tel Aviv he would buy materials for this guy for his other projects. One day he told my husband that he was thinking about taking another wife. What do you say to that?
>
> KN: What was your husband's reaction?
>
> Keren: Well, he's American, so his reaction was different—I can only imagine what it would have been if he was an Israeli man! But this is a conversation *at our house!* [The roofer] never calls first, he's always just stopping by and coming for coffee. It's not like when I was growing up and people would stop over—there's an "Arab" knock at the door. It's a different kind of knock. If I open the door he stays out of the house, even if my husband is home. I know that if he wants coffee I have to go upstairs or into my room, otherwise they'll have to take coffee outside. Politically it's very difficult.[31]

Related at length, Keren's account initially moves from considering her children's safety to an acknowledgement of fear, terminating with a statement of necessity and felt frustration. Strikingly, Keren proclaims familiarity with the "Arab side," as knowledge and experience are enabled by the relaxed labor codes that facilitate the construction and growth of her settlement community. Keren cites the exceptionality of Har Adar in this regard and articulates that those Palestinian workers permitted entry to the settlement from villages in the West Bank are overwhelmingly male. Yet rather than recounting gendered or sexualized physical threat, she describes feelings of political discomfort at the imposition of what she perceives to be Palestinian (read: Muslim) moral codes and gender norms on the space of her home and private life. Harkening back to "what they do to their women," Keren feels herself in an awkward position as she tries to relate to the Palestinians with whom she comes in contact, supporting her husband's friendship, while at the same time finding the prospect of multiple wives and gender segregation a personal affront. Warned by the telltale "Arab knock," Keren chooses her degree of engagement with the anxiety that accompanies the Palestinian roofer's appearance in the space of her home. Yet rather than ending on the fear, (in)security, and necessity born of labor practices and government policies, Keren's account replaces this tension with larger questions of morality and custom.

In these narratives of labor-based encounter, recurring themes center on the entrance of male Palestinian workers into the space of the Jewish Israeli family. Whether perceived as threatening to sexual, personal, and communal security or the bearers of repressive gender norms and moral codes, these Palestinian laborers from within or beyond Israel's border are nameless and largely faceless, with details related in absence. At the same time, their low-cost labor remains essential to the construction and growth of Jewish Israel, its territorial expansion, and even its claims to moral supremacy. Importantly, here families become the locus of insecurity, comprising the frames in which scenes of encounter unfold.

Who Maintains Us? Keeping Israel Tidy

In the realm of maintenance, Palestinian workers again enter the spaces of Jewish Israel in ways consistent with the perceived gender norms of both "here" and "there." Whereas Palestinian men appear at construction sites often separated from their Russian, African, Asian, and Jewish Israeli counterparts, Palestinian women laborers often clean private homes in the stead of "other" women, namely those from Eastern Europe and Asia. Yet, rather than bolstering the seeming division between "public" and "private" realms—where men maintain the former and women the latter—the range of laborers tasked with cleaning and tidying Israel frequently blurs the margins of these spatialized domains.

As recounted during interview exchanges, normative patterns of gender often prevail even within this blurring of boundaries—Palestinian men largely enter the private domain of the Jewish Israeli family via maintenance in positions as gardeners, plumbers, mechanics, and day laborers, while Palestinian women appear most often as domestic cleaners. However, in instances when male Palestinian workers arrive in intimate spheres of everyday life, security concerns rise to the fore in a manner similar to construction-based instances of encounter. Sonya, an elderly activist living near Tel Aviv in Jaffa, related how the onset of military occupation in 1967 intersected with labor practices in the family domain:

> Our farm was the last on the road before the *moshav*'s collective orange grove. The Palestinians were brought in every morning to work in the communal orange groves, and at two or four P.M. they would come back from the groves and gather on our lawn. They would wash up using our spigot for watering our lawn, they would spread out their prayer mats, pray, and eat lunch. They never left any dirt. They took everything with them and left the lawn as clean as they found it. They never made any problems. My youngest daughter would even come home from school and let herself into the house alone, and there were no problems. I had no fear. We felt that everything was all right—I really thought that the occupation was OK, it was all right.[32]

Though Sonya protests that she experienced "no fear," her sentiments clearly highlight the extent to which, as a Jewish Israeli mother of a school-age girl, she was expected to feel a sense of danger as the day laborers sat literally on the edge of the private sphere around her family home. Sonya's description of the Palestinian workers' positive qualities—clean, tidy, and well behaved—points to the unarticulated characteristics more commonly attributed to these men at the time: filth, chaos, and trouble. With their presence further regularized through good comportment, not only did the Palestinian day laborers maintain the village's orange groves at a low cost, but also their conduct granted legitimacy to early Israeli claims that the occupation was in part a *mission civilisatrice*.[33] Perched on the boundary of the family home, here the presence of Palestinian workers signals not only the degree to which labor practices normalized disparate relations of power in the years immediately following 1967, but also how an overwhelming sense of faith in the occupation and its aims potentially rendered the dangerous "other" (man) innocuous.

In the present day, laboring Palestinian women differently maintain Jewish Israel and enter deeply into the private realm of the family. As noted by Keren in her narrative above, Jewish Israeli contact with Palestinian women from the Occupied Territories is less frequent than encounters with men from the same areas. Here, gender norms collude with the policies and practices of occupation to further limit the mobility and opportunities afforded to women living in the West Bank, Gaza Strip, and East Jerusalem (Abdo 2011). Yet even as restrictions prevail, Palestinian women living within and without Israel's internationally recognized borders contribute to the informal economy through the provision of domestic labor, further normalizing relations of domination.³⁴ In the instances in which Palestinian women enter the spaces of Jewish Israeli families, encounter occurs largely between women and at times highlights perceived commonalities. Keren, whose home in Har Adar was constructed in large part through (male) Palestinian labor, additionally spoke of her house cleaner:

> I have a lady who helps to clean the house, an Arab woman, once a month. She lives inside the border in a village near Abu Gosh. Recently she was asking me "Are the *matzas*³⁵ in the stores now?" They love *matzot*! Her kids love it and she was anxious to have it. She tells me that her kids buy dresses for Purim too—her daughter loves Purim.³⁶ She said that this year she bought so many masks for them! They don't have a holiday for kids to dress up, for Muslims. It's too bad. So she waits for Purim and Pesach each year! Her family visits sometimes from Jordan—they're originally from Jordan, I think. They come to stay and tell her that she has become "too Jewish." They don't see it with a good eye that she is close to this country. She's big in body, but she has big fear. I feel that she needs it more, the money—she needs the money more than I need her help. I guess it's a contract by heart between us.³⁷

While the cleaner she employs lives within Israel's recognized borders—and so is deemed "Arab" rather than "Palestinian"³⁸—Keren's narrative situates this woman clearly in the realm of the "other," deserving of pity as she appears repressed by religion and castigated by family. Here, "what they do to their women" enters the realm of "our" women as Keren responds emotionally and materially to the perceived privation and fear of her employee, to the extent that she presents domestic labor as a particular kind of indulgence. As Keren enters into a "contract by heart" with the Palestinian cleaner in the space of her home, the encounter indeed occurs between women and appears to engender solidarity, although the relationship remains suffused by power and paternalism. Living in a Jewish Israeli settlement east of the Green Line, Keren employs a Muslim Palestinian woman from inside Israel—though for the sake of conscience the woman's family may be "originally from Jordan"—and maintains the relation of domestic labor largely in an act of sympathy. Yet the ostensibly pitiable conditions of the cleaner's life and labor in part make Keren's existence both livable and normal, pointing to a relationship between domination and social class.

The entry of Palestinian women laborers into the space of Jewish Israeli families cannot be typified as an always sympathetic encounter, however, particularly as exchanges between women are framed by relations of power beyond shared gender. On entering the home, female Palestinian domestic workers are not automatically deemed "neutral" based on biological sex; rather, national, race, and class belonging additionally inform the judgment of threat. In the instance of domestic labor, appraisals of danger and safety are not limited to physical well-being but extend into other aspects of personal and communal security. After an afternoon of shopping together outside Tel Aviv, my friend Ilana mentioned her house cleaners in passing. We had just removed our bags of goods and locked the car doors in the parking garage, running back to the vehicle to double-check the latches. As we ascended to her flat in the elevator, Ilana told me that recently quite a few cars had been stolen from the new development where her family now lived. In fact, on the previous Saturday a car was stolen from the lot, replaced by the company hours later, and then stolen again! I asked whether she knew whom the thieves might be and she replied, with eyebrows raised, "They come from Qalqilya, Taybeh—these are our neighbors." I responded that perhaps her neighborhood should hire a roving security guard if theft is such a frequent occurrence, but Ilana said that no, this would be expensive; though prized, security can be cost-prohibitive. As we unpacked our bags and boxes in the flat upstairs I asked Ilana whether she had the next day off from work, which garnered a sharp look—as she is responsible for the majority of the housework, in addition to caring for her children and working full time, her day could never be fully "off." Rather than free time, one of the items on the next day's list was the arrival of two cleaners recommended by a friend. Ilana told me that she had hired both as "two can do the work of one in half the time for the same price." With cost the same for either two laborers or one, I was puzzled as to why expediency would be a concern, given that Ilana would presumably leave the house during the cleaning. However, Ilana relayed that she felt compelled to stay with the women as they worked, claiming, "You can't trust anyone." I then inquired as to where the cleaners were from, and Ilana replied, "Tira or Taybeh—I can't remember which."[39] By virtue of their residence in towns on the border between Israel and the West Bank, the domestic workers cleaning Ilana's house share the frame of insecurity with the thieves who prey on cars in the parking lot below. As Ilana explicitly calculates the value of her time against that of the items potentially stolen in her absence, security here relates to the sanctity of home and the objects within. Similar to the entry of male Palestinian workers into the home through construction trades, this encounter is one of seeming necessity coupled with vulnerability, now a question of material property rather than physical or sexual threat—gender is indeed no guarantee of solidarity.

Thus, various practices of maintenance sew Palestinian women and men into the fabric of Jewish Israeli everyday life, as cleaners and gardeners from inside, beyond, or on the border with Israel gain entry into the intimate realms of family and domesticity. Through the entanglement of gender roles and norms with racialized and classed relations of power, cheap Palestinian domestic labor consistently enters into Jewish Israeli homes, maintaining the material conditions of normalcy. Yet clearly this normality retains aspects of insecurity, reflecting the wider political realities in which experiences and understandings of encounter remain embedded. As with building and construction, gender, race, and class structure modes of contact through maintenance, determining entry to space and shaping the conduct of relations therein. While at times opening sites of imagined solidarity, as shared space may indeed positively impact social relations, these ostensibly neutral exchanges largely entrench the sense of threat fostered by prevailing popular and political discourses. Whether resting on the margins of an orange grove in historical memory or entering deeply into the private realm in the present day, the presence of Palestinian men and women then reproduces not only the material conditions of everyday life in its ideal form—bountiful harvests and clean homes—but also the normative precarity central to Jewish Israeli society.

Who Feeds Us? Nourishing Israel

Through construction and maintenance, experiences of exchange and understandings of contact clearly blur the constructed division between public and private spheres, entangling Jewish Israelis with Palestinians. So too narratives of nourishment and sustenance span this porous boundary, as the explicate realm again takes shape through implicate relations. Here the reciprocity between space and social relations not only shapes patterns of gender but also gives rise to dynamics of resistance and complicity, building on the tense dynamics of imagined solidarity recounted above.

As with maintenance and construction, the family remains central to narratives of nourishment, whether within the space of homes or outside the domestic realm. In Jewish Israeli society, desires for nourishment and experiences of sustenance are informed by the weight of both intimacy and security, invoking the narratives of survival and the politics of living so central to Zionism. Ronit Lentin (2000, 17) retrospectively observes this dynamic in childhood experiences with her own grandmother, who narrowly escaped

Europe during the Holocaust or *Shoah*, noting "the compulsive attitudes to food, feeding us too much, worrying when we did not eat enough." As nourishment thus becomes entangled with security, this time in the form of full bellies, food practices differently reproduce the precarity at the core of Jewish Israeli society. Speaking once more of her position atop the hill in Har Adar outside Jerusalem, Keren conveyed this intimate relation through the figure of her daughter.

> KN: How do your children react to the conflict? To living so close to the fence?
>
> Keren: Well, each kid reacts differently. My daughter is really into fantasy—it's a kind of running away. I was like this too, growing up. "We live here now, but not forever"—maybe it's a Holocaust thing or a Jewish soul. I always thought I would live somewhere else, in a better place. But I've travelled around and now I think there isn't a better place. I try to tell her that, but.... For her *bat mitzvah* we're taking her to Ireland. She said that she wants to go to the land where all her dream writers write ... she wants to fly away. Har Adar is like that, it's an in-between place, especially for her. It's like being on the border of the sea, but you can't go there. We look over the fence and I *know* there are great *hummus* places there, I just know it! But we can't go.[40]

This passage is notable for Keren's admission of her daughter's dream of escape, along with the extension of that desire to wider society—not only are national narratives shaped by historical experiences of the Holocaust, so too are collective emotions and imaginaries. The account is brought "down to earth" or "back to reality" by recognition that escape can only ever be ephemeral, as tomorrow's trip to Ireland remains embedded in the political reality that separates "here" from "there" and explicitly divides "us" from desired nourishment. In her account, Keren clearly relays familiarity with the cuisine attributed to her Palestinian neighbors, desiring the quality and authenticity of their *hummus* through an Orientalist gaze, certain of its presence "there" beyond the fence. Although her stated desire is to consume—craving *hummus,* the object of consumption—encounter is implied by the wish to "go," even if absent or denied. Speaking in the "we" of family, this nourishment just beyond reach comes to stand for security on two levels: a political promise denied and a state of being pursued. Were Israel-Palestine "safe" *we could go there,* a Jewish Israeli woman and her daughter; in the meantime, *we remain here,* safe behind the fence.

Yet at the same time as desires for nourishment entrench the primacy of security, so too modes of encounter might generate resistance, structuring space and social relations in unanticipated ways. Through a narrative which again invokes "their food, there," Ron, a thirty-six-year-old musician and journalist from Tel Aviv, associates contact with Palestinians with his own position as an "outsider" among Jewish Israelis. Often picking up odd jobs to support his artistic pursuits, Ron related how actualized encounters produce resistance:

> For a while I was working in Roche Ha'Ayn—actually it was Kfar Qasem [a Palestinian town in Israel]—in the orange industry. It's on the land of Kfar Qasem, but the area belongs to Roche Ha'Ayn, which is a Jewish town. The area in Roche Ha'Ayn looks like a shopping mall, it's very Israeli. It's amazing—it's on the Green Line, but it's like a cliff. On the other side is the Occupied Territories.... It's like being in Ariel [a Jewish Israeli settlement in the West Bank] looking out. But there isn't any cliff, that's the point. The Israeli side looks like a mall, but the industrial area of Kfar Qasem is all garages, it's very poor. There are *hummus* places in Kfar Qasem, so I would eat there at lunch—it's literally just down the road. It was such a difference going from this mall, corporate environment to the *hummus* place! It was very interesting, very exciting.
>
> KN: How did the people you work with react to you going for *hummus* down the road?
>
> Ron: People already thought I was a weirdo, so.... This was during the Lebanon operation [in 2006] and for some stupid reason I got involved in talking about it with someone at work. It was totally useless. The guy almost hit me! There were young people who would come to work with us and they'd work for a day, a couple of weeks, and leave. There was one guy, Amir, who was really quiet. He was sitting near the computer with his head down, not showing his face. One day I said hello to him and I realized that he was an Arab. So this violent guy said, in the room, standing next to this guy, that he hates Arabs. I tried to.... The guy was trying to piss me off.[41]

Recalling Keren's imagery of a fence that forcibly instates social division, Ron relays the construction of a metaphorical "cliff" dividing Jewish Israel from Palestine, this time through scenes of industrial materiality. Positioning his body as catalyst, Ron actualizes encounter through his pursuit and consumption of *hummus*, creating moments of contact that prompt exchange; notably, as opposed to Keren's ostensible passivity and longing, Ron acts. In this, like Keren, Ron performs his normative gender role, resisting one set of power relations while at the same time reaffirming another, based on the registers of action available to him. Yet in keeping with the complexity of gender norms and constructs in Jewish Israeli society, Ron's actions fail to fit the parameters of hegemonic masculinity. Labeling himself "already a weirdo," Ron's border crossing "just down the road" is framed by his apparent strangeness vis-à-vis the Jewish Israeli men with whom he works. Ron belongs to "us"—Jewish Israeli society, national identity, and space—but remains a kind of "other" within, even as an altercation with a macho Jewish Israeli co-worker allows him to perform protective and aggressive masculinity. However, despite the resistance implied and performed in his pursuit of nourishment and exchange, in some ways Ron's actions are trapped within the structures of normativity. Here political encounter appears as the domain of conflict and men; Kfar Qasem remains located "there," beyond a cliff, "poor" and "other"; and an act of protection—this time on behalf of Amir—catalyzes Ron's performance of masculinity.

In the narratives recounted above, nourishment yields encounters typically removed from intimate personal contact, more remote than the accounts of builders, cleaners, gardeners, and plumbers who enter into Jewish Israeli homes. Within Israel's borders, food-based contact occurs most visibly in city streets and restaurants, where Palestinian labor makes possible a thriving Jewish Israeli culinary culture associated in part with Arab cuisine assimilated into the category of "Israeli food."[42] Though *hummus, falafel,* and chopped salad remain prime sites of (national) contest (Stein 2008, 97–127; Kamin 2013; see also Dean 2013), Palestinian men continue to staff Jewish Israeli kitchens in Tel Aviv and West Jerusalem, whether in pizza parlors or establishments known for "Arab" cuisine. While the fusion of cultural practices and products might be seen as a potential road to "peace" (BBC 2011), food-based labor, exchange, and encounter remain embedded in the relations of power and privilege that shape Israel-Palestine. Gender again emerges as a central element of structure: while those laboring in the kitchens of the Jewish Israeli public realm are largely Palestinian men, presumably Israeli citizens or with security clearance, within private domestic space Jewish Israeli women often reproduce this fare and craft.

In private practices and spaces, the reproduction of Palestinian cuisine may become a mode of opposition, an expression of desire, and a performance of precarity, simultaneously resisting, reflecting, and shaping prevailing narratives and relations. On May 10, 2011, Jewish Israelis marked Independence Day (Yom HaAtzmaut), as many Palestinians prepared to commemorate the Nakba (Arabic: catastrophe) five days later, bringing to a close the intense two-week cluster of holidays which includes Yom HaShoah (Holocaust Remembrance Day) and Yom HaZikaron (Memorial Day). On Israeli

Independence Day, which is observed annually with fireworks, parties, and barbeques, I was invited to attend a themed gathering at the home of a wealthy older couple on the outskirts of Tel Aviv. The theme was "What Made Us Laugh in the First Ten Years, 1948–1958"; guests were asked to bring stories, artwork, recipes, poems, songs, and letters to the gathering to share with those assembled, actively (re)creating historical and collective memory. Amid landscaped gardens, yellowing propaganda posters, and tables laden with a bounty of dishes, I engaged with the aging (Ashkenazi) leftist intelligentsia of Tel Aviv, meeting artists, academics, and collectors. "Do you see her?" I was asked, and my eyes followed a finger extended toward a particularly elderly guest, her face strikingly stern beneath a floppy hat. "She was in the Palmach—she even killed an Englishman!"[43]

At lunch, among the many platters of salads and sauces a heaping dish of rice and chicken appeared, shaped like a massive upside-down pot. "Ooh! What's that?" a woman asked our smiling hostess. "Something Arabic," came the answer—this was *makloubeh,* a Palestinian dish, now being served at an Israeli Independence Day celebration. How was the symbolism lost? Throughout the presentations of "what made us laugh," gestures had been made toward (absent) Palestinians and Palestine, as many speakers demonstrated their leftist politics through the particular photographs, narratives, and letters chosen. Though their stories and objects testified to a shared position opposing Israel's occupation of Palestinian territories and populations, conversations and expressions were tinged with a kind of benevolent regret, which strangely resonated with the appearance of the *makloubeh.* "Oh, wow," the first woman continued, clearly delighted by the dish, "I haven't had this since the time when I was in Neve Shalom!"[44] Aghast, I too filled my plate with succulent chicken and rice, aware that I would be consuming Palestine like those around me.[45]

Though notable for the apparent hypocrisy in eating *makloubeh* among a group of Jewish Israelis on Israeli Independence Day—a contradiction that, like many, sits all too easily—this narrative highlights a different way in which Palestinians and Palestine nourish Jewish Israelis and Israel. Here encounter is again distanced or displaced, as no Palestinians ate with us at the celebration; rather the preparation and presentation of this dish within the space of a home nourished the political identity of our hostess and her assembled guests. As Palestine gave rise to Israel, celebrated on Independence Day, so too the presence of and continuing conflict with Palestinians makes possible a Jewish Israeli political "Left." The collective consumption of *makloubeh* becomes a way of speaking about and illustrating personal politics, wherein modes of prior encounter are animated and demonstrated through familiarity with Palestinian cuisine. Also known as Wahat al-Salam (Oasis of Peace), Neve Shalom is significant to the narrative and its political work. In highlighting her knowledge of both cuisine and village, this guest signaled the general contours of her politics, as did the hostess when choosing to serve the dish. Yet more important than the positions conveyed and encounters implied is the exact phrasing of the guest's recognition—her surprise and delight relate a sense of temporal distance. Not having eaten *makloubeh* since her last trip to Neve Shalom, the intensity of this reaction makes clear that prior consumption and contact are happy memories. Why has she not returned to the village? As we sat chewing and exclaiming over the deliciousness of this prized dish, the assembled guests participated in a kind of remembrance made possible only through the infrequency of encounter—many recalled and again desired both cuisine and contact, yet knew the limits seemingly imposed by "conflict" and the distance of "peace." In this, Palestinian food reaffirmed precarity and insecurity among these Jewish Israeli leftists, brought into the sanctity of home and literally to the table by a Jewish Israeli woman. For the party guests, unable to freely meet and eat due to the wider political reality, the *makloubeh* ultimately nourished a longing for normality.

CONCLUSION

Through everyday practices of nourishment, cleaning, and building, and by the mundane processes of moral coding, racialization, telling, and mapping, in the context of Israel-Palestine space and social relations (re)produce not only one another but also domination. On the explicate level, divisions and separation prevail both socially and spatially: cities are carved into folds and zones; belonging is borne on bodies read as physical texts; and morality and progress are marked by (perceived) cultural codes and customs. In this a society divides itself, creating and mirroring hierarchies of power and privilege that generate a particular kind of biopolitics. Indeed, making visible the ways in which "relations of subjugation manufacture subjects" (Foucault 1997, 265), these modes of division and differentiation actively create a category of "us" and along with it "here," spatially bordered and symbolically guarded.

Yet the reciprocity between space and social relations reveals how "we" remain dependent upon "them" and "here" becomes fused with "there," as power and norms require maintenance and repetition. In keeping with Foucault, within a given society mechanisms of regularization "establish an equilibrium, maintain an average, establish a sort of homeostasis" (246)— here "regular" must be continually recast against the ostensibly irregular, as an inside is made possible through its outside. Thus Israel takes shape through Palestine—fed, tidied, and built through the physical, emotional, and symbolic labor of "others," which paradoxically catalyzes processes of boundary marking and practices of border guarding.

As the explicate realm both fashions and relies on the implicate, gender structures those experiences and understandings which regularize and massify, divide and entangle. As is evident in the range of narratives in this chapter, gender constitutes a significant generative social order that permits individuals to "socio-spatially order their lives" (Portugali 1993, 57), while reproducing and entrenching existing hierarchies predicated on race, class, nation, and ethnicity. Here, gender provides a foundation for the seeming divisions between broad categories of (Jewish) Israelis and Palestinians, while generating the social value of space; yet at the same time space produces patterns of norms, codes, roles, and relations that inform specific kinds of sociality. In keeping with Doreen Massey (1994, 179), the meanings of spaces and places in Israel-Palestine indeed "reflect and affect the ways in which gender is constructed and understood."

Yet the work done by the relationship between gender, space, and social relations extends beyond creating domains of public and private, realms of political and intimate, or zones "here" and "there," along with categories of "us" and "them." On the one hand, this nexus continually reaffirms the normative precarity so central to Jewish Israeli society, casting normalcy as just beyond reach. On the other hand, the evident spatial and social entanglement of Jewish Israelis with Palestinians and Israel with Palestine sheds light on how political apathy takes work to produce—here, a state of "knowingly not knowing" (Cohen 2001) requires active willingness to disavow the social, political, and economic realities that make everyday life livable. Memories must be selectively recalled, experiences understood through particular logical frameworks, and exchanges either rationalized or diffused using specific social mechanisms. As this chapter has illustrated, Palestine and Palestinians are very much present for many Jewish Israelis, not solely in news accounts that relay conflict threatened or actualized, but in daily interactions and spaces. Thus apathy takes shape as a form of "active disengagement," rooted in a gendered spatial dimension where lives are entangled and communities are distinguished, with significant political effects.

THREE

Normalcy, Ruptured and Repaired

JUNE 10, 2011. WE SIT ON THE SMALL LEDGE of pavement beneath a dingy white apartment building, thankful for a break from the sun and a moment of rest before the scheduled festivities begin. Just after noon, the temperature in Tel Aviv has climbed to near stifling and the humidity rests heavily about our shoulders, shining in beads of perspiration on the bodies of those passing by. Guy and I have momentarily escaped the day's growing intensity as we wait for our friends to meet us for the main event: Tel Aviv's annual Pride Parade. We join this celebration hesitantly, unsure of what our participation signals politically—tacit support of pinkwashing or a joint struggle against discrimination. The bags of shopping at our feet testify to this ambivalence; we spent the morning hours at the nearby shopping center, buttressing our "activism" with domestic multitasking. En route to our shady sanctuary we had glimpsed the weekly cluster of activists representing Women in Black, today a group of four elderly women holding vigil with their signature black hand-shaped signs reading *"Dai la Kibush"* (End the Occupation). In the soaring heat these four activists had attempted to find relief in the shade of an anemic palm tree, looking almost pitiable in their persistence, as colorful, boisterous young crowds flowed merrily in the direction of Gan Meir and the impending parade.

As we wait, I notice that we are not alone. Nearly thirty black African men sit in the adjacent patch of shade, talking in pairs or resting quietly on the ledges of concrete and green spaces that comprise a common area for the buildings above. Each man, young or old, wears the blinding yellow-green bib of the sanitation department, a familiar sight in central and north Tel Aviv, where the street cleaners are often legions of African migrants or the elderly. As we exchange glances and a few smiles in our respite from the sun, it strikes me that perhaps these men are sweepers hired to clean behind the parade as it winds along its route. A more thorough survey of the street supports my theory: three enormous green street-cleaning machines sit idling at the ready.

The band of cleaners moves on, and our friends arrive, beaming with excitement at the prospect of taking part in the parade. We stand and gather our bags, attempting to transition to participation. The parade shows signs of motion, and together we walk toward the park under the punishing sun, accompanied by strains of dance music that mix with the unmistakable sounds of revelry. Approaching the nearest corner, we encounter the group of cleaners again, though now their ranks are reinforced by a number of young Palestinian men; all those assembled hold rolls of plastic bags or large wheeled garbage bins as they receive instructions from a man likely to be their supervisor. After nearly nine months of fieldwork I understand that expressing political views among friends and family risks causing tension, but I cannot help making a comment. Angrily, I draw attention to the group of cleaners and voice my frustration that this particular class of men are tasked with cleaning up after the display of "freedom" and "equality" in which we are about to take part. Our friend laughs and seems surprised, turning to me with a genuine smile. "But it's their parade too!" he says. I ask how this could be true, hoping for some kind of clarification. He gestures toward the group of men in response: "Isn't it a kind of parade? Some carry flags and others carry bags!" Laughing, he hurries off to join the glitter, rainbows, and thumping bass; in an instant he has unseen what is in front of him, rationalizing and diffusing the scene, effectively rendering it palatable for his conscience.[1]

What transpired under that hot summer sun was nothing short of political, as the play of power emerged from a gray space between the public sphere and personal experience. Here normalization occurred not passively but actively and consciously, as joking allowed participants in Tel Aviv's annual Pride Parade to effectively unsee the city's African and Palestinian sanitation workers, or at the very least bypass the issue of their presence. In this instance, multiple factors converged to produce a kind of visible invisibility that materially supported the celebration and national embrace of an often-marginalized community—yet the felt experience of inclusion was made possible in part through the continuing practice of exclusion. Here, the invitation to "belong" promises parade participants a sense of strength and solidarity that does not elide wider relations of power but rather renders them normal as a condition of acceptance.[2]

As the episode above makes clear, the seemingly unconscious acceptance of inequitable social and political realities often occurs not through force or indoctrination but in tandem with deeply personal experiences of everyday life. Following critical scholarship of power in the everyday (Mitchell 1990; Abu-Lughod 1990; Navaro-Yashin 2003; Chalfin 2008; Hoffmann 2011; Ochs 2011; Richter-Devroe 2011), this chapter explores the sites and practices of normalization that make Jewish Israeli lives livable in a context of sustained conflict. In detailing how intimate relations give rise to a particular vision of normalcy, the wider relations of power that shape Israel-Palestine emerge as most effectively produced and maintained precisely where they seem barred, absent, or least visible. Here, everyday moments and sites of least resistance demonstrate exactly how normalization works, how specific mechanisms function to both guard and blur the boundaries between conflict and normality, creating a relationship of mutual dependency. Importantly, gender roles and relations actively shape processes of normalization, weaving the personal with the political, the intimate with the public, and the everyday with domination. Thus framed by gender, intimacy becomes central to a sense of normality desired, pursued, and performed, revealing unexpected sites of action and investment that bind communities of varying size and composition. Ultimately, as diverse social mechanisms produce and maintain collectivities, the passive assent in part underwriting domination (Gramsci 1971) takes shape as the product of action. Problematizing conceptualizations of apathy as a political practice and emotion associated solely with absence or lack, this chapter reveals how action and investment are not entirely rejected by many leftist Jewish Israelis but rather selectively pursued in manners and arenas deemed meaningful and effective.

BARGAINING WITH POWER

> Israelis are descendants of a long longing to normality, to live your personal life. Not who is wrong or right, what I do that defines me as a person.... Just living a quiet life is a *longing*. It's why they established the state of the Jews. So you don't have to think about what to do to make things better. It's a way to analyze collectively—longing for a normal life is thousands of years old. It's tiring. If you are a person with a consciousness for the collective there are so many wrong things—on all levels and on all sides—that you just can't deal with. If you give a little contribution, no one will notice. So what's it for? I can go to the park with my kid and at least my kid will be a good person.[3]

Summarily binding normality, intimacy, and apparent passivity in a familiar site of the everyday, thirty-five-year-old Dalia spoke these incisive words late at night in her Tel Aviv flat alongside her partner as their daughter slept in an adjacent room. Rich with commentary about shared history, state building, and community, Dalia's account reflects how processes of negotiation and compromise are set into motion when participation in politics meets not only with seemingly little or no substantive return but also with the intimate realm of the family. Yet while Dalia describes how normality prevails seemingly despite the presence of "so many wrong things," her account masks the extent to which the sense of certainty and stability promised by the park, that site in which her daughter can become a "good person," relies on the continuing presence of insecurity.

Not set against but constituted through wider political realities, normalcy among Jewish Israelis depends on the very relations of power, conflict, and violence that it seeks to erase. As Natalie Konopinski (2009, 92) demonstrates in her ethnography of security perspectives and practices in Tel Aviv, within scenes of normality "violence always threatens, always the possibility, always the potentiality, to break through the surface of security." Here "security" may actually reproduce and amplify the fears and suspicions it claims to anticipate and thwart (Ochs 2011, 5), sewing conflict deeply into everyday life.[4] Among Jewish Israelis, appraisals of both normality and reality remain largely framed by the continuing threat of violence, whether absent or present. In this, violence becomes overwhelmingly associated with "reality," as reflected in the prevalent opinion that life in Tel Aviv is "unreal" due to its relative insulation from attack;[5] yet at the same time as violence constitutes reality, it presents the greatest obstacle to the attainment of normalcy. "I spent all my life between wars, terror attacks," fifty-seven-year-old Ronit recounted as we sat in her living room in Mevasseret-Zion. "In the Yom Kippur War two of my best friends died. But after all these terrible conditions I don't know how people grow up normal. It is *abnormal,* exhausting, depressing."[6] In her statement Ronit clearly demonstrates how violence can dissociate normalcy from reality while at the same time binding them together, as the wars that frame her life experience produce a desire for and imagination of a different (better) mode of living. Through this dynamic violence evades complete normalization or even "routinization," failing to become understood as ordinary or experienced habit (Konopinski 2009; Ochs 2011; but compare Allen 2008).[7] Rather, in keeping with the precarity of Zionism's normative narratives, violence continues to interrupt everyday life, maintaining worlds and communities as it paradoxically reinforces and stabilizes constructions of normality.

Returning to Tel Aviv's annual Pride Parade, the specter of this stabilizing violence is relatively absent save the presence of minimal security personnel, recognizable in uniforms that mark particular bodies as vehicles of the state. Yet, other traces are indeed present, if harder to detect, as protracted violence yields various social mechanisms for "getting by" (Allen 2008) the discomfiting awareness of reality. In a society stratified across and fragmented by complex divisions,[8] the production of normalcy entails seemingly passive assent to bargains with power, such as "knowingly not knowing" (Cohen 2001, 24), so that one might lead an "ordinary life" amidst conflict.

Within the microcosm of the parade, three mechanisms emerge to reveal how individuals bargain with, or normalize, power on a daily basis: joking, unseeing, and bypassing. In addition to making these mechanisms visible, the brief encounter with friends demonstrates how joking, unseeing, and bypassing are necessarily relational processes and practices. Responding first to my anger over the racialized division of labor plainly visible before us, my friend laughingly diffused the tension with a joke: "Isn't it a kind of parade? Some carry flags and others carry bags!" This joke transforms the laborers into parade participants, collapsing racial, social, and economic exclusion into the celebration of diversity. Clearly, the African and Palestinian workers are not invisible, yet the speaker incorporates their presence into a rational grid that allows him to unsee the power relations at play. While physical bodies and assigned tasks remain visible, the laborers are (falsely) credited with a kind of unconstrained agency shared by the revelers. With discrimination disguised and rationalized as inclusion, the conversation ends, and we effectively bypass the wider reality that surrounds the day's events.

Throughout the process of research, this trio of reparative mechanisms frequently recurred when political realities ruptured the careful construction of normalcy, as in the incident recounted above. These moments of interruption emerge as central to the production and preservation of normality, making an ostensible "inside" possible through the continued presence of its "outside." Yet this necessity in no way diminishes the intense discomfort that accompanies the destabilization of order. In the context of Jewish Israeli society, processes of normalization function to their remarkable degrees of efficacy precisely because of their intimate dimensions, or the ways in which they join the personal with the political and in doing so generate tension.

Joking, Unseeing, and Bypassing

Within Jewish Israeli society the family constitutes a key site in which processes of normalization unfold, binding politics with largely (hetero)normative units of assumed stability and belonging. Though granted primacy within Jewish Israeli society (Halperin-Kaddari 2004, 229), the position of the family in the literature on Israel-Palestine is contested, often cited as central to state-building and nationalist projects (Sharoni 1995; Yuval-Davis 1997; Herzog 2005 [1998]; Johnson and Kuttab 2001; Kanaaneh 2002; Halperin-Kaddari 2004; Jacoby 2005), while at the same time yielding accusations of overemphasis turned cultural reductionism (Abdo 2011, 3). Yet these analyses converge in highlighting how the family constitutes a significant social institution due to its location at the nexus of multiple borders, facilitating the transmission of ideology while providing a central unit of support. In this, the family emerges as a point of confluence, a central location of boundary collapse, wherein individuals come to understand and negotiate the intersection of everyday life with wider political realities, as depicted in earlier chapters.

This conceptualization of the family—as a site and institution wherein tensions intersect—then counters the image of a bounded "domestic" or "private" sphere characterized by depoliticization. Yet as a primary locus of normalization, understood here as the process through which "an undesirable situation (event, condition, phenomenon) is unrecognized, ignored or made to seem normal" (Cohen 2001, 51), the Jewish Israeli family is often identified as a site from which politics is purged. Now eighty and living in Jaffa, outside Tel Aviv, with her husband, Sonya spoke at length about the ways in which her political identity creates familial tension, catalyzing processes and mechanisms of normalization.

> KN: Are your daughters politically engaged like you?
>
> Sonya: One shies away from politics completely. Her now ex-husband is right-wing.... We never talked about politics together, not the occupation or anything like that. They have four sons: eighteen and a half, seventeen and a half, fifteen, and twelve. They never wanted these arguments in front of the children, they wanted to keep it as far away as possible. My daughter knows what I think, and I'm sure she agrees that the occupation is not a good thing. But she's not in any way radical—she won't stand in the street with a sign saying "Down with the occupation!" Because she won't let us discuss it, the boys know approximately what I think.... Like at last Pesach, the oldest asked

a question about the occupation. Their family likes to do the whole thing [Passover ritual], to read the whole reading, with a break for dinner in the middle. So I answered, my husband answered, and it became a big discussion. It lasted about forty-five minutes. And my daughter got upset and said, "We have to finish [the reading]!" So we had to leave the discussion, but we said [to the grandson], "When you want to ask again, do so." The opportunity doesn't come often, as the boys are older. They're busy and it isn't like we get them on Saturday afternoons to go to the park anymore. They have their own lives. But they're very much aware of my way of thinking and that where I stand is very different from where their father stands.

Our other daughter and our son-in-law actually met in Peace Now[9] at the university. But she doesn't want any political discussion when we're visiting—she hates arguments! Her husband would disagree pleasantly with me all the time if he were allowed. For instance, there was one discussion and their son was twelve years old at the time. He started asking "Why are they angry? Why is *aba* [Dad] yelling at *savta* [Grandma]?" and that was it—she doesn't want him to see this. Her in-laws are very far right. We have to be careful when we visit with them. But she understands where I am. My daughter is running away, but I can't force her.

Our oldest daughter is in Los Angeles, and she is totally with my way of thinking, she agrees. But what can she do? She lives in LA! Our youngest, who is at home with us, agrees with me about the occupation, but she is very sensitive. She won't do Machsom [Checkpoint] Watch[10] because she doesn't want to see. She will sign a petition, but she won't be active. She actually laughs at me—she says, "Who are you going to make peace with tonight?" when I go out the door. I told her that "Tonight I'm going to make peace with Katie!"[11]

Highlighting a range of political subjectivities, from her own identification as a radical leftist feminist anti-occupation activist to her former son-in-law's right-wing stance, Sonya articulates the ways in which the family seemingly inevitably constitutes a repository of politics.[12] Yet each daughter differently attempts to fend off and mitigate against the intrusion of the political into the familial and intimate, revealing how mechanisms of repair emerge through episodes of rupture. Through means of joking, bypassing, and unseeing, the politics that frames and facilitates Jewish Israeli normalcy is seemingly displaced, rendering the impossible, discomfiting, and unknowable manageable or digestible. As Sonya's youngest daughter jokes about her mother leaving the house to "make peace," she summarily hyperpoliticizes her mother's actions while making them surreal or ridiculous, despite their shared political views. The first daughter to appear in Sonya's narrative also shares her politics but effectively bypasses the resolution of a conversation about the occupation with an appeal to the completion of ritual or tradition. The middle daughter, who met her husband at Peace Now, again demonstrates a common politics, yet she shields her son from the sight of familial disagreement and fends off future conversations, helping the child unsee the dispute. Not without a touch of sad irony does Sonya relate the absence of her most politically like-minded daughter, the child who would do something but cannot by virtue of geographic distance.

While these mechanisms of joking, unseeing, and bypassing became evident through interviews such as my exchange with Sonya, their explicitly gendered dimensions are perhaps best clarified through experiences within my own family, a small unit split between Tel Aviv and West Jerusalem. While providing a network of support, my secular middle-class Ashkenazi family provided a register in which to check the dynamics uncovered during the process of research. Holding an American passport and possessing a desire to travel the entirety of Israel-Palestine, I understood physical borders differently from my Jewish Israeli family and friends—for me, these lines and constructs were passable and open to traversal. These acts of border crossing and limit testing were framed by my positionality as a white, middle-class, non-Jewish American woman; this social location informed not only my imagination and mobility but also the reception of my perceived transgression.

For June 2011, I planned a three-day trip to Ramallah and Nablus to visit friends, join a hiking group, and travel to the origin of *knafeh,* a famed dessert in the region. Hoping to maintain accord, I had kept a previous trip to Ramallah and Birzeit a matter of secrecy to all but a small number of close friends; and, not wanting to cause worry with my border crossing, I had decided against telling the family my intentions, effectively bypassing the issue and its wider political context. This time, however, I felt more confident in defying limits, emboldened the day before by an interview participant who spoke about the importance of destabilizing perceptions. Framed by my impending absence at a family birthday party and the reassurance that, no, Guy would not be going with me to Ramallah, I looked forward to this trip for both the new experiences it would offer and the satisfaction of transgression—I would knowingly rupture the guise of normalcy within my own family.

Surprisingly, no one expressed concern that I would be going to the occupied West Bank as a woman traveling alone; it was preferable that I venture solo into a territory popularly associated with violence and insecurity, rather than taking my male (Jewish Israeli) partner with me. Clearly, ethnicity and nationality trumped gender in this appraisal of safety, though I was often mistaken for being Jewish, if not Jewish Israeli, inside Israel. Was there some intangible aspect of Jewishness that Palestinians could read, some way of "telling" unknown to me? But more pressing at that moment, would my "rupture" interrupt anything at all?

During my absence that weekend, Guy kept a record of how friends and family responded when learning of my location as the topic inevitably arose in various contexts, from a beach gathering to the birthday party and an art exhibition. Acting as both partner and research assistant, Guy answered openly when asked about my whereabouts and relayed the reactions over the phone, revealing how my act of rupture met with diverse modes of repair. "Why does she have to go there? Isn't there enough to do *here*?" This sentiment was frequently repeated among female friends and relatives, whose rhetorical queries bypassed my location and the politics surrounding my absence through turning inward. Similarly, a male relative asked, "Why would she go there?"—this time expecting a response. Guy replied with questions in kind: "Why wouldn't she go there? If it was Paris, would you ask why she's there?" The interlocutor apparently considered this for a moment before declaring that he would like to visit Ramallah himself, were he not concerned for personal safety. At a beach gathering among childhood schoolmates, a male friend responded to my absence with another sort of query: "What? She has an Arab boyfriend now?" Simultaneously a joke and an accusation, this response to my location not only diminished the politics of my absence but also called into question my morality through invoking sexuality. Perhaps feeling badly about his reaction, this friend continued by admitting that he would actually like to visit cities in the West Bank and Jordan as he feels "more comfortable in Arab cultures." Though he feels this desire stymied by fears for safety, in reality he lives in a settlement in the West Bank with his wife and children—he is surrounded by a desired "Arab culture," though unable to access its "comfort" by virtue of the politics that makes his life possible within the settlement.

Interestingly, these reactions as recorded and recounted emerge in specifically gendered terms, which largely reaffirm prevailing norms, codes, and relations. As practiced primarily by female relatives, bypassing remains rooted "here"—why can't I stay put?—while joking by male relatives and friends morphs into admitted desires to go "there," to act and move. Though bypassing and joking are not strictly limited to women and men respectively, these mechanisms (re)confirm prevailing dualisms of stasis-as-feminine and action-as-masculine through expressions of incomprehension and desire. Here, "military-masculine hegemony" and the masculinized construction of normality in Israel (Lentin 2000) provide a significant social frame for understanding reactions to transgression, as together joking and bypassing effectively serve to avoid and reduce in ways that diminish and invalidate actions.

While mechanisms of joking and bypassing locate acts of transgression within a familiar social grid, a third mechanism of normalization, unseeing, is activated not through absence but through physical presence. For example, as I sought to share gifts, photographs, and experiences from my trip to Ramallah and Nablus, materiality forced recipients to acknowledge what lies beyond the seeming limits where Israel and possibility end. Carried through the Old City of Nablus, ferried to the top of Ibn Tulkarm's palace, stashed under dusty bus seats, x-rayed and crushed in the machines at Qalandia checkpoint, and finally driven tiredly to Jerusalem and Tel Aviv, a plate of sticky sweets and bars of olive oil soap met with unexpected reactions. "We don't like Arabic sweets—they're too sweet. You can take them with you when you go," I was told after presenting the Palestinian treats. While my photographs of the hiking trip—images of fog and breaking sunlight, terraced hills and exquisite flora—prompted a request to see pictures of Ramallah, these disappointed the viewers as they revealed a bustling and crowded city no more exotic than other areas outlying Jerusalem. The olive oil soap was received first with genuine appreciation; yet gratitude was followed closely by a joke: "Wow. So if I wash with this will I become—" The sentence hung suspended in midair. "Clean?" I offered. "Pro-Palestinian?" came the end of the query with a quick laugh.[13] In these ways, gifts and images from Palestine were actively unseen by their intended recipients, rejected or reduced in their materiality and symbolism. Operating in tandem with joking and bypassing, here acts of unseeing acknowledge a discomfiting presence while barring it from entering too deeply into home or psyche—before being set aside in a sink for use, soap is first cleansed of its politics. Importantly, these intimate exchanges occurred among women within domestic spaces, pointing to how mothers and wives might regulate the presence of politics in family life. In a dynamic that emerged as key to the efficacy and durability of normalization within family units, here women meet politics head-on and set the terms of visibility and engagement.

Silencing

As joking, bypassing, and unseeing take shape within intimate settings and interactions, resoundingly clear is the silence that prevails after incidences of rupture. In its function as a mode of repair, silence emerges not only through the absence of articulation but also through how particular issues are spoken about, or rather *around*—silence may thus include speech, albeit that which "has had no political 'voice' or impact" (Berlant 2011, 232). However, if normalcy depends on the presence of politics and the continuation of conflict, as argued throughout this chapter, these repairs can only ever be partial—whether rendered insignificant or silent, the political cannot be fully erased in its necessity to everyday life.

Then what is preserved by acts of silencing, and for whom? Returning to Sonya's narrative recounted above, through she was forbidden to speak about politics to protect her grandchildren from the emotional upset caused by conflict among relatives, here silencing does not instill a sense that "everything is all right" for adults, nor for children. Rather, silence reconstitutes and enshrines a knowing approximation of childhood normalcy, where reality—political disagreement among adults—becomes displaced by desire. As such, the resulting normalcy is largely aspirational, reflecting "the desire to feel normal and to feel normalcy as a ground of dependable life, a life that does not have to keep being reinvented" (Berlant 2007, 281). Similarly, the silence that prevails in my own family after episodes of rejection or diminishment does not sit easily, yet it nonetheless remains—we wish it could be otherwise, as if somewhere else "normal" might be recreated by our stepping gingerly around obvious hurts and disappointments.

Though Sonya, her husband, and myself appear victims of silencing as a reparative mechanism, those silent and silenced often play an active role in their apparent muteness. As illustrated by critical scholarship on political violence, silence may indeed be a matter of active consent in response to violent acts witnessed or watched (Last 2000, 324; Cohen 2001, 145, 166), just as it may constitute a protective strategy for victimized individuals and communities (Das 2007, 54, 87; Lawrence 2000, 178; Lentin 2000) or a sign of protest and reassertion of commitment among the politically depressed (Eliasoph 1998; Berlant 2011, 231). Within this range of silences (Lawrence 2000, 178), some forms retain aspects of agency despite their seeming imposition by external actors. Not one to shy from confrontation, Sonya frequently marches in anti-occupation, anti-racism and pro-democracy demonstrations, in addition to participating actively in multiple feminist anti-occupation organizations, from Machsom Watch and Women in Black to the Coalition of Women for Peace.[14] Then her consent to silence among family is quite significant. Indeed, my own silence after the reception of sweets and soaps must be read in conjunction with my academic research and frequent participation in demonstrations and protests—holding politics and family in tension, I actively recreated the dynamics at the heart of my own study. Rather than indicating denial, as commonly associated with silence (Cohen 2001, 9), our muteness constitutes an affirmation, a subscription to the sense of normalcy that seems requisite for familial accord. While silence indeed interrupts the transmission of meaning on which communities rely (Daniel 2000, 351), our reticence actively stabilizes a most intimate constellation of collectivity.

Within these family units from whence silence emanates, gender again functions as an element of structure, a vector of normativity, and a relation of power, though perhaps unpredictably so. The behaviors and attitudes produced through the entanglement of private with public and intimate with political resist generalization, as an individual's location, experience, and perspective as "woman" or "man" are embedded in multiple relations, at once personal and familial, social and political, material and emotional (Brah 1996). As the narrator of episodes, Sonya's voice trumps that of her husband and she appears an authoritative matriarch. Yet in moments of silencing, political clashes that initiate closure occur explicitly with her daughters' more conservative male partners—in Sonya's opinion, her daughters all agree with her on matters relating to the occupation, while the men around her express opposition. However, in each of the final moments of judgment, these very daughters are the actors who forbid the intrusion of politics into the intimacy of family life; they emerge as the keepers of normality. "*She* won't let us discuss it [with] the boys"; "*she* doesn't want any political discussion when we're visiting"; "*she* doesn't want to see"—Sonya's daughters guard the gates of normalcy and family harmony, exercising power over political debate and engagement. Though acting differently within the ostensibly apolitical domestic sphere, political passivity cannot be ascribed to any of these women. Rather, despite their male partners' clear exercise of political voice, Sonya's daughters appear as de facto heads of household, invested in the preservation of familial sanctity against their mother's tide of politics. Thus, while the existing literature highlights the connections between political speech and "knowledge of security" in Israel—primarily available to men through their history of participation in combat (Mazali 2003; Lentin 2004; Jacoby 2005; Rimalt 2007; Sasson-Levy, Levy, and Lomsky-Feder 2011)[15]—these accounts reveal more subtle gendered relations in operation at the level of the family, where women regulate visibility, discussion, and engagement in the interest of normality.

Then family units uniquely reveal how the production and maintenance of normalcy entails active modes of bargaining, which seemingly preserve the sanctity of intimate communities. Speaking from the position of a woman whose child, a son, opted against serving in the military, sixty-one-year-old Aviva differently illuminated how gendered modes of silencing are key to the bargains made:

> I can say that because my son didn't go to the army, in that way it [the occupation] didn't touch me. But when your son is in the army I think it touches you very badly, again in a paradoxical way. I have friends who came from the Left, who were activists in their young ages. I cannot say that they rationally changed their minds—it doesn't mean that they didn't, maybe they did. But the fact that their sons serve in the army, in the [Occupied] Territories, makes them blind. Maybe this is normal, I can't tell you.
>
> KN: This isn't something you experience with a daughter in the army?
>
> Aviva: You don't experience it with a daughter because she doesn't go to combat. I don't think I would experience it anyway, I can't change my mind. But I can't say. My daughter challenged my limits, she said "Maybe I will be a combatant." I said, "No way. No way." We had great discussions about the army in our family. First with our son—my partner didn't go to the army and he didn't want our son to go, but he let everyone make his own decision. He said that I didn't allow our son to go to the army. It's *true,* he's right, but I think that we *shouldn't* allow our son to go to the army! Here is the discussion. With our daughter we were more permissive because she's a girl, but she was more rebellious also. It was clear that I didn't want her to go. But I supported her, I took food, I went to the ceremonies. Here is where you have—the army gets into your house. The main way the occupation gets into your house is through the army.
>
> Now it's less, but I was very busy with one issue when my daughter was eighteen years old and her boyfriends came to the house. We'd have dinner together, chat, the usual thing. These boys are in the army. And you don't ask questions, you try not to. I knew that if I asked questions I would be in a situation where I have to decide if I let them into the house. On the other side, they are responsible, but they are eighteen years old—eighteen years old. They are kids. There also, you close your eyes to the occupation.[16]

Gender pervades Aviva's account as she raises issues of sight, speech, and silence in response to my question about whether she encounters the occupation in Jerusalem. While daughters appear to constitute "less worry" in their relative safety from combat assignments, these very "safe" beings actually usher the military into the domain of family, dispelling the notion of sanctity from occupation and violence. Yet, according to Aviva's narrative, normalization operates on two levels that remain associated with sons: the shift toward conservative politics or "blindness" among parents of male soldiers, and the self-censorship that accompanies certain knowledge of what those soldiers do. In Aviva's account, the decision taken by her son to avoid military service provides escape from the "touch" of the occupation—a respite from violence—rather than instilling in her a feeling of alienation from the collective. While Aviva immigrated to Israel from Argentina as a teenager, her sense of belonging to Israeli society somehow resists the destabilization of a son failing to fulfill mandatory service. Yet, with her daughter's enlistment, Aviva actively performs national belonging on multiple levels despite her acute sense of political and personal discomfort, bringing food to the military base, attending ceremonies, and acquiescing to silence and approximating normalcy as conscripted male friends join the family for dinner. Here, the destabilizing yet normalized entry of the military into the domestic is borne by daughters, who introduce violence into "private" and "home" in ways that simultaneously complicate and reinforce prevailing norms.

The Ties That Bind

As in the narratives of numerous research participants and indeed in my own experience, silence indeed resounds at the close of Aviva's account. Yet, again, what does it preserve? An approximation of normalcy, similar to the stakes with Sonya's teenage grandchildren? Whereas Sonya brings with her the "abnormal" politics that threatens accord, at Aviva's dinner table the catalyst appears to be external: her daughter's friends bring the military to family mealtime. In this instance, rather than producing an overwhelming sense of normalcy, the individual silent or silenced feels tension, anxiety, and frustration; there exists no false sense that everything is truly "all right." Yet in a context of aspirational normality, these sensations point to surprising, if familiar, terms of belonging. Here, the insecurity of the moment's calm, the mantra of "live for today because you can't count on tomorrow," reaffirms the community of trauma and perseverance at the core of Zionism. Then as tension and silence feed into normative precarity, these dynamics secure belonging to the nation, a collective invested in recasting normalcy as if "against" and "despite" but in so many ways through conflict.

These tense terms of belonging were underlined by Yael, a fifty-six-year-old Jerusalemite with four children above conscription age, as she reflected on the cohesive capacities of anxiety within Jewish Israeli society:

> The minute a child—a child! A *child*!—goes to the army it becomes all-encompassing for that person who goes to the army. And also for the parents. It's very different to send a daughter versus a son—it depends on what the daughter is doing, of course. When you're a mother, even living in Tel Aviv, and you send a child to a combat unit, your life isn't the same. You live on a different level. If Tel Aviv kids aren't going to the army, then they [the parents] are excluded from worrying about the security of their children and the nation.[17]

Embedded in an explanation of how she experiences the occupation in daily life as a "modern religious" woman with friends and family living in West Bank settlements, Yael frames her observations as a difference between Jerusalem and Tel Aviv. While dissociating Tel Aviv from reality due to a perceived lack of violence experienced and duty fulfilled, Yael raises the possibility that continued detachment is not the highest price paid by parents of service evaders and conscientious objectors. Rather, these parents "miss out" on the worry that coheres a collectivity, particularly during times of conflict and war; their disconnection from the needs of military and nation becomes a basis of *non-belonging*. Unlike her Israel-born children, Yael does not take social and national belonging for granted, having emigrated from Australia at age eighteen; the inclusion of her children in the fabric of military, nation, and society verifies her own belonging. As Nira Yuval-Davis (2011, 18) writes, "Belonging . . . is not just about social locations and constructions of individual and collective identities and attachments, it is also concerned with the ways these are assessed and valued by the self and others." By highlighting the varying levels of anxiety that accompany the deployment of daughters and sons—young women, like Aviva's daughter, must volunteer for combat positions, while young men may be openly conscripted—Yael makes a further distinction between the degrees of investment and perhaps prestige that accompany belonging to the national worry. Yet, when the symbolism of the military appears on the body of her child in the space of the home, these distinctions matter little; as Yael said of her youngest daughter, with obvious concern trailing into silence: "When my baby comes home with a big rifle and puts it in her clothes closet..."

Thus, Yael's account underlines how normalization occurs through the simultaneous disruption of stability and production of belonging, highlighting how tension frames the bonds between military and family—when children report for duty, lives collectively fail to remain the same. Here, an experience of rupture grants social capital and political voice, as those families whose children refuse or evade military service face silencing and exclusion due to their lack of participation in both national security and worry. Daphna, a research participant in Tel Aviv, corroborated this claim as she spoke of an explosive conversation with her brother-in-law, which involved the accusation that she and her fellow leftist activist husband were *ochrei Israel* (haters of Israel). "You hate your country, you hate your people—send your daughter to the army and then you can talk to me!" the brother-in-law reportedly yelled, before marching to the car to await his wife's departure from the ruined family meeting. Having previously agreed to a pact of silence with a female cousin in Jerusalem who "refuses to talk about politics with anyone in the family because of the huge damage it can do," Daphna and her partner now entered into a similarly tense voluntary truce with this relative.[18] In this case the gender of the should-be soldier seems to matter little, as a daughter's enlistment is the source of contention, despite her lack of access to the social and political capital ascribed to male combat soldiers (Sasson-Levy 2003; Sasson-Levy and Amram-Katz 2007; Levy and Sasson-Levy 2008). As indicated by Yael, what is at stake in this exchange about military service is not solely political speech and familial accord but also, and perhaps more importantly, belonging to a wider collective.

Together, these accounts highlight the centrality of the family to social relations and political realities, as both take shape through the tension between precarity and belonging. Within family units normalcy entails active modes of bargaining, generating processes of rupture and repair that set the stage for a particular vision of normality—one that permits the practice of living *as if* all is "normal." Living this politics of 'as if' may cement or even widen the gap between awareness and action, as here fantasy does not replace material reality but rather ensures its continuation (Wedeen 1999; Navaro-Yashin 2002; Allen 2013). As Yonathan Mendel (2009) argues, fantasy continues to shape material realities in Israel-Palestine: "The way of fantasizing another Israel—peaceful and moral, Jewish and democratic, not perfect but not harmful—has brought into being a virtual reality in which historical and contemporary events are blurred by wishful deceitful and blinkered thinking." Through producing and maintaining these precarious relations, intimate practices of joking, bypassing, unseeing, and silencing ultimately *make us belong* even while closing down avenues of trust and understanding assumed guaranteed, opening fissures of anger, disappointment, and resentment in their stead. As a member of my own family summarized succinctly after a particularly upsetting exchange, "Now we're a *real* Israeli family, having an argument about politics in front of the television on a Friday night."[19]

SMALL WORLDS, SIMPLE LIVES

In these ways, mechanisms of normalization are enacted in family units during and after moments of rupture, providing a toolkit for repair shared by those invested in the preservation of normalcy. Here, joking, bypassing, unseeing, and silencing emerge as modes of stabilization in the necessarily precarious conditions that produce belonging, finding function through intimate political relations. Yet, after its repair, what does this normalcy look like? How does it feel, and for whom? As seen above, rupture and repair can be profoundly tiring enterprises for all involved, particularly as these processes involve intimate realms and relationships (Berlant 2011, 27, 48).[20] Thus, for many Jewish Israelis, personal energy is best invested on levels in which life can be made to feel immediately normal, relative to the enormity and seeming intractability of wider political realities. Just as mechanisms of normalization render the politics of occupation and discrimination palatable, so too does the creation of small worlds make life more livable.

Though varied in size and composition, small worlds signal a "becoming-private" (Berlant 2011, 259), which suggests that the guise of normalcy cannot be adequately maintained on larger scales. Here it is important to distinguish between modes and layers of normalcy. In part, this book illustrates how conditions of conflict, occupation, and discrimination have become so normalized as to constitute the basis of everyday life for many Jewish Israelis. With concertina wire and security checks experienced as routine and Palestinians understood to work largely in particular trades, material and corporeal reminders become ostensibly "normal" to the extent that they remain visible. Yet at the same time visibility is seemingly rescinded as the performance of "normal" liberal, Western, modern, capitalist life in Tel Aviv and West Jerusalem creates a stage for the enactment of "just like you, like anywhere (else) in Europe." Thus, while domination and subordination consistently underwrite and maintain the everyday, these relations remain unevenly normalized.

As sociologists Stanley Cohen and Laurie Taylor (1992, 113) write, "We simultaneously occupy several worlds and move into different activities each of which may be distinguished by the degree of individuality, at-homeness, freedom from constraints which can be experienced." In the context of Israel-Palestine, these coexistent worlds may additionally provide familiarity, awayness and connectivity, as experiences of sustained conflict are compounded by the fragmentation and privatization that accompany rapid liberalization (Shafir and Peled 2000, 2002; Semyonov and Lewin-Epstein 2004; Yiftachel 2006; Abdo 2011). Into this tension feminist and queer theorists insert a provocative claim: the normative and aspirational dimensions of these worlds apart may produce an economy that secures existing relations of power and privilege. Couched in affective terms by Sara Ahmed (2004) and Lauren Berlant (2007, 2011), worlds large and small are built and maintained through attachments—to others, to objects, to scenes, practices, and desires.[21] Here, intimate relations and reciprocity yield the experiences of "unconflictedness, belonging, and worth" (Berlant 2007, 282) imagined to underpin normality and "ordinary life," where existence ceases to be a project and is instead exercised as fact (291). Constructed differently by Jewish Israeli women and men, these small worlds of intimacy take shape as gender intersects with hierarchies of class, race, religiosity, and geopolitical location, producing approximations of normalcy that indeed preserve the status quo.

Elsewheres, Here, and There

> The mentality is Hobbesian here. Fuck Hobbes! You can't build a society based on Hobbes unless you want no equality, depression, aggression. Like Buffy the Vampire Slayer said, "I say my power should be *our* power!"—that's the fandom I come from. In sci-fi and fantasy Henry Jenkins did research and studied the link between involvement in sci-fi or fantasy fandoms and political action. There's a strong link, like how Donna Haraway writes about the creation of "elsewhere." The problem is that most people think, "We have to do this," to be X is the only solution. Well no, we live it and we can live it differently if we choose. I believe in small steps, very small steps, not symbolic steps which are huge. Of course it's complicated and huge, but if we don't start, who will?[22]

Meirav, a twenty-five-year-old feminist blogger and political activist, first raised the possibility of "elsewhere" as we sat together in Jerusalem's Machane Yehuda market, watching evening shoppers from our position at a popular cafe. The founder of an online initiative aimed at ending street harassment, Meirav invoked Donna Haraway's (1992, 295) conceptualization of "elsewhere" multiple times during our interview, citing it as a positive space of possibility and meaning. Of debates around the differing plights of Palestinian and Jewish Israeli women in Israel, Meirav claimed, "The argument [of who has it worse] usually gets stuck at a dead end, but there's always an 'elsewhere.'... Real change can come from women on each side." Similarly, in discussing Israel's ongoing occupation of the Palestinian Territories and annexed East Jerusalem, she concluded, "It is what it is, you get angry and frustrated. You break down and then you see the options ... if you're lucky enough to have an 'elsewhere.'" For Meirav, "elsewhere" exists as a realm of political action, as suggested by Haraway, a site of imagination that leads to transformation, where the ability to access fantasy might change reality.

Contesting claims to biological determinism, "naturalization," and postmodern "hyper-productionism,"[23] Haraway (1992, 299–300) proposes the existence of "elsewhere" as a space of difference and diffraction, a site of interruption and interference that creates the possibility of change. Home to "inappropriate/d others" (Trinh Minh-ha 1986, 1989 cited in Haraway 1992, 299)—those multicultural, ethnic, racial, national, and sexual subjects excluded from hegemonic (Western) narratives of biology, nature, and social construction—the third space of "elsewhere" promises combination, interface, implosion, collapse, hope, and action, a place where "my power" may indeed be "our power." What binds this realm of possibility and engagement with the clear avoidance enabled by the Pride Parade depicted at the opening of this chapter, a microcosm of celebration and community that arises seemingly despite the very conditions that inspire Meirav to act? In a context of sustained conflict, rather than ushering in novel forms of resistance "elsewheres" may provide escape or respite, becoming small worlds of normalcy and immediate influence in a sea of uncertainty, fear, powerlessness, and despair. Promising stability and belonging, these worlds may constitute enclaves or "free areas" in which "we don't experience any massive tension or disruption between fantasy and script" (Cohen and Taylor 1992, 113); so too they may be linked with denial, or the maintenance of social worlds that render undesirable situations invisible, avoidable, or usual (Cohen 2001, 51). As highlighted by Meirav above, while "elsewheres" expand the scope of thought and deed, the "very small steps" taken within these realms may replace large and symbolic actions, fostering not transformation but stasis.

Rather than transcendental politicized realms evolved beyond prevailing conditions or conventions, the small worlds of Jewish Israelis emerge as liminal spaces—sites held in tension between aspiration and reality. Similarly to how processes of othering and exclusion directly produce "elsewheres" (Haraway 1992), these small worlds take shape through the surrounding environment, resonating between extremes as they offer both escape and action—as Meirav acts to thwart street harassment, so too she escapes the violence of occupation and conflict. Bound to both "here" and "elsewhere," small worlds remain rooted in material conditions, dependent on reality for content and intelligibility—in part what a small world is *not* and in part what it seeks to transform. Yet in a context of political violence, the inverse relationship is equally significant: how existing conditions might rely on the production and maintenance of small worlds, both escapist and oriented toward political hope.

A Theory of Systemics

> What's keeping me sane is the microenvironment—family and friends. I see families and I think, "Where is this going? What will we leave to our kids?" I feel things are getting worse. Neighborhoods are a microcosmos. At [age] eleven, I saw that my daughter couldn't be free. They built a student dormitory—four-story-high buildings that were fancy and new. Many students live there. Then the Arabs in the neighborhood became aggressive, they started attacking girls. The students built their own security groups and patrolled, they were the *mishmar ezrachi* [civilian guard]. The neighborhood had groups on patrol too. I decided that if I was alone I would stay, I have no energy to make the changes! But because of Maya, not only was she growing up in this crazy country, but her development as an independent child [was at risk], the ability to go to her friend's safely and come back safely. So we left the neighborhood because of Maya. And I'm so glad we did! Maya is independent, she goes to school and returns on her own, safely. It's not only being in an Arab environment, there are many people around who make life impossible. I still have the feeling that I need to protect her—Maya calls me when she gets to school, when she gets home. But I'm not hysterical.[24]

As we sipped tea and ate cakes in the cool of Ronit's apartment outside Jerusalem, my host outlined the contours of her particular small world, presented as a "microenvironment." Here Ronit constructs a multilayered scene of threat and intimacy: a once-safe neighborhood "microcosmos" whose changing dynamics jeopardized the core of her small world, her young daughter Maya. From neighbors to friends and ultimately family—a unit of two, as Ronit raises her single child alone—the narrowing rings of Ronit's microenvironment indeed reveal sites of both action and stasis, clearly constructed through and bound by intimacy. While Ronit admits to having felt "no energy" to move from her first neighborhood in Jerusalem's French Hill area, a de jure settlement across the Green Line in the Occupied West Bank, she is impelled to action when her daughter's development and security appear at risk. By moving to escape conflict, violence, and harm—acting to secure her small world—Ronit preserves a sense of stability, manifest in the apparent safety of a new neighborhood and the "normalcy" of childhood freedom.

In this, action becomes a vehicle for seeming passivity, ensuring a mode of "coasting" (Berlant 2011, 18) that allows Ronit to invest in her microenvironment and avoid feelings of constant struggle, danger, and survival. As our conversation ended, Ronit mused, "If one is happy in one's microenvironment, one will be used to the macro—this is keeping me sane. In science, if the micro takes hold it becomes systemic." Yet, to read Ronit's words carefully, the happiness, security, and stability of her microenvironment remain tenuous, in need of continual maintenance and reaffirmation. Despite moving from French Hill to Mevasseret-Zion, where Maya can walk through the neighborhood without fear, Ronit still requires her daughter to phone on reaching the nearby school. During the course of our interview Maya called to say that she was leaving school, and arrived at the house some time later to a warm reception from her mother. Rather than a performance of acute relief, an indicator of the extraordinary, Ronit and Maya's interaction conveyed routine—this call and response constitute a daily interaction. Instead of creating accord with the wider environment, the "systemics" of Ronit's small world clearly operate within particular boundaries to produce normalization. One grows accustomed to the macro rather than including it in the scope of action and everyday life.

Then, even as her microenvironment promises stasis and offers respite from wider cycles of violence, trauma, and conflict, the stability of Ronit's small world requires constant repetition. As demonstrated by feminist and queer scholars including Judith Butler (1993, 1997b), Lauren Berlant (1997, 1998a, 2007, 2011), and Sara Ahmed (2000, 2004), world-building and world-maintenance necessitate the reiteration of particular norms that grant "matter" "boundary, fixity, and surface" (Butler 1993, 9). Within Ronit's small world, normativity not only shapes the substance and structure of everyday life but also links her "elsewhere" to material reality in its provision of simultaneous "at-homeness" and away-ness. Most clearly, Ronit's microenvironment underlines norms of protection, challenging prevailing gender norms while reinforcing sexualized racial norms. Produced through militarized patriarchal nationalism in combination with an ongoing settler colonial project (Abdo and Yuval-Davis 1995; Lentin 2000), the normative relations of Jewish Israeli man-as-protector and woman-as-reproducer are undermined by Ronit's account of lived experience. As a single mother and sole income earner, Ronit assumes the dual responsibility of security and nourishment/care. Here the (gendered) divisions between "homefront" and "battlefield" (Sharoni 2005 [1994]; Herzog 2005 [1998]; Jacoby 2005) collapse, even as Ronit seeks to maintain division, physically moving home to a locale beyond—yet near—the Green Line, through mobility enabled by her membership in Israel's middle class.

Yet in pursuing a sense and site of security on behalf of her young daughter, Ronit reaffirms a racialized and sexualized category of "other" in Israel's settler colonial project: the "Arab" imagined to lurk menacingly at the physical and metaphorical borders of her microcosm. In a manner strikingly similar to discourses of colonial projects past (Anthias and Yuval-Davis 1992; McClintock 1995; Stoler 2002), Ronit's narrative (re)produces a normative image of the "other" as an aggressive (brown or black) native-man-turned-invader preying on innocent (white) daughters, salient symbols of the nation. Thus while Ronit performs protection and subverts prevailing gender roles, the reiteration of sexualized racial norms confirms the position of the "abject being" (Butler 1993, 3) whose continued presence materializes the border of her small world—a site simultaneously secure and precarious in its proximity to "other" bodies and violence. Then systemics transmit not happiness and security but rather a sense of danger and fear, reproducing the impetus for protection. Indeed, after describing the contours of her small world, Ronit said: "Katie, you can't imagine how they *hate* Arabs... Maya grew up—you can't *imagine* how she hates Arabs. In this house, in this family, you won't hear these words. She has so much hate, fear. I say, 'Maya, you can't generalize! We have [friends] Amal and Khalid, we're invited to their house!' She tells me, 'They are exceptional! You can't trust [Arabs].'"

I asked, "How old is she?"

Ronit said, "She'll be thirteen in October."[25]

Spiritual Escapes: Of Self and Circles

As is evident in Ronit's account above, the small worlds of family units provide a site in which the repetition of norms might stabilize prevailing discourses and hierarchies, while at the same time providing opportunities for subversion. On a broad level, though a daughter remains the object of protection, her mother assumes the (masculine) roles of defender and provider along with that of (feminine) caretaker. Yet family institutions do not provide predictable patterns with regard to small worlds and the normative relations therein; rather, specific factors intersect to give rise to diverse realms of escape and action. In Ronit's case, living as a single mother in the occupied territory of French Hill converged with perceptions of (Palestinian) race and the opportunities afforded by (middle) class status, producing her "microenvironment" as a site worthy of cultivation and action. For others, the family draws together individual interests and social locations in different ways, generating realms of varying shapes and sizes that again complicate and reinforce overarching norms.

For thirty years, Yael has lived in the same modest limestone home in West Jerusalem's German Colony, separated from the tense environment of French Hill by the Old City, Hebrew University, and what feels like a cultural chasm. Now retired from work as the manager of her husband's clinic and with four children grown and moved away, at fifty-six Yael cultivates her interests in dance, pottery, yoga, and meditation through courses offered at the cultural center behind her house. Prefacing our exchange with the claim that she is "not a political creature," Yael outlined her position and practices thus: "Let me paint you a picture. Every morning the paper is delivered to our door, my husband picks it up and goes through it, clucking his tongue in disappointment. Ido is very left and he can't believe what's going on here. I can't get my head around it. I have to put my head in the sand like an ostrich to live here, because I don't believe there's a solution."[26]

After immigrating from Australia Yael chose to raise her own family in Israel, exchanging one reality for another that, for her, necessitates conscious disengagement. Defining her family as "modern religious," for Yael "what's going on here" extends beyond the divisions of nation and ethnicity described in prevailing narratives. "We are modern religious, so we're very exposed," Yael related as we sat in her kitchen. "In Jerusalem as modern religious people we don't have one group of friends, we have all kinds. My husband has lots of family here from Denmark and Sweden, all of his cousins immigrated. And they're all religious. We also have a lot of family living in hard-core settlements. For us it's not 'them' and 'us.'" With family living in occupied territory, Yael's experiences and understandings of "otherness" are shaped by religious practice, belief, and affiliation as abject beings appear internal to her society, "others" along lines of not race but ideology.

This intimate relation to Israel's illegal settlements then informs Yael's perceptions of the world around her, as family ties and religious belief propel her and her loved ones across territorial boundaries. Indeed, with two of her children wounded during a shooting in the West Bank as they drove along a "settlers only" road, Yael views macro and micro scales in distinctly political terms. For Yael, "macro" takes shape as "the Arab countries," settlements, and her children's military service—matters of "security and survival" which preoccupy the country—set against the "micro" of friends and family. "Yes, my kids were shot at in the car, but it wasn't a personal attack on me," Yael explained. "And my son had an army accident, but it wasn't the Arabs. I don't take this on board—the way I divide life is that the problems, bad, negative is 'out there,' and what is personal..." Trailing into silence, this disjuncture between "out there" and those matters deemed "personal" creates the boundary of Yael's small world, a site of escape, connection, and action:

> I'm a person who connects things! I always say to the kids, *"Hakol kashur"*—everything is connected! They don't see how, but it is. But I disconnect because I look for the spiritual life. I feel how I can bring the spiritual to the ground, into the here and now. I only believe that what I can do in the world is to do what I can, to do good within my small circle. I begin with myself—when I'm depressed it's not good for anyone. Then I go to my relationship with my husband, build a wonderful family, reach out to friends. I don't do community work on an organizational level, going to organizations and demonstrations, but on a *personal* level. All I can do is on that level, in my small circle.

Disengaging from the macro level despite feeling irrevocably connected, Yael outlines a small world constructed through spirituality, which is brought "to the ground" through particular sites and means. Again demonstrating a subscription to systemics—the ability of change, happiness, and stability to transmit from small circles to those larger—Yael positions herself as central to her small world; from here "goodness" radiates outward, yet "all [she] can do" remains within the personal level delimited by the presence of "bad" beyond. Yael's small world then becomes a multilayered sphere of influence, intimacy, and consistency, a space of simultaneous connection and disconnection that allows her to live in Israel.

As in Ronit's microenvironment, repeated norms form the basis of this world unique to Yael's spirituality, social class, race, location, and gender, while at the same time allowing for subversion. Here, the overtly racialized normative "othering" of "us" and "them" as Jews and Arabs becomes displaced by internal exclusion born of religious belief and practice—instead, "we" (secular Jewish Israelis) are meant to remain within state borders, while "they" (religious settlers) live illegally beyond. However, while complicating conventional understandings of "otherness," Yael's distinction between "out there" and "the personal" again mirrors the normativity of protection, in both racialized and gendered terms. "Macro," "bad," and "there" are bound with Arabs, conflict, and politics, while "micro," "personal," and "here" become a source of sameness, read in terms of intimacy, calm, and the presumed whiteness of Australia, Denmark, and Sweden. Thus "here" emerges in need of protection from "there," reproducing the sexualized, racialized, and gendered norms generated by and productive of conflict. Relatedly, while Yael directly experienced political violence as visited on the bodies of her children, she avoids politics in a manner reflective of the norms that link knowledge of security with political voice in Israel (Mazali 2003; Lentin 2004; Jacoby 2005; Rimalt 2007; Sasson-Levy, Levy, and Lomsky-Feder 2011). Through avoiding "the bad there" even as it intrudes on "the good here," Yael actively constructs herself as "not a political being," unqualified to speak about the world around her, even as she demonstrates a nuanced understanding of its machinations. Yael's spiritual small world of action and influence then reaffirms "the political" as a realm of men—as described in chapter 1, the exercise of power by these "gangsters" produces in her the desire to flee ever deeper into spirituality, a hybrid practice made possible through (middle-)class belonging.

"Together in Pain, Together in Hope"

Troublingly, the narratives above seemingly point to a phenomenon of depoliticized or apolitical small worlds produced explicitly by Jewish Israeli women, as gender norms meet with geopolitical location, social class, race, and religion. Left uncomplicated, this depiction comes dangerously close to reproducing binary orders and gendered oppositions that assign silence and passivity to women and the feminine. However, in the context of a conflict society and conditions of pervasive militarization, prevailing norms and patterns of social relations indeed often reinforce dualisms that render the world intelligible through stark "black and white" categories. While this book complicates these tidy divisions by introducing and exploring "gray areas" and spectrums, binary constructions of us/them, here/there, active/passive, man/woman, political/intimate, and public/private remain a key grid for interpreting the experiences of everyday life. However, this is not to say that Jewish Israeli men collectively dwell in the wider world of politics and action, while women reject this realm in favor of small worlds—rather, Jewish Israeli men also construct microcosms of belonging, influence, escape, and action vis-à-vis wider realities of conflict and violence. While differently emerging through the confluence of norms and intersecting hierarchies of power and privilege, these worlds again centralize intimacy and connectivity.

Both a practitioner and a leader of a movement-based meditation practice, forty-year-old Yair's small world resonates with the circles built by Yael, in part through spiritual practice. Now living near the Knesset in Neve Sha'anan, northwest of Yael's home in the German Colony, Yair credits his father's extreme politics with shaping his own current beliefs and practices: "My father was very right-wing politically—he was part of the original settlement movement Gush Emunim[27] and part of the group that supported [former prime minister Ariel] Sharon when he ran for the first time to the Knesset. He wasn't religious or anything, but he had a hard-core right-wing orientation. This was also me through high school—I was involved in the ideological right wing until the army.... It is the outcome of my father's education that I support the opposite."[28]

While military experience catalyzed a period of questioning and personal transformation for Yair, a post-service trip to Japan and the eruption of the second *intifada* during a retreat in France radicalized his politics, bringing Yair to participate in what he terms "Dharma activism." "The basic tenet of Dharma is that there is suffering in the world and we should be involved in ending or finishing the suffering," Yair explained. "The goal is not to solve, but to understand the conflict." Activism among this small community of practitioners aims at self-understanding as a foundation for wider processes of change. "What does the conflict do to me?" Yair related as the central question posed by Jewish Israeli Dharma activists. "Not even to *us,* but to *me.* We want to create a safe space and gently insist on exposing this pain." Again the individual takes up a location at the core of a meaningful world, this time based on "universal" suffering which must be "ended or finished"—though, paradoxically, the continuation of violence makes this very "safe space" of action possible.

In contrast to Yael's small circles, expressly political action becomes manifest in Yair's world of self-reflection, greater understanding, and reduced suffering. Yair describes "advanced practice" as a time in which the work of Dharma activists "extends," mirroring the principle of systemics outlined by Ronit and internalized by Yael, as all view security, stability, and happiness as radiating outward from a core. However, Yair admits that the "immature practice" in Israel focuses on "inner work"; as such, while leaders seek to integrate their students' self-cultivation with the wider context, many students identify conflict as the root of their suffering yet do not understand it as a target of their practice. From workshops with teenagers nearing military service to consciousness-raising meditation walks and solidarity actions in Palestinian villages, Dharma activist leaders actively attempt to bridge self and society through explicit engagement with politics. Yair recounted one long-term initiative and its ambiguous results thus:

> The New Age community is a group that you could say doesn't have any political awareness, but for the last eight years there has been a ceremony commemorating Memorial Day, Independence Day, and Nakba Day together.[29] The reason you don't know about it is because it's initiated by New Age people. At the start it was a Jewish renewal group that celebrated all the holidays. A friend who belonged said, "We're celebrating everything that happened here, but not Nakba Day—there are people here to whom that is important." It was a two-day event and the theme was "Together in pain, together in hope." The first day is Memorial Day—it's about pain: the Holocaust and the *nakba* story. The second day is Independence Day—it's about hope: how do we see a joint state or a joint way of living together? . . . But the New Age group doesn't understand the political implications of what they're doing. Very healing things happen: Jews listen to Palestinians tell their story, they sympathize, and then the same thing happens in the opposite direction. . . . The New Age group, their minds don't go there, they're happy with their personal moment of deep catharsis. But I support it, of course.[30]

Bringing together divergent national narratives under the banner of a single event, Yair and his fellow Dharma activists centralize suffering as a means of fostering connectivity across borders. In doing so, they aim to formulate a sense of shared history and common future, even as the practitioners who take part fail to move beyond "personal catharsis." Repeated in this world are the prevailing intersecting norms of race, class, and gender: categories of "us" and "them" again take shape as the racialized categories of "Jew" and "Palestinian"; privileged social class facilitates access to a spiritual practice requiring time and mobility; and the "safe space" for reflection and understanding remains embedded within conditions of violent conflict associated with militarism and masculinity. Yet, significantly, the central repetition underwriting this small world is the normative narrative of Zionism. As Idith Zertal (2005, 3) writes, "Through a dialectical process of appropriation and exclusion, remembering and forgetting, Israeli society has defined itself in relation to the Holocaust: it regarded itself as both the heir to the victims and their accuser, atoning for their sins and redeeming their death." These terms of victimization and redemption resonate deeply with the suffering, pain, and hope centralized by Jewish Israeli Dharma activists, as Nakba Day converges with commemoration of the Holocaust and celebration of Israel's "independence."[31] Enmeshed with gender, class, race, and the geopolitical location of Jerusalem, Yair's small world recycles the very narrative at the core of Jewish Israeli state and society, linking "me" with "us" in ways which halt at the borders of self and nation. Here sympathy does not engender movement beyond the boundaries of collectivity but guarantees trauma its position of primacy in worlds both small and large.

As related throughout this chapter, this central ideological narrative generates the norms repeated in worlds of varying shapes and sizes, spaces of escape and action that become the setting for everyday life. While ostensibly free from the violence of "politics," these safe realms are those same sites in which "whiteness" takes shape through the masculinized and sexualized threat of "Arab others," where class and location enable the accumulation of "sameness" in constant need of protection. Then at stake in the loss of these worlds is less their sense of normalcy, knowingly suspended between fantasy and reality, than the very selves and intimate relations at their center.

CONCLUSION

As mechanisms and microcosms of normalization provide ways of bargaining with reality and (re)ordering everyday life, their dynamics reveal how divisions between intimacy/politics, homefront/battlefield, and normalcy/conflict are both reified and collapse in ways that sustain domination. Securing wider relations of power through acts of protection, investment, and care, intimate practices among friends, within families, and inside small worlds make visible how action indeed underwrites seemingly passive assent. While constructions of normality resonate and circulate in the public domain, they find foundation in the private, bridging the gaps between nation, state, and self. Here gender not only emerges as "a structure of social relations" (Connell 2002, 10) but acts to structure those very relations and the resulting political realities in complex and at times contradictory ways. Here, shifting norms, codes, roles, and relations ensure that desired normalcy remains aspirational as, following Zionist narratives, everyday life entails constant hardship, pursuit, and transcendence. As mechanisms effectively mask this dependency on rupture and violence, surprising regimes of regulation and sources of domination emerge to highlight how intimate constellations of community might be indicators of power as much as sites of belonging.

Within families, microenvironments, and small worlds, seeming inaction emerges from the tension between reality and aspiration, as intimate relations provide modes of "escape from" and "resistance to" wider political realities. These attachments reveal that political apathy among Jewish Israelis cannot be understood as an absence of action but must be regarded as a kind of selective practice, where experiences and understandings of politics shape expectations of where engagement and investment might reap the greatest rewards. Searching for a sense of relief or escape from social, political, and economic realities, many individuals retreat into intimate sites and communities. Yet everyday life cannot be completely dissociated from conflict—rather, this chapter has described precisely how conflict and violence become sewn into the fabric of normalcy, generating mechanisms of maintenance and repair that seemingly protect intimacy from politics. Together, these sites and mechanisms point to how investment on micropolitical levels generates disengagement and inaction in broader spheres of influence, fashioning a particular kind of apathy.

Through intimate sites and relations, apathy as "active disengagement" gains not only spatial and social grounding but also ties to belonging. Offering normativity, security, and forums for action, small worlds become microcosms of normality, an "inside" of seeming calm and dependability made possible through the perpetuation of conflict "outside." While joking, bypassing, unseeing, and silencing function to maintain and repair normalcy when these are ruptured, the necessarily interpersonal dimension of these mechanisms reminds us of *who we are* and what binds us together. More precious than the fostered sense of normalcy acknowledged by many as fleeting and unreal, intimate sites and relations offer moral consistency, meaningful participation, and realms of optimism and hope. This is not to argue that leftist Jewish Israelis take action in families or small worlds "instead of" politics, but rather to point to what their investment is oriented toward: intimate communities of belonging. Again resonating with the prevailing ethos of Zionism, actions largely aim to ensure preservation and protection of community, producing social bonds, generating apathy, and sustaining conflict.

FOUR

Embedded (In)Action

A LANDSCAPE OF BROWNS AND GREYS spreads out before me from my position at the fence line, high atop the hill. When I first decided to join in the olive harvest with Rabbis for Human Rights, I pictured myself near Nablus amid a grove of olive trees, laboring with volunteers and villagers as the shadowy presence of settlers and soldiers haunted the slope below. However, a call from the organization on the day before the harvest brought into focus a different image, as I learned that we would be going not to Nablus but to the area of Jayyus, near the Green Line. We were set to harvest in a "buffer zone" of sorts, positioned between the village and the fence with its military patrols. According to the woman on the other end of the line, we would be helping a widow and her two young sons to bring in their harvest for processing, a feat impossible for them alone in their relative ages and small number. It was less romantic than the thought of myself among gnarled trees high above the valleys of the West Bank; I adjusted my expectations to a barren dust track, turnstile gates, and patrolling soldiers whose latent violence threatened the widow and her children. Slightly more nervous than before, I slept little that night, particularly as a relative expressed her shock on hearing my plans for the next day: "This is not an ordinary thing for people to do, you understand?" Flushed with the excitement of transgression, on harvest day I was surprised to find that our ultimate destination would actually be not Jayyus but a site behind Qalqilya, technically across the Green Line yet on the "Israeli side" of the fence.

Bumping along dirt roads in a minibus peopled with retirement-age Jewish Israelis and international activists, our leader—a female rabbi—briefed us on violence and how to position our bodies between Palestinian harvesters and the military or settlers—our task was explicitly to "act as a buffer," not solely to harvest olives as I had imagined. Previously unaware that this was part of the job, I felt a creeping anxiety as we came to a stop seemingly in the middle of nowhere; the Palestinian driver kindly instructed us to disembark and wait for our contact, who would lead us to the harvest site. However, a quick look around revealed no Palestinian villages, inhabitants, or olive trees. The only recognizable sight meeting the eye was a Jewish Israeli settlement that oozed over the sloping hillside above us, with its red roofs and orderly streets enclosed by a formidable perimeter fence. After a time we were indeed met by our "contact," two Palestinian boys no more than ten years old, who turned and led us up the dirt track toward the settlement—could this be right? Along the path other harvesters worked in the valley: small groups of Palestinian women and children with sticks, mules, and carts, some singing as they whacked the olive branches, others resting under shade in the growing heat of morning. As we came to a stop at the fence, it was clear that we would be harvesting inside the settlement—my sense of the surreal grew on learning that we must wait for the armed settlement guards to allow us entry. After more than twenty minutes and numerous phone calls to parties inside the settlement, two men appeared in a large truck, with black guns slung over their shoulders, their bright white smiles shining with benevolence. They granted us entry along with a group of university students and the small number of Palestinian harvesters who had joined our retinue, slowly making note of passport numbers on a pad of legal paper. Amid the activists in the queue, the Palestinian women remained silent as their children practiced English, and the single Palestinian man present revealed that we would be harvesting his trees—not a widow with two small children, but a middle-aged male filmmaker with property in Ramallah. Nothing was as expected, a reality that left me feeling uneasy but other volunteers seemed to take in stride.

The harvest proceeded, with volunteers picking by hand and rake, while the Palestinian children and women used long sticks to reach the higher branches with force. "The Palestinian methods are backward and primitive, but we are their guests, so we do it like they do, even if we can think of a better way," our rabbi leader told me as we moved slowly among the twenty trees which sat directly behind a row of red-roofed houses, the area littered with garbage thrown over private fences. If I climbed even one meter into a tree I could see over the fences and into the lives of these settlers, their yards manicured and adorned with lawn chairs, children's bicycles, and brightly colored slides and swing sets. Turning my head 180 degrees, my eyes met another fence, that of the perimeter behind the patrol road. Slowly, slowly we worked, with many volunteers taking breaks to practice Arabic and commiserate. Why weren't we rushing? It was *Shabbat,* and we needed to leave by early afternoon in order for those observing the Sabbath to be home by sunset. I asked about our unhurried pace and received the answer that really this harvest allowed the Palestinians with us "to feel good," that some measure of accomplishment came from merely tending the trees. In truth it seemed more symbolic. The filmmaker and his family had been denied access to the trees for at least three years and did not expect to make much from the actual olives, yet our presence and actions were a means of articulating a claim to the land. Perhaps this desire to "feel good" more accurately applied to the volunteers and settlement guards than it did to our fellow harvesters.

A short time later, we broke for a lunch of hot tea, breads, dips, cheeses, and vegetables prepared by the Palestinian women. Eventually, we began to gather our belongings before returning to the waiting minibus, and I decided to walk alone for a moment, following the patrol road uphill toward our entry and exit point. As the warm sun and dust slowed the day to a crawl, I found my lookout. I closed my eyes in an effort to just be, to imagine my original fantasy, and instead became increasingly aware of a loud, rhythmic pounding. Opening my eyes and turning my head, I matched sound with image: a nearby construction site promised a bloom of new red roofs, private yards, and orderly streets atop the neighboring hill. Only days earlier, the construction ban in the settlements had expired, and clearly no time would be wasted. I turned back to the vista, this time with my eyes open, taking in exactly what I was doing, where it was being done, and under what circumstances, feeling much less the resistance and resistor of my imagination.[1]

Outside yet glaringly inside, my participation in the olive harvest with Rabbis for Human Rights brought multiple limits and layers of power into focus. East of Qalqilya yet somehow still within Israel, inside a Palestinian olive grove yet enclosed by a settlement, transgressing the borders of *what people do* yet requiring permission from security guards—could my act honestly be framed as resistance? In this context, acts of transgression sit in tension with their limits, entangling opposition with power. As Michel Foucault (2003 [1963], 446) writes: "Transgression carries the limit right to the limit of its being; transgression forces the limit to face the fact of its immanent disappearance, to find itself in what it excludes (perhaps, to be more exact, to recognize itself for the first time), to experience its positive truth in its downward fall. And yet, toward what is transgression unleashed in its movement of pure violence, if not that which imprisons it, toward the limit and those elements it contains?"

Following Foucault, here limits and transgression contain one another, proving inseparable as each becomes possible through the continued existence of the other. As the exclusion of nonconforming acts, objects, and others makes limit lines clear, so too transgression relies upon a standard of ordinary *things people do*; a given order arises through the presence of both.

Just as I stood inside the settlement fence line considering its multiple boundaries as the hammering of renewed expansion rang out, layers of power shape decisions around action and inaction in Israel-Palestine, binding the two together. As transgression indeed raises the limits of a particular order (Foucault 2003 [1963], cited in Fadil 2009, 440), actions taken and withheld constitute indicators of embeddedness, revealing how power is produced and overlayered in a given context (Abu-Lughod 1990). In response to the rhetorical query *Ma la'asot?* (What can we do?), this chapter illustrates the multiple means through which individuals take action, how they engage with the politics of conflict and occupation through modes of resistance and transgression. In doing so, a range of limits informing oppositional political action in Israel-Palestine becomes visible, producing a complex dialectic between resistance and power that again takes shape through patterns of gender. Moving from practices of "everyday resistance," to the normalization of feminist anti-occupation activism, to the routinization of radical protest, this chapter reveals a continuum linking political action and inaction among Jewish Israelis, adding complexity to both apathy and domination.

EVERYDAY CONFLICT, EVERYDAY RESISTANCE

As argued in chapter 3, in Jewish Israeli society everyday life takes shape relative to an approximation of normalcy that attempts to bar the reality of conflict, while at the same time holding this violence close as its condition of possibility. The task of this chapter is not to judge or evaluate modes of oppositional action, to assign labels of "good" or "bad," "effective" or "ineffective," but to consider their economy and effects—what they *do* in frames wider than individual everyday lives. No longer an *event* in the sense of "a drama which shocks being into radically open situations" (Badiou 1999, cited in Berlant 2011, 5), Israel's occupation of the Palestinian Territories has become a *situation*, "a state of things in which something that will perhaps matter is unfolding amid the usual activity of life" (Berlant 2011, 5). Overlapping with and often producing the event's staccato punctuation, the situation constitutes "a state of animated and animating suspension" (5) that resonates with the precarity explored in the preceding chapters. Here, resistance sits in constant tension with routinization, risking absorption into the everyday or translation into habit (Allen 2008) as actions simultaneously subvert and reaffirm the extant order.

For many Jewish Israelis the everyday remains a site of meaningful action, even as resistance risks becoming routine—"You have to consider people like my cousin, who refuses to drive over the Green Line," I was told adamantly during the early days of fieldwork. For months I actually understood many of my own actions to be a form of "everyday resistance," in keeping with scholarship by James C. Scott (1985), Diane Singerman (1995), and Asef Bayat (1997), feeling myself part of a "prosaic but constant struggle" characterized by "passive noncompliance, subtle sabotage, evasion, and deception" (Scott 1985, 29, 31). In the name of resistance, I refused to travel Route 443 through the occupied West Bank, a "shortcut" from Jerusalem to Tel Aviv. However, on traveling the highway in a shared taxi I realized that my previous act of boycott had colluded with power, in some way rejecting sight, experience, and knowledge of where Israel's occupation is and what it creates.

Far from uncommon among politically leftist Jewish Israelis, everyday resistance takes shape across a diverse range of subject positions, as "nonactivists," "would-be activists," "should-be activists," "couch activists," "passive activists," "one-eighth" or "one-quarter activists," "office activists," "radical activists," and "former activists" practice innovative modes of opposition.[2] Here, *what we can do* is constantly articulated and performed in the everyday in both positive and negative terms—through doing and not doing. Yet as each account of everyday political action and resistance unfolds within the limits of a given order, it may also become implicated in layered modes of power. Echoing Lila Abu-Lughod's (1990) work on power and resistance, here oppositional action must be understood as embedded, as an act of resistance against one particular relation of power potentially reconstitutes or affirms another. Urging scholars to invert Foucault's (1998 [1978], 95–96) dictum "Where there is power, there is resistance," Abu-Lughod (1990, 42) looks to "signs of human freedom . . . to tell us more about forms of power and how people are caught up in them." If we appraise oppositional political action among Jewish Israelis through this lens, resistance indeed diagnoses power as patterns of gender emerge to shape the spaces and contents of action.

Here, the multiplicity of domination becomes visible, produced and maintained in diverse sites and practices through overlapping and at times contradictory relations of power.

Resistance at Home

As seen in the preceding chapters, the intimate spaces of domestic realms remain central to understandings and experiences of politics among Jewish Israelis—in this, "home" might also become a site of resistance. For Boaz, a long-time Jerusalemite living in the Beit HaKerem neighborhood, home is a physical space marked by experiences of ownership and autonomy: "Living here, being part of the society, I feel that I cooperate with the occupation whether I like it or not. I evade taxes for the most part. Here it's moral, in this situation. I evade taxes by not working—I don't bring a benefit to society and I don't pay much tax. It's also because I'm lazy. But it's a resistance! I don't feel that I fit in with society. Also I'm not married and I don't have a family—also maybe this is resistance."

Conveying awareness of his own embeddedness in wider political realities—"I cooperate with the occupation whether I like it or not"—Boaz describes a mode of oppositional everyday action that targets the economic foundations of the Israeli state: he refuses to pay taxes, as an explicit act of resistance. Yet as Boaz articulates and practices opposition, he simultaneously declares a fondness for capitalism, "surviving" on the rental income generated by the multi-unit building that he owns and lives in. "Now let me tell you about the renter who was smoking on the bench over there," Boaz said later, as he motioned toward where an older man had been sitting quietly on the edge of the garden, a lush green space with chestnut trees transplanted from the Golan Heights. "He's a Palestinian from the north, from 1948. Being a Palestinian looking to live in West Jerusalem is not so fun. He works as an economist in the budgeting department at Hebrew University—he's been there for years. To me, he has a regular paycheck. That's the only thing I look for."[3]

Here, resistance in the space of the home diagnoses power as Boaz protests Israel's occupation and state policies in explicitly capitalist terms, subscribing to the logics of neoliberalism—individualism, profit, privatization—that underwrite the political conditions of economic and social life. This layering of power produces in Boaz a sense of benevolence as he accepts "a regular paycheck" from a Palestinian lodger in an act morally consistent with his participation in East Jerusalem protests, even as it elides the politics of capital gain; here, resistance simultaneously subverts and reaffirms. Not without significance is the way Boaz relates his act of protest and egalitarian ideals to marital status and (hetero)normativity—these registers of resistance are *available* to Boaz, as a single Ashkenazi man, providing him with both an expression of political voice and a source of financial profit. After our interview Boaz admitted that he will need to reconsider his present lifestyle if he begins a family in the future: "There will be more money going out in expenses and I'll have to expand the flat—this means less rental income coming in. In the end, I will have to work." Thus Boaz acknowledges that his resistance to state policies and practices through withholding tax and providing accommodation is necessarily ephemeral, as when he shifts to a normative lifestyle, moving to "fit in with society," both will cease.

Significantly, Boaz invokes the normativity of the family unit assumed to be heterosexual and nuclear in his description of political action at home; however, this constellation should not be taken as given. Rather, alternative family formations reveal further ways in which resistance might become caught up in power. Also single, Ashkenazi, and a property owner near Jerusalem, as a single mother Ronit lived in French Hill prior to moving to Mevasseret-Zion, on the outskirts of Jerusalem. For Ronit, her prior residence in French Hill constituted an explicitly political act:

> I looked in many Jerusalem neighborhoods, but I liked French Hill so much. At the time I was very ideological about peace, and living in a mixed neighborhood attracted me. So I decided to buy a small apartment with three bedrooms and I took a mortgage. My living room and bedroom windows faced the desert and the Dead Sea, the hills of Jordan. The road below my windows went to the Dead Sea and the desert—it was very pleasant. I was very happy at that time period.... After, in 2000, I had Maya.... We were very happy, we had cats.
>
> Then the *intifada* started. It was so tough—I'm telling you about Maya because of this. When there was no nanny... the nanny didn't have a car, so they would walk home, carrying a cell phone. The kindergarten was a square building, facing the road, with five classes—there were 150 kids in the kindergarten. It was nice, there were different ages and classes. When I went to pick up Maya [one day], everything was curtained, closed, and dark. There was no music. Normally it was a loud place, open, with lots of music. The guard also wasn't there—you need to knock and then the guard walks toward the gate from inside the building. He told me that the army said that terrorists were moving around the neighborhood, and one of their aims was to kidnap little children from the kindergarten.... I don't know how I didn't run away.[4]

Ending on a familiar note of perseverance, an ordinary act of resistance is again embedded in layers of power as Ronit recounts living in a "mixed" neighborhood, which is in fact a Jewish Israeli settlement beyond the Green Line. Surveying the Dead Sea and the occupied territory below, from her vantage point in French Hill Ronit experienced the satisfaction of resistance without explicitly acknowledging the politics engaged and hidden by her actions. With the arrival of her daughter Maya, Ronit's everyday oppositional act—living among "others"—is revealed to be fleeting, as her experiences and understandings of coexistence reaffirm racialized constructions of threat. Here, home becomes a site of both security and precarity, at once the safe space to which Maya returns and the seemingly sole place of stability in a sea of danger. In this space Ronit acts to both nurture and protect, as recounted in the previous chapter, upending gender norms as a woman raising her daughter alone. Yet as Ronit doubly resisted power in her daily life in French Hill—attempting to practice coexistence as a single mother—her experience simultaneously reproduces prevailing norms and narratives: a daughter in need of protection is ferried to the heights of Mevasseret-Zion, where violence seemingly cannot shatter the music of childhood and the sanctity of home.

In these varying ways, home provides a site of everyday resistance struck through by contradiction as it produces, reflects, and subverts modes of normativity. Through their narratives, both Boaz and Ronit make visible multiple forms of opposition that overlap while seemingly standing in tension. Neither conforms to the prevailing gendered norms that centralize family in its nuclear constellation as man, woman, and (multiple) children—Boaz remains single, and Ronit raises her daughter alone. Yet in their non-normative lifestyles both reproduce different sets of gendered norms through their chosen registers of opposition. In keeping with hegemonic constructions of masculinity Boaz projects authority and concerns himself with earning income, while Ronit describes her experiences of mothering and an attendant sense of vulnerability. However, even as Boaz performs aspects of hegemonic masculinity, his non-normative lifestyle and activism imply a kind of social marginality; so too Ronit might affirm hegemonic roles associated with women within Jewish Israeli society, but at the same time she provides income and protection for her family. Then as patterns of gender shape everyday acts of resistance within the home, prevailing norms, roles, codes, and relations are simultaneously contested and confirmed, revealing their embeddedness in power.

Resistance through Labor

Beyond the intimate spaces of home and family, resistance is further threaded into the fabric of everyday life through labor, as employment practices create opportunities for contact and exchange. Again, here patterns of gender reveal embeddedness in multiple layers of power, creating the possibility of simultaneous subversion and affirmation. On beginning our discussion in a Tel Aviv restaurant, Dana, a thirty-two-year-old occupational therapist, described herself as politically "avoidant," yet demonstrated throughout our exchange that political awareness and engagement are not limited to reading newspapers, watching television broadcasts, or listening to radio programs:

> I work with Palestinians, you know. I work as an occupational therapist at the hospital in Tel Aviv, with children who have cancer and have to stay in the hospital. There is a whole floor of Palestinian kids from Gaza—a whole floor. This is the only way that I can be a pacifist, the only way that I can think of myself as contributing to the conflict. I'm learning Arabic, "*shwaya, shwaya*" [Arabic: slowly, slowly]. But I don't feel the conflict with them.
>
> KN: How do you mean?
>
> Dana: My boss has to do a presentation about this floor at a meeting now that more people are finding out about the Palestinian kids there—they want him to talk about what "dilemmas" we face working with Palestinians, how we get along, etc. But I don't feel the conflict, although there are lots of other issues. There is no stress, no expression of it. The other issues are medical, mostly—about treating the children. Will they die if they are sent home to those conditions?—we can't get their medical histories, it's difficult to communicate, cultural differences, their families have no means, no resources—these are medical issues.
>
> KN: So is this a way that you feel you can be proactive about the conflict?
>
> Dana: No, it's not proactive. But treating them as equal, really trying to learn Arabic.... This is the only thing I get being peaceful—I judge them as a person, no less.
>
> I also learn things about their society, things that make me question their behavior. Before working with the children at the hospital I definitely would have said "It's all our fault" or "What options do eighteen-year-old boys in Gaza have besides terrorism, becoming a terrorist? I would probably do the same in that situation." But I had a Palestinian friend, he's from the West Bank, and he would sometimes blame Israel for everything. Everything! Like family pressure, and they had means—they weren't rich, but they had means—and narrowed options. There is no argument about his position in

life and the fact that Israel has something to do with it, but it's not *all* Israel's fault. I have pressure from my mother to be responsible, to have a family and a job, and it's not to do with the conflict. He would transfer everything to the conflict. But it also has to do with the conflicts you have in life—yes, you have fewer options than us, but also you have to take responsibility for growing older.[5]

Recounted at length here, Dana's narrative is notable for its self-reflexivity and clarity as she articulates the layered relations of power in which her work unfolds. Crucially, though Dana works with Palestinian children from the Gaza Strip, she openly relates *not* "feel[ing] the conflict with them" and instead focuses on seemingly separate "medical issues," underlining how normalization and "unseeing" may be actively practiced among Jewish Israelis. Yet Dana's account remains framed by her pacifism and desire to act or "contribute to [ending] the conflict," shedding light on the ways in which considerations of social class, race, religiosity, physical ability, and geopolitical location inform her interaction with Palestinian patients. Here resistance emerges not only as providing care and learning Arabic to overcome technical obstacles to her work, but also in terms of learning to treat these patients as equal—"as a person, no less." However, while this egalitarian practice enables Dana to practice resistance, it simultaneously generates an unexpected sort of clarity that moves her away from radical politics and critique. Through "learning about their society," Dana arrives at a more politically centrist position that moderates her perception of how occupation, annexation, blockade, and control impact the lives of her Palestinian patients and friends. In this, her everyday resistance—practiced literally each working day—gives rise to a political sentiment aligned with the status quo.

Interestingly, the experiences of Gil, a thirty-five-year-old social worker in Jerusalem's lower-income neighborhoods, underlined this phenomenon where political conservatism emerges through labor-based encounters. In his work with "at-risk" Jewish Israeli adolescent boys, Gil spends increasing amounts of time in the neighborhoods of south Jerusalem, an area in which he includes Gilo despite its status as an illegal settlement overlooking Bethlehem. As Gil related:

It was always because of this thing, of oppressed people and groups, that I was always very left-wing, but in the process of the last few years of life ... I'm getting to understand other opinions as well. Right-wing politics—I'm not talking about economics here—I'm getting to understand their concerns. The fears, the complex situation, the need for security.

KN: How? Because of the families you work with? Are they more conservative?

Gil: Not because of work and those communities. Because I'm getting more involved in society—my opinions are getting more based on reality, not on a basic idea of oppressed and oppressors. I feel it is happening with my friends, too. It also comes with age, you get to see a more complex view. Specifically for me, because I felt in a way oppressed, in a way pushed away from society— how do you say *leshatef peula*? "Cooperate." I used to go with this, seclude myself from society. In the last few years, especially since I started with social work, started working... I felt in a way that society was fucked up, I didn't want to deal with it—society was fucked up and I didn't want a connection with it, I didn't want to deal with it. In the last years I am involved more with society, I get to understand the complexity. I understand that I have to influence in a limited way—I *have* to. It's not worth it to stand on the side... even though it's not perfect and it isn't going to be. So it comes from more involvement in society. I didn't go to the army, I was doing my stuff, music. Jobs were just things that interested me, jobs didn't influence. In a way they do [influence] because I always liked art—it's a more abstract, free way of influencing, of being part. I'm trying to be involved in more concrete ways.[6]

On first reading, this narrative seems internally contradictory, as Gil rejects work as the reason for his shift in political opinion while simultaneously detailing how his job as a social worker provides an avenue of awareness, resistance, and influence. Here, experiences of encounter and subsequent understandings emerge not from exchanges with Palestinians but from meeting Jewish Israelis who possess scant access to social, economic, and political capital. Like Dana, Gil sees his work as everyday resistance, this time providing a means of acting against the prevailing relations of power that shape privilege and belonging internal to Jewish Israeli society. Yet these ordinary oppositional actions remain embedded in wider realties, including relations of domination. Through resistance Gil comes to understand the complexity, fears, and security that drive politics more conservative than his own, effectively moving toward the center as he draws closer to the society from which he felt previously estranged.

In these narratives of resistance based in labor practices, patterns of gender again shape and reflect the different registers for action available to women and men. Both Dana and Gil work in trades associated with caregiving, and both articulate a shift from stances described as more radically political to "understanding"; in keeping with the gender norms that frame Jewish Israeli society, this might be perceived as a process of feminization even as it conveys a kind of equity. However, the actions, resistance, and complicity of Dana and Gil must be read through the intersection of norms and hierarchies. Here Dana relates her understanding of responsibility, something that she admits to personally struggling with, to acceding to normative pressures, including the drive for family and reproduction—this seemingly equalizes the life experiences of Jewish Israelis and Palestinians. For Dana, these imperatives are divorced from their wider context of conflict and occupation, as all men and women are subject to family pressures purely as a matter of "growing older." In her eyes, what Dana negotiates as a young Ashkenazi Jewish Israeli woman should be met similarly by a young Palestinian man from the West Bank, nothing more and nothing less. For Gil, resistance enables proximity to a society by which he has felt rejected both as Mizrahi and as an artist. In terms of gendered normativity, Gil's non-normative masculinity is implied by his avoidance of mandatory military service. This vector of difference intersects with Gil's Iranian ethnicity, producing in him the impulse to "go along" with his own marginalization, which simultaneously yielded Gil's formerly radical politics and disengagement. Now refusing to cooperate in his own oppression and resisting the hierarchies of power and privilege that shape Jewish Israeli society, Gil chooses a register of action in which he might have more influence as a nonconformist; yet in doing so he paradoxically draws closer to the dominant group. As made visible by both Dana and Gil in their accounts of labor, the layering of power in Israel-Palestine creates complex and seemingly contradictory conditions in which everyday resistance provides a site of subversion while at the same time reproducing present political conditions.

Structures of Practice

As considered here, accounts of everyday resistance demonstrate the extent to which acts occur not in isolation but within the wider context of "living on" in conditions of conflict. However, this embeddedness does not imply that actions taken or withheld are collectively futile, nor that individuals are victims of false consciousness; rather, this overlayering of power directs attention to its economy, how these acts combine and what they do together. Implicating resistance in capitalist accumulation, illegal settlements, and conservative politics, here everyday oppositional action gets caught up in wider matrices of power. While individually these actions might resist the "mode of coasting consciousness within the ordinary" (Berlant 2011, 18) that characterizes small worlds, they also provide the moments of rupture necessary for the stabilization of normality, as argued in chapter 3. Thus oppositional action may indeed fortify relations of power beyond those targeted through resistance. In this manner, actions against occupation, injustice, and discrimination become entangled with neoliberal capitalism, nationalism, and political conservatism, all integral aspects of contemporary Zionism.

As such, those forms of political action often deemed most accessible and least incendiary—everyday acts of resistance—serve to diagnose power, enlarging the frame of reference to reveal how "resisting at one level may catch people up at other levels" (Abu-Lughod 1990, 53). As depicted in the passages above, these actions not only reproduce the precarity of everyday life through potentially catalyzing cycles of rupture and repair but also bolster domination through a range of social practices (Mitchell 1990, 553). Gender becomes central to these dynamics, shaping the roles available to women and men along with avenues of action and access to political voice. Yet as argued throughout the preceding analyses, these patterns of gender remain dynamic even as they structure resistance, adapting to changing relations of power. In this, the role of (Ashkenazi) woman-as-mother sits easily with mother-as-earner as both intersect with the dominant national narrative. So too a Mizrahi man who refuses mandatory military service might increasingly identify with the role of man-as-protector, reaffirming the very construction of masculinity from which he felt excluded. Together these textures point to a diverse range of gendered roles, norms, codes, and relations that in part determine registers for action in everyday life.

Yet, as argued earlier, while everyday resistance makes complexity and contradiction visible, these problematic actions cannot be reduced to "false consciousness," or the ideological persuasion and misrecognition that implicates individuals and communities in relations of domination (Scott 1990, 72). Rather, the individuals narrating the passages above knowingly articulate their embeddedness: Gil acknowledges that refusing to cooperate in oppression paradoxically brings him closer to the mainstream and domination, just as Dana admits that treating Palestinians from Gaza as "equal" means passing judgment on individuals whose "position in life" is shaped through violence perpetuated by her own state and society. Thus diverse actions intended as resistance or expressions of solidarity openly implicate individual actors in layers of power, dissolving the border between structure and practice. As Mitchell (1990, 561) well cautions: "The distinction between particular practices and their structure or frame is problematic not simply because it may not be shared by non-western traditions, but because ... the apparent existence of such unphysical frameworks of structures is precisely the effect introduced by modern mechanisms of power and it is through this elusive yet powerful effect that modern systems of domination are maintained."

HEGEMONIC ENTANGLEMENTS

In the context of Israel-Palestine, acknowledgement of "catching up" in power becomes a means of expressing how one "lives on" or "gets by" in conditions of conflict, as evident in the admission, "I am part of it whether I like it or not." As demonstrated throughout the preceding chapters, domination arises not through the division of coercion from persuasion or the separation of the physical realm from behavior and consciousness (Mitchell 1990, 545, 559) but in large part through social maintenance and production. Then participation in domination cannot be appraised as imposed or enforced by state or military actors on an unwilling or unknowing populace but must be understood as rooted in interpersonal and intimate dimensions of sociality, inclusive of resistance. While this creates a seemingly untenable position for oppositional actions and actors, resistance continues to be significant in part due to its embeddedness, as individuals and communities insist on the possibility of a better future despite inevitable flaws and failures.

However, given this degree of entanglement with power, resistance risks generating its own resistance, or movement away from its promise of opposition. In a manner similar to transgression, which "allows the limits to arise, in their blank nakedness, while simultaneously being transgressed" (Fadil 2009, 440), opposition to resistance despite a shared politics betrays much about the workings of power, providing an alternative reading of Abu-Lughod's (1990) imperative. Here reticence toward or rejection of oppositional actions and agendas might be cast as a "nonpositive affirmation," a contestation that "does not imply a generalized negation, but an affirmation that affirms nothing, a radical break of transitivity" (Foucault 2003 [1963], 446–47). While modes of "resistance to resistance" might contest power in varying ways, (non-)actions and (non-)actors simultaneously become implicated in domination as their practices of apparent passivity again weave into wider structures.

The Banality of Activism

On the most readily apparent level, individuals who resist resistance are responding to the overwhelming normalization of organized activism in everyday life, particularly those initiatives associated with the political Left in Jewish Israeli society. From municipality-approved demonstrations in Tel Aviv and Jerusalem to independent activist organizations, various forms of political protest have become stitched into the fabric of ordinary life, many in specifically gendered terms. As my fieldwork progressed, my participation in frequent Tel Aviv demonstrations began to feel routine and formulaic, if not oddly "normal." Even as I understood that greater numbers of bodies in the street drew attention to opposition, I was aware that my actions somehow contributed to the prevailing sense of anemia. Dana, the occupational therapist who earlier characterized her degree of political engagement as "avoidant," described this phenomenon, saying, "Most demonstrations are in Tel Aviv, but you barely feel it. Every Friday at Ben Zion there is a quiet demonstration."

"Women in Black?" I asked.

"Yes," she said. "No one notices it. It's on a major route for shoppers and, okay, they [Women in Black] are there, but it's the same with the puppies of SOS.[7] One Friday people were yelling at them, but there is indifference here."

Grouped with the pitiable puppies leashed to a city fence in hopes of adoption, the weekly protest of Women in Black stands as a marker of normalcy rather than a provocation, though it presumably evokes different emotions and reactions than the pets nearby. Indeed, the presence of four Women in Black activists clustered in the shade of a small palm tree set the stage for my experience of Tel Aviv's Pride Parade, the comparatively boisterous and popular action that opened chapter 3. While often ignored or unseen, these primarily elderly women protesters at times elicit aggressive responses, emotional reactions that stand in contrast to the women's "quiet demonstration" and the overwhelming "indifference" to their acts of protest. Yet this very volatility of encounter becomes subject to normalization, as it occurs within a political and social environment characterized by conflict, aggression, confrontation, and heated debate. When asked later in our interview about the possibility of mass mobilization, Dana remarked on the conduct and emotion imagined to spur action:

> The problem is that the left wing is impotent—where the right wing has loads of people and shouting, the left is civilized and singing. They don't get

noticed. There is practically no left wing. Sadly, when the people will rise for change it will be because of internal problems, not because of the conflict. Problems like the corrupt government, financial judgment, and criticism of education. When [prime minister Yitzhak] Rabin died he was supporting the peace initiative—if there is any serious initiative there will be followers. But to rise against the situation as it is now? No. The activists, the Anarchists, the Women in Black—it will be the same actors and the same percentage. People won't rage against it.[8]

In this passage, the indifference facing oppositional actors becomes a product of their own doing, an apparent deficiency in critical mass, political voice, and visibility contrasted by the political Right.[9] Critically, these "same actors"—explicitly listed among them the Friday protesters from Women in Black—are deemed lacking in rage, the same ingredient I felt was missing from the organized protests of Tel Aviv and West Jerusalem, save when met with right-wing counter-protests. Interestingly, this subscription to rage— also on my part—replicates the denigration of women's and feminist protest groups in Israel, as it validates a belief in the transformative potential of masculinized anger infused with the threat of violence. Numerous commentators note the prevalence of women's anti-occupation and peace activism organizations in Israel from the 1980s through the early 2000s (Mayer 1994; Sharoni 1995, 1996; Helman 1999a; Cockburn 1998, 2007; Freedman 2002; Misra and Rich 2002; Svirsky 2002a, 2002b; Lentin 2004; Fuchs 2005; Jacoby 2005; Powers 2006; Kaye-Kantrowitz 2008; Segal 2008; Sasson-Levy, Levy, and Lomsky-Feder 2011; Lavie 2014), detailing how women activists became associated with particular protest agendas. While the historical links between women and peace potentially serve to feminize anti-occupation organizations and initiatives, Dana's narrative points to a sense that the *wider* culture of leftist political protest has become feminized, extending beyond women's and feminist groups. Thus Dana's political avoidance emerges in part as a means of resisting the normalized and pacified specter of organized political protest, an ostensibly feminized mode of action deemed "impotent" in the face of masculinized right-wing fury. Here, as anger seemingly constitutes the ultimate political motivator—an exception to the banality and perceived passivity of "getting by" conflict—the presumed emotion of opposition effectively affirms prevailing norms and values.

However, in keeping with the complexity and contradiction of resistance, this belief in the positive transformative capacity of rage halts at the limits of the Jewish Israeli collective. Intersecting with race, class, and national belonging, here too protest provides an avenue for opposition while entrenching norms, codes, roles, and relations, if differently so. As seen in reactions to demonstrations by Palestinian citizens of Israel, African refugees and asylum seekers, and domestic caregivers, the normalization of specific forms of protest in turn creates "abnormal" or "dangerous" modes of action, coded along lines of race and gender. With protest sites intentionally positioned in the center of Tel Aviv, a Palestinian demonstration against Hosni Mubarak's regime in Egypt and two marches involving the city's African migrant population were characterized by a high level of male participation, high relative visibility in the core of "white" Tel Aviv, and a striking degree of audibility. In attending the Palestinian-Egyptian solidarity demonstration in Basel Square,[10] I was struck by the way "Israeli Arabs"—a category clearly differentiated from "Palestinians" in nearly every interview—suddenly became *Palestinian* even to the "hard-core" Jewish Israeli activists who stood watching the demonstration across the street. "They don't understand Arabic, they don't know what they're saying," a fellow researcher explained to me after speaking with these activists, many of whom were participating in her project. "People are scared—they see a big group of angry young Palestinian men, shouting in Arabic and waving Palestinian flags."[11] Although young Palestinian women were also in attendance, their voices were subsumed within the majority-male mass as the specter of rage and threat of violence transformed not only the "Israeli Arabs" but also the radical Jewish activists who in their trepidation became "Israeli."

Playing drums, chanting in English, and appearing in numbers previously unknown to the Jewish Israeli residents of central and north Tel Aviv, African refugees and asylum seekers elicited similar shock and anxiety during the 2010 Human Rights Day march and a demonstration against the construction of the planned African-only detention facility.[12] Appreciating the size and strength of the Human Rights Day march, Dimi Reider (2010) of *+972 Magazine* wrote, "Until yesterday, Israelis have never seen the refugees march together, as a coherent, unapologetic group, not merely speaking their claim not in the slums and the periphery where they have been pushed, but chanting it on one of Israel's most affluent shopping streets." While viewed by participants and organizers as a welcome addition to the ordinarily predictable annual Tel Aviv event, the presence of (primarily male) African migrants on Human Rights Day was more ambiguously received by onlookers. Ilan, a thirty-two-year-old Tel Aviv resident, recounted: "I was in Pilates on the day of the International Human Rights Day march and we watched out the window as hundreds of blacks walked past on Rothschild [Boulevard]. They just kept coming, and people found it really alarming."[13] Months later, I took part in a protest against the Holot detention facility, which was specifically designed to house African migrants who entered Israel illegally.[14] Again massing in central Tel Aviv and traveling the length of Rothschild Boulevard, the protest's vibrant energy and collective claim to human rights electrified the surrounding environment. While newspaper accounts cited the presence of a large number of "Israeli activists" (Lior 2010), the overwhelming majority of participants belonged to south Tel Aviv's African migrant community. As I walked amid the crowd, Ilan's words came to mind, and I wondered how the appearance of large numbers of African demonstrators—many from Sudan, Eritrea, and Congo—would impact their struggle, given the climate of virulent, and increasingly public, racism.[15] While these events allowed the African migrant community to become visible and audible, at the same time a perceived "threat" materialized and became suddenly tangible to a wider Jewish Israeli society.

This sense of threat consistently frames the masculinization and racialization of non-Jewish protests, articulating through sexualized discourses of penetration and "infiltration" applied similarly to Palestinians from the Occupied Territories and to African migrants (Ettinger, Hasson, and Lior 2010; Khoury, Pfeffer, and Ha'aretz Service 2011; Dana 2011; Sheen 2011a; Lis 2011; Reuters 2013). Then rage cannot be so easily associated with transformative potential in political protest—rather, race, national belonging, sexuality, and gender intersect to shape perceptions and experiences of political action. During my fieldwork this claim was underlined by a protest against the institution of an immigration law which tied health workers and domestic caregivers to a specific family. Again problematizing an easy association of anger with political or social change, this relatively subdued action garnered far more public support and far less anxiety or fear. Though the law—dubbed the "slavery law" by activists—was eventually passed (on May 16, 2011— ACRI 2011a), in March 2011 relatively large numbers of (white) Jewish Israelis attended a quiet, orderly demonstration in support of the individuals tasked with caring for their elderly relatives. One interview participant explained the support for this demonstration as a testament to the successful "integration" of these workers, primarily women of Asian origin, within Jewish Israeli society. However, this demonstration also followed the template of "normalized" political action, characterized by the same perceived lack of rage and relative calm apparent in many leftist demonstrations.[16] Interestingly, these same qualities granted the health workers' initiative markedly greater legitimacy than protests by Palestinians or African migrants, even if all three demonstrations ultimately had little impact on discourse or policy. Tamar Hermann (2009, cited in Sasson-Levy, Levy, and Lomsky-Feder 2011, 746) makes a similar observation with regard to the Arba Emahot (Four Mothers) campaign, which resulted in the withdrawal of Israeli troops from Lebanon in 2000: "The movement gained legitimacy and public attention because of its framing as an apolitical group within the acceptable framework of motherhood."

Marked by the specter of masculinized and racialized rage, the Palestinian and African migrant protests were cast as abnormal vis-à-vis the normalized leftist protests in Tel Aviv, which the care providers and their supporters invoked to an advantage. Again pointing to the embeddedness of protest and resistance in wider relations of power, the political actions undertaken by Palestinian citizens of Israel and African migrants living in Tel Aviv underlined perceived "threats" while at the same time substantiating the Israeli state and society's claims to democracy—as these minority populations publicly exercise freedom of speech and right to assembly, resistance becomes "caught up" in power. However, the significance of these accounts to perceptions of *what we can do* lies in their relationship to normalization, as a particular mode of protest—seemingly pacified, impotent, and feminized—is reaffirmed as the standard for "acceptable" political action. Yet despite often achieving greater legitimacy, in wider Jewish Israeli society these normalized expressions of protest become subject to active resistance, as conveyed through Dana's remarks above. Here, opposition to political action emerges as a move against their overwhelming sense of passivity, calm, and balance projected by these actions, paradoxically the very qualities strived for in the pursuit of normalcy.

However, this dynamic does not go unacknowledged by the activists whose initiatives and organizations become normalized and associated with the hegemonic qualities of leftist political action. Yardena, a seventy-five-year-old Jerusalemite formerly active with Bat Shalom and currently working with Machsom Watch, the Israeli Committee Against House Demolitions, Women in Black, and Sheikh Jarrah Solidarity,[17] became politically active in England during the anti–Vietnam War and anti-apartheid movements, returning to Israel in 1970 in time to join the first demonstrations against the then-nascent West Bank settlements. As we spoke together on Naksa Day,[18] Yardena recounted her experiences and perceptions thus:

What was interesting was the *sociology* of things—I find that very interesting. The first time when I was arrested, in 1970, [for protesting] against the settlement of Kiryat Arba, we were all stuck in a big cage of the Russian Compound prison, men and women together. The guards brought us coffee ... the environment was relaxed. We were not taken seriously—the occupation had not settled in. We weren't the enemy. But in '73, we were the enemy. I was not in a cage with other people, I was put with women. Some women there didn't like me because when you're low down on the social scale you have to be "better than" [someone else].... With Women in Black—I can't remember the start date ... it was the first *intifada*.... The drivers would go past and say, "Women go home! You have a child waiting for you! The Sabbath dinner is waiting!" A few months later it was, "Arab lovers! Prostitutes!" And a few more months later it became, "Traitors!" Women's place as political beings, who don't follow their men into the army, was very interesting.... Then, there were a lot of women at the demonstrations, but now there are fifteen, with many women from abroad. Then there were forty to fifty—it's fifteen now. On the Friday nearest the 6th of June [Naksa Day] we used to get more than a hundred people, Israelis, men and women. Last Friday we had forty, with many from abroad.

Highlighting how gendered tensions suffuse her experiences of arrest and political protest, Yardena's narrative recalls a transition from the social inclusion of the early 1970s to the sexualized and nationalized exclusion caused by episodes of violent conflict—the 1973 October or Yom Kippur War and the first *intifada*—culminating in the relative indifference and inaction of the present day. The narrative arc is particularly significant within her secondary discussion of Women in Black, as Yardena traces a shift from dismissal, on gendered grounds as mothers, to accusations of betrayal as women mounted an increasingly serious challenge to Israeli state and military policies. Yet Yardena ultimately reflects on women's position as "political beings" in the past tense, linking their failure to be "taken seriously" with declining participation. Then the process of normalization can be read as silence, as the gap between vehement accusations and low participant numbers; in the interim, Yardena implies that women have been nearly erased as political actors.

An intersectional reading of Yardena's narrative sheds even further light on the normalization of protest, complicating the reading above through vectors of race and class. Throughout our exchange, Yardena referred to the racial, ethnic, and class composition of what she deemed Israel's "social scale," invoking this spectrum as she recalled time spent in prison. At one point, she related an experience of marching with the Israeli Black Panthers, a Mizrahi protest movement active in the 1970s:

> They had a big march, several, in Jerusalem. At this one I was separated from the main march and surrounded by North African Jews. They said, "What are you doing? You're Ashkenazi! You're rich, you have an apartment!" I wasn't [rich], but the assumption was that because I'm Ashkenazi I'm rich and I have an apartment to go home to. I said, "Okay, let's assume I was [rich]. Why wouldn't I march with the Black Panthers?" It was like a march with the blacks in the southern US when the whites came, except the blacks [in the US] accepted it.[19]

In this second narrative, Yardena's actions aimed at social and political transformation are met with what she perceives to be class- and race-based antipathy, rather than solidarity—in both the Black Panthers march and the women-only prison cell, Yardena is unwelcome. She is identified as Ashkenazi (white), affluent, and female, and in this account fellow citizens who possess less privilege, influence, and capital receive the figure of the hegemonic Jewish Israeli protester with hostility and derision. Strikingly, in both instances the "social scales" invoked by Yardena are inverted, as if in a state of exception—though a white Jewish Israeli activist, she is treated as if positioned beneath her interlocutors in social hierarchies and clearly left feeling unwelcome. In this, Yardena's historical narrative of activism makes visible not only gendered dynamics of normalization but also how varying acts of resistance again remain embedded in power, balancing opposition with affirmation.

Resistance to the Game

In addition to engendering resistance, the normalization of activism also yields new modes of political action, even if they are judged "abnormal" or threatening, as related in the passages above. As made evident by Palestinian citizens of Israel, African migrants living in south Tel Aviv, and the Mizrahi Black Panthers of the 1970s, protests arise through and at the limits of present hegemonic forms, including those actions deemed impotent or pacified. Then established forms of activism set "rules of the game" to be contested and reformulated by subsequent initiatives and organizations.

As "games" of resistance unfold within more veteran protest vehicles—those now-normalized modes of political action, including highly visible women's initiatives and organizations—their diverse codes of conduct influence the perception and performance of new modes of activism. These games take place not only within the borders of Israel proper but also in the spaces of the Occupied Territories. Indeed, the normalization of older forms of anti-occupation activism within Israel's recognized borders has in part informed Jewish Israeli participation in groups such as Sheikh Jarrah Solidarity in East Jerusalem and popular resistance initiatives in West Bank villages, including Na'alin, Bil'in, and Nabi Saleh, which have shifted to the forefront of organized political action. Ofek, a twenty-six-year-old activist from Jerusalem, detailed the rules of one such earlier game of activism:

> In the south I was part of Machsom Watch—they're a human rights group to watch entry. Usually there aren't young women, it's more like old aunts because they can be easy, relaxed with the soldiers. When they had enough [older] women to balance me, I took part. It was becoming a practice at this point: three women arrive, the soldier closes the checkpoint, no Palestinians can go in or out because of Machsom Watch. It's like a game. Then we'd go to the hill and they [the soldiers] would notice, they come back and close the checkpoint again.... Until we go, the Palestinians suffer.[20]

Well documented and researched, similarly to the Israeli Women in Black, Machsom Watch was founded by Jewish Israeli women in 2001 at the onset of the second *intifada*, as the function and proliferation of checkpoints in the Occupied Territories became increasingly visible (Kotef and Amir 2007, 974). The organization has been critiqued both internally and academically in terms of its gender, ethnic, class, and generational dimensions, as membership consists primarily of retirement-age middle-class Ashkenazi Israeli women whose "desexualized" femininity and maternal appearance is seen as granting a degree of protection from and influence over the young (male) soldiers stationed at military checkpoints in the West Bank.[21] While Machsom Watch activists practice an innovative mode of action relative to sanctioned demonstrations occurring within Israel's recognized borders, Ofek highlights the game-like qualities of the interaction between these women and the soldiers; in this, she illustrates the extent to which both action and reaction have been regularized over time. Characterized explicitly as "a practice," this game of political protest and intervention follows particular rules, generating values and codes. While the declared intention of the organization is to observe and document the operation of the checkpoints and the treatment of Palestinians at these sites,[22] in Ofek's narrative—and indeed the accounts of other research participants active with Machsom Watch—the exchange unfolds almost strictly between Jewish Israeli actors; the Palestinians subject to this exercise of power are consigned to waiting and suffering. Paradoxically, and in keeping with the embeddedness of resistance in domination, Machsom Watch has been explicitly criticized for its role in ensuring the continued function of the checkpoints by measuring their failure to protect human rights.[23] Potentially contributing to the extension of military control, the actions of Machsom Watch not only produce another mode of normalization but also usher in the depoliticization that often accompanies a shift to the language of human rights in this context.[24]

While more radical and marginal than the sanctioned demonstrations of Tel Aviv, oppositional political actions such as those undertaken by Machsom Watch continue to produce rules of the game, providing new standards for future initiatives. Positions adopted by the latest generation of radical activist initiatives—such as Sheikh Jarrah Solidarity and the Friday protests in Bil'in, Na'alin, and Nabi Saleh[25]—challenge these shifting rules and standards, actively contesting the regularization of political protest while creating new games and value systems. Intrigued by the demonstrations in Bil'in,[26] presented to me as "hard-core" political actions during numerous interviews, in May 2011 I decided to join a Friday protest. I was encouraged by the small number of interview participants who had participated in the action, yet I felt puzzled by comments made by Nadav, a thirty-one-year-old activist from Tel Aviv:

> You should go because if you're a decent person you will get mad—about the activists, the army, all the ritual. Of course there are reasons it is like this. It's hard to keep it in mind. For an Israeli to go to Bil'in is something necessary. For the first time in your life you're in the Palestinian Territories, surrounded by Palestinians, Arabic, Arabic music coming from speakers on a large truck ... it's like something from a Reuters photo. You're sure you will get killed. The army is no longer an eighteen-year-old douche bag with a rifle—it's the enemy. You try to remember that the army is an eighteen-year-old guy whose vacation is screwed up because of you. But the Palestinians have more to lose. It doesn't change your views, but it does change some of the elemental fear Israelis have of Palestinians.
>
> Most of it is like tourism. Like, I met four Italians in Ma'asra[27] who were singing, shouting something at the soldiers. I speak Italian, so I understood what they were singing—it was children's songs. They were singing excitedly, furiously at the army ... they were having a very nice time. This is what happens. Last time I was in Bil'in, I was surrounded by tear gas, shock grenades, people weeping ... and you can hear "Jingle Bells" coming from the ice cream truck on the road. It's a hot day and the truck is there, like usual, selling ice cream to people and playing "Jingle Bells." You sit and watch the truck with

the driver... it's something you have to see. Some Israeli activists do it for adventure, for tourism... for righteousness.[28]

On the day of my participation in the protest at Bil'in, "Jingle Bells" was not to be heard, nor was the mythical ice cream truck in sight, but Nadav was present, along with fellow Jewish Israeli bloggers relaying the events in real time on Twitter. The predicted sense of ritual and fantasy began on the forty-five-minute drive from Tel Aviv to the village, during which passengers in the vehicle played friendly "name games" by means of introduction as we hurtled along Route 443 past Modi'in and across the Green Line. As we drove and introduced ourselves, Sean, a young Jewish American man studying at the Arava Institute,[29] summarized his perception of the Bil'in protests with a reference to American popular culture: "It's like *Fight Club*: 'Once you've been in fight club the volume on everything else is turned down.'"[30] Our driver, Nina, nodded in agreement, and Sean continued excitedly with a declaration that, having been to Bil'in four times, the next week he planned to attend the demonstration in nearby Nabi Saleh, explicitly because these actions were more violent. "The army goes into the city there!" he told us, highlighting the hierarchy that orders these West Bank demonstrations according to levels of danger and assigns degrees of bravery to the participants therein.

After crossing through the checkpoint—"Everybody look Zionist!" Nina commanded with a laugh as we passed the Israeli soldiers—the game of protest continued to unfold in the village, and its rules became obvious as the event began. On joining the main group, I was assigned a "babysitter," a veteran (male) Jewish Israeli activist who would guide me at the demonstration and ensure that I stayed within my personal comfort zone vis-à-vis the anticipated violence. We chatted as I waited for a safety briefing to begin and, with some surprise, I actually recognized particular houses and a number of faces from the film *Bil'in Habibti*, having viewed the documentary months earlier.[31] Eventually, members of Anarchists Against the Wall[32] called new participants to a shaded garden, and the safety briefing commenced in serious tones. Here we learned what kind of violence to expect and how to (re)act. Clearly there was a customary order of escalating events: first stun grenades, then skunk water and tear gas canisters, possibly followed by Ruger rifles and rubber-coated bullets, or even live fire. Next came instructions on what to do on injury, arrest, and—for women—sexual harassment by male protesters. Finally, alcohol wipes, replete with their own set of instructions, were passed around the group as a means of quelling the effects of the inevitable tear gas. I felt increasingly unsure of this game, yet as the demonstration began I fell in behind the line of yellow flags and youths with faces wrapped in *keffiyeh*, joining a group of nearly fifty Jewish Israeli and international activists.

Following a cardboard coffin,[33] we walked in a broken line to a small peninsula of land ringed by fencing and Israeli soldiers. The real game began here. My babysitter explained that as the official nonviolent procession advanced toward the far end of the fence—where soldiers stood at the ready with guns and a skunk-water truck behind the buffer zone—the *keffiyeh*-clad youths would break to the right and begin throwing rocks, though it was always unclear who acted first in violence, the soldiers or protesters. As we followed the demonstration at a distance, the first stun grenades were fired, at the young men, who had indeed broken off from the group. Then the tear gas began, rising in clouds of sulfurous vapour. When the gas momentarily dissipated we retreated to a small rise, watching the game from a safer vantage point. Youths stood inside the fence among low scrub grass and rocks as soldiers pelted them with tear-gas canisters—both "sides" baited and responded. In the distance, the official demonstration nearly reached the fence before being sprayed with skunk water and enshrouded in tear gas, trapped between concertina wire, soldiers and guns, and a haze of noxious smoke. Shouting, crying, and vomiting, the protesters retreated and lit small fires in their wake; only a single man, in a wheelchair and wearing a gas mask, was able to withstand the intensity.[34] I stood watching, at times coughing or weeping due to the gas, realizing that for many of the Jewish Israelis and international activists around me the demonstration was a "choose your own adventure" affair, like a children's story with multiple plot lines and alternative endings. These protesters were constantly testing their personal limits as they and their Palestinian counterparts challenged those of the Israeli military. For others, the scene of conflict spread out below as if on television, though at times it surrounded all who played the game. It was indeed "like a Reuters photograph"; in their brightly colored vests the press stayed close to the young Palestinian men and boys near the fence, with their slingshots, rocks, and *keffiyeh*, engulfed in tear gas and "looking for blood," according to my minder. Amid the popping of newly fired gas canisters, we turned back to the village close behind. As we walked, I asked whether villagers protested on other days of the week; my babysitter shook his head and replied in the negative, "They have to work, live their lives, so no. The game is on Friday, and everyone knows it."[35]

Exhilarating and confusing, surreal and hyper-real, my experience of Bil'in that day indeed unfolded in a game-like manner, one marked explicitly by violence expected and enacted. In these few hours, I began to understand the extent to which violence can be shattering and unifying, terrifying and productive of intense solidarities. Yet this was all part of the game, very much in keeping with the values, codes, and myths created by and defining our political action. While standing apart from the regularized, normalized, and seemingly impotent modes of protest commonly associated with leftist Jewish Israeli activism, participants in this recent generation of initiatives construct new rules, drawing fresh lines of inclusion and exclusion. Tali, a thirty-year-old feminist gay rights activist from Tel Aviv, painted a complete picture:

> At the big demonstrations I can see that they are run by men. Even when women are the organizers, the people on the stage are men—Ashkenazi Jewish men at that. This is frustrating and annoying to me. It makes me feel that even though these movements are against the occupation, they are also against me. In the radical Left there is more discussion about gender, so there should be more awareness. But there you can see subtle oppression, like in Sheikh Jarrah a few months ago when the women protesters were asked to wear "decent clothes." You can also feel the physical aggression, the machoism. For example in Bil'in you can feel the machoism of the Palestinians—only Palestinian men are there—and also the machoism of the Jewish demonstrators too. Women are pushed aside.
>
> KN: Does that change how you feel about participating?
>
> Tali: I don't want to be part of it. It makes me angry that in order to promote justice for Palestinians, we don't want gender equality. There is a song from the '80s by Pollyana Frank called "Dykes and the Holy War"—the refrain says, "Revolutions are alike, none will enter my door / Guess what they'll do with us dykes when they win that holy war?" It's true.[36]

As articulated by Tali and other interview participants, the rules of this new game cannot be read through a lens limited to the relations between "Israel" and "Palestine" or "Israelis" and "Palestinians"; rather, an intersectional approach again makes visible the layering of power within and around resistance. Marked by stages, speakers, and rallies, for Tali the normalized demonstrations that accompany organized political protest in Israel remain the bastion of (particular kinds of) men, highlighting the prevailing relationship between politics, voice, power, and privilege in this context. While paradoxically these (white) men speaking on stages participate in the very same actions perceived as "feminized" and "impotent" among many younger activists, Tali outlines a point of overlap with the new generation of protests: both are "run by men" despite the participation of women. In this, she charges Bil'in and Sheikh Jarrah, two of the most popular Friday protest sites, with a kind of "machoism" that mitigates against gender equality and the realization of gay and queer activist agendas.

In addition to gender and sexuality, clearly Tali's account may also be read for the ways in which race intersects with conflict-derived norms in the space of protest, adding a further layer of complexity. As Tali identifies forms of "subtle oppression" in operation at the Sheikh Jarrah events, race, religion, and ethnicity go unspoken. However, the request that women, in practice largely Jewish Israeli and international, wear "decent clothes" came at the behest of Muslim Palestinian participants (Issacharoff 2012). Additionally significant is her emphasis on the absence of Palestinian women at the protests and the active subordination of those other women present. While the sexual harassment briefing provided in Bil'in was free of commentary on race or ethnicity, those providing and attending the training shared an understanding that the warnings pertained to the targeting of Jewish Israeli and international women by Palestinian men (Issacharoff 2012). For feminist activists like Tali who remain invested in realizing anti-occupation and gender-equity platforms together, these dynamics generate substantial tension. Yet for many would-be participants the treatment and position of women in the protests constitute a significant deterrent to action, particularly as rumors, experiences, and understandings evoke fears based on prevailing stereotypes. Indeed, the Israeli internal intelligence agency, Shin Bet, has used the publicity surrounding instances of sexual harassment to pressure Jewish Israeli and international activists, demonstrating how new rules of the game might generate novel methods of state deterrence (Hass 2012) and again underlining the embeddedness of protest within telescoping layers of power.

Soldiering

On hearing my tale of the Bil'in demonstration, hours later in Tel Aviv, Guy confessed, "I want to go even less now—it feels just like the army, with the security briefing, the strategizing, the gas, and the violence. It's a game, but also it's the military."[37] Though perhaps a guilt-assuaging excuse as to why he declined to join me in the West Bank that day, Guy's reticence highlights another mode of hegemonic entanglement that frames Jewish Israeli political action: the overlap between military service and activism.

Among Jewish Israelis, resistance to "soldiering" becomes a way of talking about the assertion of individual identity in a context of conformity, a means of insisting on the salience of subordinated interests, and a critique of existing hierarchies of power and privilege internal to the Jewish Israeli collective. As militarism collapses the boundary between military and civil society to facilitate the production of violence (Geyer 1989, cited in Levy and Sasson-Levy 2008, 353; Jacoby 2005, 42–43), soldiering extends into everyday life with its affective regime, modes of practice, and value system. Arguing that Israel is characterized by conditions of "total militarism," which encompass professional and civilian dimensions, Baruch Kimmerling (2001, 215) writes: "This characterization is amply underscored by the overt and latent social significance that is attributed to military service, and by the way in which the society orients itself toward constant preparation for war, a kind of 'militarism of the mind.' In this case, the socio-political boundaries of the collectivity are determined and maintained by participation in military service and manipulation of the collectivity to sacrifice in order to support the spheres classified as belonging to national security."

While much academic research substantiates these claims regarding the influence of militarism over collectivity boundaries, national belonging, and social hierarchies in Israel (Sharoni 1995; Yuval-Davis 1997; Lentin 2000; Shafir and Peled 2002; Sasson-Levy 2003; Jacoby 2005; Yiftachel 2006; Segal 2008),[38] by invoking "manipulation" Kimmerling positions Jewish Israelis as largely subject to rather than productive of the discourses and practices that prioritize national security. Similarly, while Kimmerling (2001, 215, 227–28) argues convincingly that Israel's particular brand of militarism creates a dialectic between war-making and peace-making, the micro-level behaviors and attitudes that bind these collective pursuits remain obscured. However, the primacy and durability of militarism in Israel remain rooted in its civilian dimension. Rather than merely absorbing and reflecting military values and objectives, here subjects and communities actively take up and extend military interests into everyday life. In this, the military enters deeply into identity formation, social relations, and collective aspirations, bearing significant implications for resistance. Indeed, as Kimmerling observes, total militarism means that preparation for war overwhelmingly "becomes part of social routine and is no longer considered a matter of public debate or political struggle" (214).

In keeping with this extension of military roles and boundaries into civil society, experiences of "soldiering" continue to impact individuals, families, and communities beyond the period of active service. Mandatory military service remains profoundly normative in Israel, shaping subjectivities and influencing political participation, national values, and institutionalized privilege. Oded, a thirty-three-year-old filmmaker living in Tel Aviv, highlighted the gendered terms of this normativity as he described the inspiration for his recent film project:

> I met an elite [unit] guy. After the army he went to India to travel and when he returned he almost lost his mind. I understood that this is a terrible thing: men are trained in combat to kill, kill, kill. The Israeli army is moral—wait, I believe that the Israeli army is less *immoral* than the US army or European armies. It's always on the surface, morals. [They say] "Don't carry out orders blindly, you are not a tool." There is actually an "absolute illegal order," which is when your commander tells you to kill, but he doesn't explain it in a way that you find logical—you can refuse. On paper this is probably as good as an army can get. The problem is that an eighteen-year-old learns "shoot and kill, shoot and kill, shoot and kill"—"oh, but wait until someone gives you a good reason." Most don't wait. They have terrible power in their hands and they're kept ready for action. I know it, I felt it. I was too much a coward to get carried away with action—I'm happy that I wasn't in a situation where I was about to kill. I feel bad enough about the experiences I had.
>
> Anyhow, I started to think, here's a good guy: kind, sensitive, intelligent. At eighteen he wants to do good. OK, so "good" goes to the elite unit to become the "man-est of men," to protect the country. He went, he killed people, it screwed his mind. He comes back to live life in society, to live as a civilian. No one prosecutes him for what he has done—in society he did the "right" thing.... At a fragile age they take your humanity and give you "manhood" instead.... You go in a child and come out a man.[39]

Oded's account is notable for the extent to which it outwardly corroborates Kimmerling's (2001, 215) claim to manipulation, as his experience of what is often called "shooting and crying" in effect displaces blame for violence onto the educating and order-issuing authority (Kidron 2004; Helman 1999b, 67 n19). Importantly, this account clearly illustrates how collective morality emerges in tandem with the construction of hegemonic masculinity, underwritten by participation in violence. "Good" not only dutifully fulfills his military service but he does so at the highest level, exposed to the greatest degree of danger, accepting the ultimate sacrifice, required to kill and deserving of prestige—ultimately "good" becomes the "man-est of men." Yet while

Oded openly voices his opposition to the normativity of soldiering, as he understands this practice to strip individuals of their childhood and humanity in pursuit of "right" and "good," he upholds the standards of militarized masculinity in deeming himself a "coward." Though retrospectively pleased with his "inability to get carried away with action" as it shielded him from moral imperatives surrounding the decision to kill, Oded simultaneously reaffirms military values as the frame for judging actions and character.

This is not to say, however, that individuals who incompletely resist the normativity of soldiering are victims of false consciousness, unsuccessful in their opposition, or unaware that their actions reproduce power. Rather, conscious negotiations, bargains, and concessions may also provide a means of self-definition. Earlier in our interview, Oded explicitly acknowledged the constant maneuvering that awareness of his embeddedness entails, particularly as he now engages in activism.

> KN: You said that you are active in human rights activism—how did you become active?
>
> Oded: It started mostly after the second Lebanon War [in 2006]—it's all part of the same process. Coming out was part of the process too.... After that I was able to make choices, it all came together. OK, so this situation is fucked up and I know it is. I might as well try to do something about it—if I don't, it won't change. And if I do maybe it still won't change, but at least I tried!
>
> So I started with gay rights, human rights, and circles of people who feel like myself about issues. The Anarchists used to have the best parties! I can't stand lots of people there—they can be as militant and aggressive as the right wing. This is the thing about Israeli society: brutality. The belief in power goes really deep. This is how Israelis define themselves as Israeli, as men. It's hard—I've only lived here half my life, I grew up in another place. But still these things got deep into me, through high school and the army. I'm still trying to squeeze it out [of myself]. Like, how can I struggle without becoming physical? It's harder for people who were born here and raised by parents who were also raised here. It defines who you are—you can't just throw it away.[40]

Paired with the process of understanding and accepting his sexuality, Oded's account of coming to action is multiply framed by militarized normativity, as seen in the narrative ubiquity of war, the "brutality" permeating activism, the overriding subscription to power, the definition of "Israeli" as masculine, and the pedagogical influence of militarized institutions. Yet as these factors collectively shape Oded's subjectivity he insists on the availability of choice, signaling agency within conditions of constraint. Initiated by the public disclosure of his sexual identity, that mentality supposedly absorbed through manipulation or indoctrination meets with struggle and resistance, and "being part of it" becomes a state that might be changed. Oded qualifies this ability to choose and act by citing his lesser degree of belonging, having grown up in Eastern Europe and arriving alone in Israel at age sixteen. Though he completed the military service requisite for "full Israeliness," Oded understands his sense of self as less bound to militarization, soldiering, and masculinized normativity than those Jewish Israelis born and raised in Israel.

Through Oded's account, the negotiation of identity and experiences of activism intersect with militarism, and soldiering emerges as a practice that might produce resistance to resistance within Jewish Israeli society. As those saturating qualities of militarism that shape constructions of masculinity, create social norms, and generate communities are rejected in the interest of self-definition, this resistance may extend to political action. Dov, a thirty-five-year-old artist and DJ living in south Tel Aviv, explicitly traced this connection: "I never wanted to be a fighter [in the army].... I'm a good boy but I don't like inclusive institutions—I don't like institutions that strip you of your identity. I thought from the beginning that I don't buy their game, I don't like to be the smallest piece on the chess board to a politician. That's what I felt.... The army fucked me up *big time*."

After serving in an intelligence unit during the Oslo Years, between *intifadas*—stationed at times in the West Bank—Dov describes his aversion to the homogenization and perceived powerlessness that accompany the military "game," confronting the limits and costs of being a "good boy." Yet so too he projects this resistance onto activism, including those initiatives that contest the military policies and practices that he opposes. In response to a query about his participation in actions against the occupation, Dov stated, "Yeah, I did something, but even in that I'm not an infantry soldier, you know what I mean? I'm not a soldier.... I read Ghandi, Martin Luther King. I don't believe in war."[41] Not only does Dov connect military service with activism through the figure of the willing and dutiful soldier, but also he critically situates both within a shared frame of conflict, violence, and war. If mandatory conscription produces hegemonic constructions of masculinity, as Oded illustrates and multiple scholars argue (Sharoni 1995; Lentin 2000; Sasson-Levy 2003; Jacoby 2005; Levy and Lomsky-Feder 2011), so too dutiful activism produces gendered subjects and hierarchies—"good boys" whose loyalty might later be questioned and resisted.

Importantly, Jewish Israeli men are not alone in highlighting soldiering and its homogenizing dynamics as they express wariness of oppositional action. Subject to deployment in combat positions and longer terms of conscription, many men experience lengthier exposure to the normative pressures of military service than their female counterparts; however, Jewish Israeli women also pass through this normative institution, which in turn shapes their experiences and understandings of activism. At thirty and now employed by a "violence reduction" NGO in Tel Aviv, Noa reflected on her former military service as an education officer in glowing terms: "This was the first time I felt *me,* that this is what I want to do." Charged with instructing soldiers in Israeli history and morals, an assignment predominantly given to female soldiers, Noa was exposed to conditions markedly different from those of the infantry or combat units where Dov and Oded served. However, later in our interview Noa invoked a familiar figure in speaking about activism and the difficulties of finding a suitable outlet for action:

> In Israel the term "activist" is an automatic label to the political sphere. Activists are people who spend their entire life at protests. I feel my work is connected to social change, yes, but not to activism. In a normal country this would be the same, but in Israel activism is *peace* activism. . . . I feel the whole country, the whole world, is concentrated on the conflict. "God damn it!" I said, "We need to do something also for ourselves." In a way it's related to the occupation. . . . It's difficult to find something that you're not a "soldier" in, something where you are yourself. I don't feel that something is really me except [the NGO] because something changed inside me. I was looking at the Palestinians and their suffering, and also our suffering. Now I'm looking inside society and doing the best I can with my tools. It's very tiring to focus on the conflict and the occupation.[42]

Echoing Dov's narrative, through her account of action withheld and pursued Noa expresses resistance to soldiering as she reacts to the entanglement of activism with conflict and peace. However, earlier in our interview Noa framed military service favorably, as this experience provided a sense of self and affirmed her burgeoning interests at a critical moment. Despite diverging in their memories of military service, together Noa's and Dov's narratives bridge the ostensible gap between war and peace in Israel-Palestine, situating both conditions in a shared context of protracted conflict. For Noa, activism in Israel is defined through, and as, peace initiatives, which constitute the hegemonic frame of political action. As illustrated throughout this chapter, these initiatives have become largely associated with passivity and impotence even as they remain the dominant mode of action. Yet in expressing her aversion to participation Noa does not emphasize these qualities but rather the location of peace activism within conflict. Thus the conditions surrounding Noa's departure from activism point to a contradiction, as she turns back to the collective which produces the very figure she had actively rejected: the soldier whose identity is lost through participation in duty. Through identifying her niche for action as "work connected to social change," Noa makes an active choice not only for herself but for Jewish Israeli society as well. As she does this, her resistance simultaneously reaffirms the prevailing patterns of gender that shape and reflect the binary order of conflict in this context, confirming the logics that divide "social" from "political" and define the latter as the bastion of men.

CONCLUSION

As patterns of gender bind conflict with peace, the too-neat distinction between action and inaction is destabilized in Jewish Israeli society. Just as war and peace might be understood as inseparable effects of power, so too actions taken and withheld—political activism and ostensible apathy—materialize as not oppositional but rather bound together as aspects of domination. As Timothy Mitchell (1990, 559) reminds us, "It is through the creation of what appears to us as the larger binary order of meaning versus reality that the effectiveness of domination is to be understood." Here, resistance both subverts and reaffirms power, and experiences of everyday life simultaneously complicate and reify the divisions that sustain conflict.

As demonstrated throughout this chapter, diverse modes of action and inaction constitute a spectrum that binds activism and apathy within the shared context of conflict, securing domination through both active and passive assent (Gramsci 1971, 52–53). Through dynamics made visible by employing resistance as a diagnostic of power (Abu-Lughod 1990) and considering practice in relation to structure (Mitchell 1990), resistance begets resistance—action begets inaction—as it telescopes within an ever-widening frame. Embedded in multiple layers of power, everyday forms of resistance may reaffirm neoliberalism, conservative politics, and prevailing relations of gender, race, and class; modes of feminist activism might produce not provocation but normalization and routinization; shifting "rules of the game" may entrench male privilege within both established and innovative anti-occupation initiatives; and practices of soldiering might generate opposition to military service and political action alike. In these trends and processes, patterns of gender importantly serve to structure experiences and understandings, providing a stable foundation while permitting change, flux, and adaptation. While actions taken and withheld by Jewish Israeli women and men may reconfirm the prevailing gendered norms, relations, codes, and roles prescribed by Zionist narratives, these patterns also respond to the pressures of changing values and conditions.

Thus the range of actions and initiatives that constitute *what we can do* for those Jewish Israelis opposed to Israel's occupation morphs into the question motivating this book: *Ma la'asot?*—What can we do? In complex and sometimes contradictory ways, individuals resist power on multiple levels and in diverse sites, yet many fail to escape the wider structure of domination—in this, both action and inaction preserve political stasis. However, short of claiming that resistance always or ultimately reconstitutes power despite the dynamic strategies and best efforts of political actors, the narratives in this chapter reveal deeper and subtler ties linking action with apathy among Jewish Israelis. Here, knowing awareness of embeddedness in power and implication in domination generates a kind of melancholia (Butler 2004; Lentin 2010), the individual sense of helplessness and powerlessness that underwrites collective political despair. Unlike mourning, which allows individuals to grapple with the loss of a concrete object, melancholia attends to the loss of a loved object as it is withdrawn from consciousness, reflecting back on the ego rather than the lost object itself (Freud 1957, cited in Lentin 2010, 50–51). Taking shape within the unconscious, the melancholic condition produces ambivalence and a depressive state of mind that emerges not from a "total loss" but from the loss of an "ideal kind" such as the vision of transformation or the promise of impact. Among leftist Jewish Israelis who *would, could* and *do* take action, experiences and understandings of resistance indeed produce such an inward-reflecting condition, as their efforts become caught up in power through dynamics of simultaneous subversion and affirmation. Then domination gains purchase not only through securing active and passive assent, blurring the boundaries between action and inaction, and falsely dividing activism from apathy, but also through holding resistance and power in tension.

FIVE

Protesting Politics

"*HA'AM! DORESH! TSEDEK CHEVRATI!*" The people! Demand! Social justice! We heard the chanting long before we saw the crowd as it surged down Tel Aviv's Ibn Gavirol Street. Curious, skeptical, and admittedly a bit cynical, Guy and I were attending the second official demonstration of Israel's nascent housing protests as observers rather than participants, for the first time taking part in a political event with some degree of passivity. Initiated by university students on July 14, 2011, in response to the rising cost of housing in Tel Aviv, the protests had electrified and magnetized Jewish Israeli society, moving to action many of those interview participants and personal friends who had until now cast themselves as politically avoidant, reluctant, or inactive. First watching the protests gather momentum from the distance of a brief trip to London, we felt at turns frustrated and ambivalent, witnessing those who we would see moved to participate in activism against conflict, occupation and discrimination join protests centered on the cost of living.

Yet here we were in the humid Tel Aviv night air, standing on the shores of a living sea that would soon engulf us too, as the tide of humanity surged to forcibly blur the boundary between participants and observers. As we waited for the protest to move from its start in Habima Square toward the Tel Aviv Museum of Art, the streets were filled with an energy, vitality, and creativity unknown to me from previous actions—the sheer numbers of participants streaming uninterrupted toward the meeting point marked something decidedly different about this demonstration. This flow continued unabated until suddenly the steady wave of foot traffic doubled back on itself, reversing direction. The demonstration had begun, and it was impossible for latecomers to fall into line behind the banners; instead, they simply turned to walk in their great numbers ahead of the organized front line.

Generating deafening, raucous, unorganized noise, the body of the crowd bore down on us. The sound of drums banging, whistles shrieking, voices screaming not words but sheer anger, hands and feet colliding with whatever made sound nearby—this filled the air to an unprecedented volume. Homemade signs were in full effect, with inspired banners and colorful posters waving high above the crowd, nearly one in every five participants carrying something original that voiced her specific demand or message. Absent were the prepared plastic signs of the political parties with their official slogans; present were tens of thousands of personal connections to this demonstration and the declared issues at hand. People were fed up, needed a release, wanted social change—and they were going make sure their concerted voices were heard. The chants began in earnest, with thousands of voices in unison rising at top lung capacity—gone were the feeble, self-conscious declarations that typified protests in Israel, including the recent Jewish Israeli–Palestinian solidarity march in Jerusalem. The night air was filled with cries: "An entire generation demands a future!" "Hoo-ha, here comes the welfare state!" "The people demand social justice!"

"Social justice—do they even know what that means?" I asked later, as we left the demonstration, walking through the remnants of what looked and felt like an enormous street party. At the moment it mattered little—social justice was what together the people wanted.[1]

As the protests hollered and crashed, laughed and sang, chanted and demanded in voices individual and collective, political actors sought transformation by targeting the policies, practices, and relations of power deemed most significant to everyday life. Seemingly more contestable and "solvable" than the matters of conflict and occupation, housing and living prices took center stage as protesters temporarily inverted the national prioritization of security during the summer of 2011. Ordinarily masked by a focus on impending or active threats of violence, domestic concerns consumed public interest and political attention in these summer months, highlighting social and economic divisions often elided by "international" politics. Yet while the collective demand for "social justice" made visible these significant tensions between national and international, the protesters' strident call for change ultimately left intact the key underlying political condition of economic and social life in Israel.

In looking at the 2011 summer of protests in Israel, the critical theorizations of Lila Abu-Lughod (1990) and Timothy Mitchell (1990) again offer tempting frames through which to consider the meaning and economy of political action. Here, resistance may once more serve as a diagnostic of power, troubling the boundary between practice and structure. Indeed, the few existing analyses of these recent actions draw attention to the limits simultaneously challenged and obeyed by protesters, from the protests' ethnic and racial composition (Misgav 2013; Lavie 2014), to their base in and reaction to neoliberalism (Ram and Filc 2013), to the aesthetic and community politics of their "protest space" (Livio and Katriel 2014). Yet the 2011 protests merit further attention insofar as they present a microcosm in which to judge how political protest may be *depoliticizing,* revealing a critical distinction between acts which are "world-making" versus "world-changing" (Berlant 2008, 269–70). This chapter considers how Israel's social protests make starkly visible a space between action and inaction, wherein resistance does not always or only reaffirm domination but again generates tension with significant political effects.

Through gender analysis, a practice of "apolitical politics" emerges as central to protesters' targets and agendas, which promised transformation and at the same time maintained stasis. Here, a carnivalesque (Bakhtin 1984 [1968]) suspension of national priorities allowed protesters to mobilize around issues normally overshadowed by protracted violence. Yet these very actions reaffirmed private as separate from public, social as separate from political, "us" as separate from "them," and "here" as separate from "there," in ways that directly sustain conflict. Critically, the temporary inversion of gender norms and codes served to structure this renewed political action—its promises, practices, and meanings—while simultaneously providing a means through which "politics" could become apolitical. Drawing together the gendered constructs, mechanisms, and dynamics detailed throughout the preceding pages, this chapter considers how a season of action aimed at social transformation intersected with domination, demonstrating anew how passive assent relies on degrees of action. Directly problematizing the distinction between action and inaction in Jewish Israeli society, this chapter investigates the contents, boundaries, and effects of the world made in between during 2011.

ROTHSCHILD, CORNER OF TAHRIR

Days after the first tent was erected on Tel Aviv's Rothschild Boulevard (Sherwood 2011; Belkind 2013)—a site that symbolizes the city's history and wealth (Mann 2001; Livio and Katriel 2014, 150, 153)—I departed Israel-Palestine for a brief trip to London, leaving behind the nascent protests with a shrug of the shoulders and the assumption that before long those assembled would disperse. Following on the heels of a Facebook-led boycott of cottage cheese, which successfully resulted in the lowering of prices for this staple Ashkenazi breakfast food (Zrahiya et al. 2011; Connolly 2011),[2] the protests claimed public spaces and relied on social media for the transmission of grievances and agendas, mirroring the mobilization strategies adopted by activists in uprisings across the Middle East and North Africa. While Israeli protesters were influenced by the Indignants movement in Spain, anarchist and anticapitalist protests in Greece, and later the global Occupy movements emerging from Canada, they adopted their rallying cry, protest name, and much iconography from the recent popular movements in the Middle East, as made clear by banners and signs reading "Rothschild *pinat* [corner of] Tahrir," "Walk Like an Egyptian," and "Go! Egypt is here".[3] As practices and organizing tactics learned in Europe and North America were consolidated under the banner of "the July 14 movement" or #J14, a name and Twitter hashtag that also evoked earlier events in Egypt, transnational political movements came together with regional events on a decidedly Israeli stage.

From one person's decision to take up living space on Rothschild Boulevard, the tent-dwellers' protest gathered momentum. Its first organized demonstration, July 23, attracted 20,000–40,000 participants, who made their way from the encampment on Habima Square to the Tel Aviv Museum of Art (Gelbfish 2011; Lior 2011; Reider 2011). Unlike the earlier spontaneous demonstration that accompanied the first appearance of tents, this time protesters followed protocol by ending their march with an organized rally, including speakers who addressed the crowd from a well-lit stage with a professional sound system. Yet, in a move that would come to characterize the housing protests, those "officially" voicing the call for change did not include politicians. Rather, the primary voices and faces of the 2011 summer of protests in Israel were students and young people. Among those organizing and leading the protests, two young women would stand out: Daphne Leef, the Tel Aviv University film student whose actions catalyzed the summer's events; and Stav Shaffir, who became the unofficial spokesperson for the protests. Though leadership was shared more widely with other young Jewish Israelis (Schechter 2012), Leef and Shaffir remained the most visible and audible protesters in popular discourse, public media, and political debate, signaling that a specifically gendered challenge to "politics as usual" would shape the summer's events (Herzog 2013).

Summarizing "Social Justice"

From the July 23 rally onward, the housing protests commanded national attention as participants demonstrated a commitment to grass-roots leadership and creative protest while articulating a collective demand for "social justice." As the protests quickly spread from Tel Aviv to cities and towns throughout Israel proper (Sheen 2011b; Belkind 2013), leaders and participants focused on two primary modes of action, supported by social networks and growing mainstream media attention: tent encampments and regular demonstrations. Yet, as the protests expanded geographically and mobilized extensively, they remained framed by the existing social hierarchies specific to Israeli society (Belkind 2013; Herzog 2013; Misgav 2013; Ram and Filc 2013; Rosenheck and Shalev 2013). Here, vectors of class, generation, ethnicity, race, geopolitical location, and gender yielded varying understandings and experiences of the protests' claims to inclusivity, complicating a perhaps too tidy portrait of the summer's events and their manner of generating individual and collective participation.[4]

Despite the overall framing of the protests as led by and largely representative of middle-class (Ashkenazi) youth, multiple meanings were ascribed to the housing protesters' demand for "social justice," increasingly binding together a diverse body of participants (Belkind 2013; Herzog 2013; Misgav 2013; Shenhav 2013; Livio and Katriel 2014). This inclusivity and appeal prompted some commentators to draw connections between the 2011 protests and the agenda advanced by the Mizrahi Black Panthers in the 1970s (Sheen 2011b; Ahronovitz 2011). Founded by Jewish Israelis of Middle Eastern and North African ancestry who recognized and opposed their treatment as second-class citizens in Israel (Massad 1996, 61–62), the Black Panthers "called for the destruction of the regime and for the legitimate rights of all the oppressed without regard to religion, origin or nationality" (Shohat 1988, 29). Significantly expressing solidarity with Palestinians (Shohat 1988, 31; Massad 1996, 63), the political, social, and economic agenda of these actors targeted not only state policies and practices but also the relations of power and privilege that shape Israeli society. Then similarly to the 2011 protests, the Mizrahi Black Panthers' platform explicitly included diverse parties with multiple claims and interests, if more radically so. Yet, unlike the recent Ashkenazi-led demonstrations, the Panthers met with violent state repression, coercion, and a government campaign aimed expressly at their delegitimization (Shohat 1988; Massad 1996; Lavie 2011). Ultimately—and again much like with the 2011 protests—rather than forcibly denying all demands, the Israeli establishment selectively addressed and appropriated concerns articulated by the Panthers, resulting in the eventual disbanding of the movement and the absorption of its leadership into existing political parties (Massad 1996, 64; Lavie 2011, 67).[5]

Despite a similarly inclusive platform, the 2011 protests assumed a less threatening façade as those demanding transformation were most visibly members of the dominant social sector (Misgav 2013). However, the mantra of "social justice" quickly became a broad "summarizing symbol" (Ortner 1973) that could indeed contain diverse and seemingly disparate interests, in part recollecting the approach of Israeli Women in Black (Helman and Rapoport 1997; Sasson-Levy and Rapoport 2003). According to Sherry Ortner (1973, 1339), summarizing symbols are "those symbols which are seen as summing up, expressing, representing for the participants in an emotionally powerful and relatively undifferentiated way, what the system means to them."[6] Operating under the pretext of generality, these symbols allow for and arise through the presence of multiple meanings. Here, rather than defining and locating a variety of precise targets for resistance, summarizing symbols generate action through remaining relatively open and facilitating membership. As Orna Sasson-Levy and Tamar Rapoport (2003, 390–391) highlight with regard to Women in Black, "The summarizing nature of the homogeneous message—'Stop the Occupation'—enabled each woman to maintain zealously her individual political interpretation and position, while outwardly preserving a united front."[7] While displaying similar dynamics, the 2011 protests paired this context-specific broad framing with recognizable regional uprisings, morphing Egyptian Tahrir Square's "the people want to topple the regime" into "the people demand social justice" (Kashua 2011a), a recognizably Israeli version of the demand for change. Having witnessed the uprisings in Tunisia and Egypt along with the reactions of distrust and fear displayed by both the Israeli government and the majority of Jewish Israeli society, many activists feared that the transformative potential of the neighboring movements might bypass Israel altogether (Ravid 2011). Thus what began as housing protests expanded to become "social protests" through employing and activating multiple sites of appeal as participants linked Israel's history of political protest with contemporary political movements.

However, beyond the appeal of summarizing symbols and recent regional uprisings, Jewish Israeli protesters needed to generate participation, principally secured through fostering a sense of commitment and investment. As highlighted by Ortner (1973, 1342), summarizing symbols bind systems of meaning with emotion, centralizing the symbol's "focusing power, its drawing-together, intensifying, catalyzing impact upon the respondent." Rather than directly organizing thought or prompting action, these symbols crystallize commitment and catalyze feelings, speaking primarily to attitude (1342–43). In part capitalizing on the enormous affective impact of regional events, both seemingly "successful" and violently repressed, participants in Israel's social protests generated participation by creating an atmosphere unique to the Israeli setting, while at the same time invoking other places, times, and struggles.

These dynamics became apparent during a visit to the Rothschild Boulevard tent encampment, two days after my experience of the demonstration that opened this chapter. During a brief prior visit to the site, I had been struck by the way organization sat side by side with chaotic revelry, as groups excitedly readied colorful handmade signs before the night's action in a public space newly rendered quasi-private. Now, in daylight, I passed the Israeli flags that adorned the main organizing tent at the head of Rothschild Boulevard, near Habima Square, noting the small poster reading *Gilad adayn chai* (Gilad [Shalit] is still alive), with its blue and white Stars of David and images of a then-hostage soldier;[8] together, these symbols provided an immediate sense of the limits that framed the protests. Beyond this logistical space—here a blackboard declared the day's schedule of meetings—the encampment's central infrastructure unfolded: the first aid tent staffed by Physicians for Human Rights, a broadcast and transmission station for the popular Army radio station Galatz, and the massive kitchen area, operated by the organized protesters themselves. From this point orderly rows of tents covered the center and perimeter of the boulevard, with largely identical gray domes branded Outdoor Revolution interrupted by pedestrian aisles, communal living spaces, and hand-drawn expressions of motivation, discontent, and desire.

While orderliness prevailed in the sections of the Rothschild encampment closest to the kitchen and organizing areas, it gradually diminished going away from Habima Square along the boulevard toward Allenby Street. In large part a product of the protesters' conviction that the encampment should be long-term, the immediate degree of organization conveyed a belief that order generated both sustainability and appeal. However, like resistance, this orderliness reflected and reproduced the wider relations of power that frame Israeli society. Indeed, the impression of tidiness on Rothschild Boulevard was also generated through the municipality's regular deployment of sanitation workers, of whom many are black African migrants. Thus the social-protest encampment clearly benefitted from and reinforced existing racialized labor patterns, if unintentionally so. This particular tension with race and labor again became apparent at the summer's end, when the remaining encampments in Tel Aviv and Jerusalem were forcibly dismantled. During September 2011, images circulating in the mainstream press depicted (male) black African contracted workers evicting Jewish Israeli protesters and demolishing their structures, potentially fuelling the fires of prejudice. Interestingly, though also orderly, the tent encampment in Tel Aviv's Levinsky Park was less maintained by the municipality and subject to frequent evacuation and demolition beginning in July (ACRI 2011b), due in large part to its location in an area of south Tel Aviv now home to much of the city's African migrant population and historically inhabited by working-class Mizrahi Jews. This disparity was likewise evident in the notable difference between Jerusalem's Horse Park and Independence Park, as more affluent protesters populated the former during the summer of 2011, while largely working-class and impoverished or homeless protest participants inhabited the latter (Levy 2011a). Then the platform ostensibly shared with the Mizrahi Black Panthers of the 1970s dissolved in these sites, as the 2011 protests left certain race- and class-based relations of power and privilege intact.

Back on Tel Aviv's Rothschild Boulevard, I made my way through the rows of dwellings and interests with camera in hand, arriving at the corner of HaHashmona'im Street. Adorned with Israeli flags, the Migdal Ha'Am (Tower of the People) faced an enormous heart-shaped arch erected by the Love Revolution and the small number of structures that constituted Tent 1948, an attempt to bring together Jewish and Palestinian citizens of Israel. In this particular space the multiplicity of messages and agendas seemed less a source of strength than an indicator of how empty "social justice" had become as a signifier, as the protests' summarizing symbol and rallying cry appeared in constant need of filling up. As I recorded images, a man in his sixties approached me and asked, *"Ma at choshevet al kol ze?"* (What do you think of all this?) Assuming that he had mistaken me for a journalist,

I responded evasively that I found the encampment interesting and somehow beautiful, with its creativity, hope, and energy. My interlocutor replied, "But there's a problem here. At night all these young people are drinking beer, dancing, singing, talking about love—I see it on television! It's starting to be a problem." He shook his head. "It's becoming like Woodstock."

"But it's also supposed to be fun, isn't it?" I asked. This drew a snort of contempt. "*It's fun*. This is no Woodstock, you understand? Woodstock was a party, yes ... but it was around the Vietnam War, it had Jimi Hendrix, it had the Doors. I've seen the Doors! These young people here don't know what Woodstock was. A friend asked me a few years ago if I wanted to go with him to see the Doors play, but how is it the Doors without Jim Morrison? That isn't the Doors! You understand? And this isn't Woodstock—they had Hendrix, Morrison..."[9]

In a heartbeat, "It's becoming like Woodstock" had morphed into "This is no Woodstock," and a statement of similarity became a charge of inadequacy that appears to reverse the previous claim. Yet, rather than revealing contradiction, this commentary highlights the deliberate act of distancing undertaken by the protesters: "politics" would remain absent from their discourse and platform. Situating the authenticity of Woodstock in the wider context of protests against the Vietnam War, this observer of Israel's largest tent encampment found the site, actors, and agenda lacking specifically in *political* terms, as he saw symbols and practices incompletely appropriated. Here the drinking, dancing, singing, and love that characterized and popularized the American protest were stripped of both meaning and transformative potential in the depoliticized space of the Tel Aviv protests, despite the presence of signs reading "*Mahapecha*" (Revolution). Equivalent to the Doors without Jim Morrison and Woodstock without the Vietnam War, the social protests assumed a form more akin to carnival, where the "pathos of change and renewal" (Bakhtin 1984 [1968], 11) became a mask beneath which politics could be expunged.

The Politics of the Carnivalesque

> Carnival ... does not acknowledge any distinction between actors and spectators.... Carnival is not a spectacle seen by the people; they live in it, and everyone participates because its very idea embraces all the people. While carnival lasts, there is no other life outside it. (Bakhtin 1984 [1968], 7)

With the boundaries between participants and observers blurred, as recounted in the opening of this chapter, Israel's protests were indeed "lived in" by the many Jewish Israelis who found space within social justice for their individual interests and claims, becoming absorbed by the life within. More carefully constructed than was readily apparent during my first experience of the demonstrations, the inner life of the protests resonated with the qualities of energetic possibility attributed to carnival by Mikhail Bakhtin (1984 [1968]; see also Shenhav 2013), replete with new modes of communication and the seeming suspension of hierarchies. However, as formulated by Bakhtin (1984 [1968], 10), the carnivalesque explicitly exists as a *"temporary liberation from the prevailing truth and from the established order."*[10] With an eventual return to the "old order" after the cessation of carnival, its promise of "change and renewal" proves impermanent (Weichselbaumer 2010; Shenhav 2013)—like Ortner's (1973) summary symbols, Bakhtin's carnivalesque works through emotion rather than targeting sustained thought or action. Then as much as the "feast of becoming" (Bakhtin 1984 [1968], 10) takes shape through promise and possibility, so too it functions through concealment, raising the question of how acts of subversion might elide relations of power (Weichselbaumer 2010; Shenhav 2013).[11]

In the case of Israel's 2011 summer of protest, concealment or masking emerged not as an incidental by-product of the emotive atmosphere but rather as an integral aspect of the protesters' strategies aimed at garnering appeal, strength, and longevity. As Bakhtin's momentary carnival can only be incompletely decoupled from the reality of the "old order," so too the Israeli protests remained bound with their wider context through discourse and practice, though selectively so. Here the deliberate splitting off and avoidance of "politics"—the erasure of Vietnam from Woodstock—created a platform from which to generate a critical mass, joining the economic concerns of the early housing protests with broader "social" interests of a dissatisfied public (Belkind 2013, 333–34; Shenhav 2013).

As indicated earlier, throughout the protests the separation of "political" from "economic" and "social" framed calls for social justice, as leaders and participants routinely renounced politics in favor of those agendas they felt were ordinarily obscured or subsumed. In gendered terms, this reversal was paramount to prioritizing issues constructed as feminine or feminized over those deemed masculine or masculinized within Israeli society. During this time calls for domestic transformation—lower costs for housing, groceries, and childcare, along with increased budgets for education, social welfare, and medical systems—trumped the primacy of international concerns rooted in perceptions of threat and security. One protester, a young man then dwelling on Rothschild Boulevard, made the wider terms of this apparent subversion clear:

> This isn't about who loves Palestinians and who hates Palestinians.... Yes, this *is* political. It is political. But it isn't political in the way that we're used to talking about politics in Israel. The biggest criticism we face is the accusation that we are all "leftists." Yes, we're leftists, but this is the *social* and *economic* left, not the political left.
>
> We're very careful to not be right or left, but we *are* social and economic left. In the end, however, it will have to become political because that's where change happens.[12]

As defined by this speaker, among Jewish Israelis "politics" relates tightly to one's stance regarding Palestinians, raising the masculinized specters of conflict and violence (Belkind 2013, 333–34; Mendel 2013). Yet even as this narrow understanding prevailed, the young man on Rothschild Boulevard demonstrates how political labels of "left" and "right" may be detached and reaffixed, transferred from politics to economic and social realms in a move that apparently leaves little residue. In creating the possibility of realizing oneself as politically conservative yet economically and socially "leftist," protesters effectively widened their popular base, increasing the numbers demanding transformation by stipulating that politics must be left at the door—here, inclusion and exclusion operate together to generate appeal. However, at the same time as the speaker reaffirms the prevailing meaning of politics-as-conflict, he ultimately evokes political process, read as governance or formal politics, as the site "where change happens" and the practice in which protesters must eventually engage. Thus, through a carnivalesque suspension and (re)affirmation of norms, politics is effectively splintered, conceptually detached from social and economic issues yet practically remaining the forum for transformation.

Gender Politics in Practice

As the events of summer 2011 developed, this bifurcation came to characterize the protesters' discourses, practices, platforms, and agendas, reinscribing the prevailing meaning and space of politics (Belkind 2013; Shenhav 2013). Importantly, these dynamics took shape through the binary orders and gendered codes that characterize divisions of masculine/feminine, international/domestic, conflict/peace, and "right/left" in Israel. As made clear in the account above, "leftist" was openly wielded as a largely pejorative term during those summer months, even when distanced from popular understandings of politics (Mendel 2013).[13] While those social or domestic matters largely considered "feminized" in prevailing popular discourses were indeed elevated during the social protests, the negative association between the feminine and leftist pro-peace platforms—"who loves Palestinians"—remained. Then in abjuring both (feminized) "left" and (masculinized) "politics" the protests effectively reproduced their very meanings, producing a form of depoliticization that maintained existing hierarchies, patterns, and values.[14]

However, these gendered dynamics of depoliticization are not unique to the summer of 2011. As seen in the previous chapter's discussion of the Arba Emahot (Four Mothers) campaign against the deployment of Israeli troops in Lebanon, depoliticization may paradoxically increase legitimacy in the Jewish Israeli public sphere, generating an apolitical politics of protest. Indeed, Women in Black's strategic deployment of their summarizing symbol "*Dai la Kibush*" (End the Occupation) also produces a mode of depoliticized politics, if differently so. As Sasson-Levy and Rapoport (2003, 391) argue, aimed at generating lasting appeal as a precursor to legitimacy, "The relatively long-term duration of Women in Black may be attributed in large part to its deliberate avoidance of any collective ideological elaboration of the political message, protest practices, or the vigil in general.... The avoidance may be regarded as a protest practice that enabled the inclusion of as many women as possible in the vigil." Then the possibility arises that avoidance may be key to mobilization, as these historical and contemporary movements highlight how deliberate depoliticization facilitates and strengthens commitment.

The gendered politics of the 2011 social protests extended beyond their association with familiar symbols, platforms, and organizations to include radical shifts in political practice. As described above, despite a disavowal of contextually defined "politics" the protests remained political in their articulation of collective interests, democratic procedure, and interface with authority. However, these practices were pursued in a manner markedly different from conventional experiences of the political in Israel. As journalist Bradley Burston (2011) wrote in *Ha'aretz*:

> From an Israeli standpoint, the most radical act of this newborn revolution has already taken place. In a country where, whether on serious television

roundtables or the Knesset floor, discourse is defined as everyone screaming simultaneously, the "Tent People" have adopted a system that sanctifies listening and respect. When a speaker is addressing the group, crowd members respond not with interjection but with sign language—raised, fluttering hands signify agreement, crossed fists show disapproval, and a rolling of both hands means the speaker is going on and on without making a point.

While temporarily suspended during the 2011 protests, active processes of masculinization and Israel's "military-masculine hegemony" (Lentin 2000, 188, 217) persist in framing modes of communication. Characterized as "everyone screaming simultaneously," political practice and expression among Jewish Israelis remain linked to Israel's conditions of "total militarism" (Kimmerling 2001, 214) and evoke the hegemonic Sabra figure, that tough native-born Israeli constructed in response to the perceived feminization of Jews in diaspora and during the Second World War (Sharoni 1995, 41; Lentin 2000, 198–201; Katz 2003, 21). Yet as Burston details above, during the summer protests political practices constructed as masculine were replaced by modes of conduct ostensibly more feminine, associated with "listening and respect." Again signaling the significance of shared discourses and practices of protest, this shift was paralleled in the Occupy and anti-globalization movements from which Israeli protesters borrowed.[15]

Yet even as this newly "feminized" political practice constituted a radical departure from prevailing norms in Israel, it was simultaneously cast in opposition to the same diasporic figure that produced the Sabra and the masculinization of politics. During the summer of 2011, this figure materialized as the *freier* (Yiddish for "sucker"), whose masculinity is called into question by his lack of wits—invoked by protesters to illustrate what/who they were not.[16] As protesters asserted an alternative mode of resistance, "*Pit'om anachnu lo freierim yoter*" (Suddenly we aren't *freier*s any more) appeared on signs posted at the Rothschild Boulevard encampment and carried in protests, and at the final Tel Aviv demonstration the popular band HaDag Nachash performed a song containing the repeated refrain "*Anachnu betach lo freierim*" (We are definitely not *freier*s).[17] Thus the reviled emasculated Jew of the diaspora was brought squarely into protest discourse and iconography.

While the association of this figure with impotence, weakness, and lawfulness gave rise to the historical construction of "native Israeliness" (Sharoni 1995; Lentin 2000; Katz 2003), its contemporary deployment raises points of complexity and contradiction. Jewish masculinity has been shaped not only by experiences of diaspora but also by the perceived hypermasculinity of *goyim* or non-Jews (Boyarin 1997, 4–5); the very cactus from which the Sabra takes its name (*Opuntia ficus-indica*) is a symbol shared by Palestinians as a marker of resistant steadfastness and resilience (Bardenstein, 1998, 11–14); and the gender roles that emerged in correspondence with the masculinized "New (Israeli) Jew" often shift during wartime in order to support the national effort (Sharoni 2005 [1994], 243). In keeping with this complexity, as Jewish Israeli protesters developed an "alternative" political practice during the summer of 2011 they insisted on shared purchase in the acceptably masculinized Sabra paradigm by rejecting the *freier* and his seeming feminization. Though practiced in contradistinction to the screaming and interjection that characterize dominant modes of political practice, this new politics then fed back into prevailing norms as the feminine remained subject to devaluation, leaving existing systems of meaning largely intact.

THE POLITICS OF BELONGING

Thus the 2011 social protests explicitly took shape through the practice of gender politics, informed by the broad appeal of a summarizing symbol and a carnivalesque suspension of norms. As political codes and gender norms were reinforced, appropriated, and selectively transgressed in pursuit of social justice, these negotiations and contestations largely reaffirmed the belief that "social" and "economic" realms could be divorced from "politics." Yet despite the seeming inclusivity of "social justice" and strategies adopted to increase appeal, relations of division and distinction progressively shaped the protest body along familiar lines of conflict.

Underlining the belief that "it will have to become political because that's where change happens,"[18] various participants and observers acknowledged a gap in need of bridging as the protests developed throughout the summer months: the protests would need to engage with politics to achieve their aims. "You can't solve this without solving the political problems—the internal can't be solved without looking at the external," a friend explained as we walked together during a late-July protest. "In the next election, whoever wins, he will need to represent this and declare it. It just isn't possible that someone will be elected who doesn't engage with the political when talking about solving these social issues."[19] Conveying his perception that the necessary connection between the social and political realms would ultimately determine the protests' resolution, this speaker directly contests claims that governance and political process may be separated from the meaning or substance of politics. Taking up a similar position, weeks later another friend and protest participant expressed her interest in Prime Minister Netanyahu's plan to engage with the protesters' demands through a series of negotiations. Rather than exploring alternative routes such as the formation of councils or joint panels, Netanyahu's vision struck Chaya as following in the model of prevailing political processes, which remain rooted in the "You're on that side, I'm on this side" logic of conflict (Lis and Bassock 2011; Verter 2011).[20] For Chaya, effective translation and successful realization of the protesters' diffuse demands depended on openly identifying and challenging the conflict-driven approach, not as a means of disavowing politics but as an integral aspect of engagement with authority. The necessity of engaging not just "in" but directly *with* politics was again echoed by Dov, the Tel Aviv artist and DJ who earlier expressed resistance to both soldiering and activism. Dov agreed that the protests had opened important new spaces of political discourse and practice, while falling short of addressing left/right divisions and their basis in conflict and occupation. "They have to [address politics] ultimately, because it *is* all about left-right issues!" he claimed as frustration with the ambiguity of an apolitical platform mounted over the passing months.[21]

As the interlocutors above suggest, protest discourses, practices, and agendas needed to retain political intelligibility and currency while working toward the realization of ostensibly apolitical demands and goals. Correspondingly, those in positions of leadership understood their substantive and material targets to be achievable through interaction with government, as "social" and "economic" issues could only be settled through the practice of politics. This need for intelligibility then influenced the limits of protest—to be heard or recognized on the level "where change happens," the protests needed to operate within prevailing political boundaries, while at the same time outwardly seeking transformation of their meaning.

Thus through these tensions around intelligibility, the protests subscribed to a "politics of belonging" (Yuval-Davis 2011) on a macro level, if indirectly so. Collective agreement around the necessity of an eventual return to politics, if largely in procedure and practice, signals the extent to which the protests' subversion and inversion of the dominant order would indeed be only temporary. Yet these macro-political dynamics were underlined by the drive for belonging on a micro level—here "politics" was apparent in the familiar fault lines that cleaved the protests nearly from their inception, threatening the carefully fostered sense of unity made possible beneath the banner of social justice. As the protest body swelled in numbers and the diversity of claims throughout the summer months, processes of inclusion and exclusion shaped its collective boundaries, complicating and contradicting its seeming broad inclusivity.

Who Are Ha'Am?

While claiming inclusivity, throughout the summer months the protests' "politics of belonging" reproduced exclusive political categories and communities, effectively maintaining the boundaries of the protest body along the lines of the dominant national body. As Nira Yuval-Davis (2011, 20) writes, "The boundaries the politics of belonging are concerned with are the boundaries of the political community of belonging, the boundaries which, sometimes physically, but always symbolically, separate the world population into 'us' and 'them.'" Thus the collective protest body gained form and substance not only through its cohesive summarizing symbol but also through the continuing presence of existing divisions and hierarchies. Rooted in the logics of conflict made visible throughout this book, in the context of Israel-Palestine broad categories of "us" and "them" relate most clearly to the distinctions made between "Jewish" and "Palestinian" residents, subjects, and citizens. Yet as Yuval-Davis notes, "The politics of belonging involve not only the maintenance and reproduction of the boundaries of the community of belonging by the hegemonic political power (within and outside the community), but also their contestation, challenge and resistance by other political agents" (20). Then resistance might once again diagnose power (Abu-Lughod 1990), this time shedding light on how the boundaries of protest overlap with the borders of nation.

Additionally shaped by the need for political intelligibility, practices of active exclusion at first appeared wholly absent from the social protests as groups and communities attempted to locate their interests in its platform and agenda. However, as actions developed over the summer months, marginal groups were assured of their subordination, in a movement aimed at equitable social and economic transformation. After my first experiences of the demonstrations and Rothschild Boulevard encampment, in early August I sat in a cafe near Tel Aviv's renovated north port area with Nili, a Jewish Israeli friend who also lived in the city. During our conversation, Nili spoke of another friend who had attended a July demonstration with a group who assembled in Tel Aviv's Levinsky Park—this was a self-professed "radical bloc" that sought to engage with politics in its fullest sense, as associated with conflict, violence, and occupation. Like myself, this friend had been astounded by the energy and anger of the protesters, feeling amazed rather than alienated, though this latter sentiment had actually spurred the formation of the radical bloc. According to Nili, her friend tended to be critical of the protests, uneasy about the *vagueness* of social justice rather than its dissociation from occupation and conflict. He was frustrated that participants wielded the term without considering its meaning. "But personally I'm more bothered by the first part of that phrase, *Ha'am*—'the people,'" Nili told me. For Nili, *ha'am* could not be separated from the ethnic and religious nation that underwrites "the people" as constructed in Israel. "This goes back to racism," she said heatedly, "social, economic, and political racism.... If it isn't right or left or center, then what do we have in common? We are Jews. 'The people' are Jewish people."[22] Underlined by the displays of Israeli flags at the tent encampments, the singing of nationalist songs from bygone eras at demonstrations, and the images and words gracing handmade signs, the (Jewish) nation indeed circumscribed the protests.

With *ha'am* clearly bound to "the Jewish people," the protests' politics of belonging took on decidedly political tones that became manifest as marginal and oppositional groups sought inclusion in its body. In particular, the participation of Palestinian citizens of Israel and Jewish settler communities differently highlighted how the political boundaries of the nation actively crosscut the protest collective. Among Palestinian citizens of Israel, the nationalized contours of "the people" were immediately recognized. Palestinian journalist Sayed Kashua (2011a) wrote in his weekly *Ha'aretz* column in early August: "'The people want social justice.' What exactly is the definition of 'the people'? Will I feel comfortable shouting those words out along with the other protesters? I know it was borrowed from Tahrir Square, where they shouted, 'The people want to topple the regime.' But in Egypt the word referred to the Egyptian people. Meaning everyone who lives in Egypt. And here? Does the term 'the people' really include all of Israel's citizens?"

Echoing Nili's concerns, Kashua's hesitancy reflects not a wariness of "social justice" but knowledge gained from his experiences as a Palestinian citizen of Jewish Israeli "democracy," where provision of and access to rights remains de facto dependent on ethnic identity (Shafir and Peled 2002; Lowrance 2004; Semyonov and Lewin-Epstein 2004; Yiftachel 2006; Abdo 2011). Highlighting how the protest body indeed mirrored the national body,

Kashua uncovers how exclusion underwrote the seeming inclusivity of the protests' summarizing symbol. Interestingly, one week after the publication of the article cited above, Kashua (2011b) was invited to speak at the second demonstration in Jerusalem and later described how his experience met with the protests' apolitical politics:

> "Talk about the place you come from," the activist said to me on the phone, trying to help. And just what is "this place that I come from," goddammit? What... like, the Arabs? That I come from the Arabs? What can I say about that? I'll get up on stage like an idiot and start talking about the housing problem in the Arab villages? What do I know about that? I come from a neighborhood in West Jerusalem. If they really want someone to talk about that, why don't they invite some Arab council head, or someone who can cite statistics? What, they want me to get up there and say that the Arabs in Israel support the protest? I should say that we too want social justice? Who gave me the mandate to speak on behalf of the place from which I supposedly come?
>
> Maybe I'll talk about the Likud, about Israel Beiteinu, about Kadima, about the National Home[23] and the racist laws the Knesset is passing left and right. No, no. I can't. This protest is not political, and who knows what the protesters think about the occupation, if they even think about it at all. This is a social protest that has an economic basis, I reminded myself. I can't talk about the settlements, the racist laws, the occupation and all that kind of stuff: It's not relevant, it's insignificant.

While Kashua's narratives point to how politicized matters of ethnicity, race, and nation effectively excluded particular individuals and communities from the protests' avowedly apolitical agenda, other Palestinian citizens of Israel found a site of resistance within social justice, however marginal. Situated at the head of the large second block in Tel Aviv's Rothschild Boulevard encampment, a small group of Palestinian and Jewish Israeli citizens took up residence at Tent 1948, as recounted briefly above. According to Palestinian rights activist Abir Kopty (2011), from Nazareth, "Tent 1948's main message is that social justice should be for all. It brings together Jewish and Palestinian citizens who believe in shared sovereignty in the state of all its citizens." The tent adorned with signs in Arabic, Hebrew, and English, Tent 1948's Palestinian and Jewish inhabitants displayed large plywood placards that detailed narratives of expulsion and dispossession, challenging the meaning and scope of social justice. As tent encampments and protests eventually spread to Nazareth, Jaffa, Haifa, and other locales that are home to large Palestinian communities, the participation of Palestinians served to politicize the protests as these participants appealed to the equity promised by both democratic citizenship and social justice (Belkind 2013; Misgav 2013).

As the appearance of politics—in meaning rather than practice—threatened the foundation that underpinned the protests' collectivity, burgeoning solidarities increasingly met with the boundaries of nation. The structures and residents of Tent 1948, which were physically attacked in late July by right-wing protest participants, signified an intrusion of the political into the sanctity of a unified world made anew, as they brought occupation, conflict, and violence into the heart of an ostensibly apolitical space. While subsequent confrontations were limited, the sea of Jewish Israeli demands and interests largely drowned discussions of Palestinian support or recognition as the protests progressed. Indeed, as Kopty (2011) wrote during her time at Tent 1948:

> For me, as Palestinian, I don't feel part of the July 14 movement, and I'm not there because I feel part, almost every corner of this encampment reminds me that this place does not want me. My first tour there was pretty depressing, I found lots of Israeli flags, a man giving a lecture to youth about his memories from "48 war" [sic] from a Zionist perspective, another group marching with signs calling for the release of Gilad Shalit, another singing Zionist songs. This is certainly not a place that the 20% of the population would feel belong to. The second day I found Ronen Shuval, from Im Tirtzu, the extreme right wing organization giving a talk full of incitement and hatred to the left and human rights organizations. Settlers already set a tent and were dancing with joy.

Here, Kopty's depiction highlights how the atmosphere and ethos of carnival did not eliminate politics from the physical site of protest but actually sewed the nation deep into the movement's core.[24]

Yet Kopty's narrative is also significant for her perception of how right-wing and ultra-nationalist factions were granted space and voice within the protest, seemingly unproblematically. As the arrival and presence of settler contingents generated controversy among many protesters, these actors differently ushered occupation, conflict, and violence into the heart of Tel Aviv. On the same day as a coalition of dairy farmers joined the main protest, right-wing activists marched from the protests' symbolic center at Habima Square, both in solidarity and as an insistence on inclusion beneath the banner of "social justice." Including factions such as Im Tirtzu—a Jewish Israeli ultra-nationalist group inspired by Theodore Herzl's dictum, "*Im tirtzu, ein zo agada*" (If you will it, it is no dream)—and the Yesha Council—an umbrella organization of Jewish settlements in the West Bank—these participants posed a new challenge to the limits of *ha'am*. Paradoxically linked to the political tensions raised by Palestinian citizens of Israel, Jewish Israeli settler contingents again tested the inclusivity claimed by the protests' ostensibly nonpolitical leadership (Levinson and Lior 2011). Along with public support expressed by Yesha Council leader Naftali Bennett and West Bank Kahanist[25] Baruch Marzel during visits to the Rothschild encampment, the move for broad-based right-wing inclusion generated a furor among those protest participants who had earlier set aside anti-occupation politics in the interest of cohesion (Mandel 2011; Frenkel 2011). Activating latent dynamics and discourses of exclusion, right-wing participants chanted, "Tel Aviv is Jewish, Sudanese to go Sudan!" along with "No left, no right, cheap apartments are our right!" (Zonszein 2011; Mendel 2013), summarily demonstrating the rigidity and fluidity of the protests' internal boundaries. As members of the Hilltop Youth—young ultra-nationalists often at the forefront of settlement expansion through their establishment of illegal outposts—pitched a tent on Rothschild Boulevard, they pushed the limits of *ha'am* even further by insisting on belonging despite their living illegally beyond the territorial borders of the state (Levinson 2011).[26]

Though ultimately expelled by inhabitants of Rothschild Boulevard after at times violent confrontations, Jewish settler groups continued to participate in the protests as encampments and demonstrations spread to the illegal settlements; indeed, organized protests in Ariel received "official endorsement" (Blumenthal and Dana 2011).[27] While they were forcibly excluded from the main protest site in Tel Aviv, the eventual inclusion and sanction of settler factions revealed tensions that again imbricated the protest body with the national body. As right-wing, ultra-nationalist, and settler groups insisted on belonging, many radically left-wing participants refused to practice solidarity and seemingly chose to exclude themselves from the summer's actions. Critically, this cause-and-effect dynamic held up an important mirror to the Jewish Israeli mainstream. Frequently scapegoated by the secular middle class for social ills, the expansion of occupation, and the perpetuation of conflict, right-wing, ultra-nationalist, and settler communities actualized the explicitly *national* meaning of "the people" and rendered visible the social and political ties that bind beyond territorial boundaries.

Though differently framed and realized, Palestinian and Jewish settler appeals to belonging reveal the extent to which the apolitical orientation of the protests remained underwritten by politics.[28] Here the divisions, convergences, and power relations specific to Israel-Palestine as an explicitly political context indeed shaped the protest body and its agenda. While both Palestinians and settlers continued to participate in encampments and demonstrations throughout the summer, the national membership and social ties enjoyed by the latter group were more readily recognized and accommodated than the explicitly political demands and appeals to citizenship voiced by the former. Then rather than being pervasive or lasting, the carnivalesque suspension of prevailing norms and orders in Israeli society was selective, obeying the political boundaries of the nation while subverting prevailing patterns of gender, if fleetingly so. Here, the politics of belonging reveal how marginal positions relative to the national body were mirrored in the protest body, reflecting and entrenching existing hierarchies of power and privilege. Though Palestinian citizens and Jewish settler communities politicized the protests through introducing the specters of occupation, violence, and conflict, Jewish settlers and ultra-nationalists living beyond Israel's territorial boundaries succeeded in insisting upon inclusion, in a way that Palestinians—non-nationals, even though citizens of the state—could not. Thus the experiences of these marginal groups reveal how limits are always already present, even within a state of suspension. While the carnivalesque promise of change and renewal seemingly invites "everyone [to] participate because its very idea embraces all the people" (Bakhtin 1984 [1968], 7), the "life outside it" defines precisely who those people are.

ISRAEL'S INTIMATE PUBLIC

As made visible through their apolitical framing, selective suspension of norms, and dynamics of inclusion and exclusion, the 2011 summer of social protests in Israel cannot be simply appraised as a movement *for* social justice, or *against* the rising cost of living. Rather, these mass actions aimed at creating, or at least improving, a world that remained circumscribed by politics. As detailed in the accounts and analyses above, the politics of occupation, conflict, and violence could not be surmounted or permanently suspended by the protesters and their supporters, even as they sought to dissociate political practice from meaning. Instead, politics permeated the sites, discourses, and body of protest, even if seemingly absent. Then the world imagined and created by protesters would knowingly be something *in between*, a space and community built in the tension between political action and inaction. As participants disavowed "politics" yet engaged in political action, if unintentionally so, their protest was simultaneously passive and active, complicit and resistant.

For many, this tension increasingly necessitated a kind of "knowingly not knowing" (Cohen 2001), in which criticism and disbelief were suspended in order to enter into the protests' promise of "the good life," or at least a better life. Yet as detailed above, the ability to imagine this life, claim belonging in it, and enjoy its desired material comforts was selective, restricted by the wider reality of conflict and protracted violence. Whether they were "leftist," Ethiopian, queer, working class, or Palestinian, during the summer of 2011 individuals and communities from every sector of Israeli society could, in theory, subscribe to "social justice," an object of desire not exclusive to Jewishness. However, while the exact content and meaning of this demand remained hazy in discussions of the protesters' aims, the imagined future emerged much in line with current realities, even if draped in new material trappings. During our portside discussion in August, Nili conveyed her impression of the protests in no uncertain terms: "The idea seems to be 'I want the most for me over here and he wants the most for him over there'—people don't all want the same thing, but the most given their position. Then, maybe once they're *comfortable,* they'll turn their attention to the occupation."[29] As a former activist who had worked in Ramallah and East Jerusalem, Nili criticized the protests for their explicit avoidance of politics in its contextually defined and popularly understood meaning. Yet her words also make visible how material desires intersected with the protests' politics of belonging, underlining the divisions between "us" and "them," "here" and "there" produced through sustained conflict. These distinctions were both internal and external, shaping different visions of "the most for me over here . . . and him over there" as visions of a better future corresponded to social location.

Then within the summer of social protests, aspiration and imagination worked in unanticipated ways, as the call for social justice produced and reflected diverse visions of the sought-after ideal world. However, the protesters' individual desires cohered on two important levels: their adherence to the strategy of depoliticization, and their aim to achieve a level of material comfort imagined to underwrite normalcy in contexts free from conflict. Collectively, these actions generated a particular kind of "intimate public," or a domain that thrives in proximity to the political yet ultimately remains ambivalent about politics (Berlant 2008, x).

Similar to the dynamics of summarizing symbols (Ortner 1973) and carnival (Bakhtin 1984 [1968]), intimate publics draw on emotion as both catalyst and agent of cohesion, creating within or beside the dominant public sphere an alternative space of belonging and action. As Lauren Berlant (2008, 10) writes: "A public is intimate when it foregrounds affective and emotional attachments located in fantasies of the common, the everyday, and a sense of ordinariness, a space where the social world is rich with anonymity and local recognitions, and where challenging and banal conditions of life take place in proximity to the attentions of power but also squarely in the radar of a recognition that can be provided by other humans." Central to intimate publics are sociality and affirmation, relational practices through which members might invest in a shared fantasy of the ordinary that promises an escape from wider structures of power while remaining subject to them. Termed "juxtapolitical" by Berlant (2008, 10), this proximate location of intimate publics provides "relief from the political" in contexts where "the political sphere is more often seen as a field of threat, chaos, degradation, or retraumatization than a condition of possibility" (11), a description echoed by many protesters in their assessments of political life in Israel.

Importantly, intimate publics straddle the porous boundary between public and private spheres, as their felt reciprocity, imagined simplicity, and sense of unity provide a deeply personal impetus for the creation of a world seemingly free from politics. Following Berlant's (2008, 3) work in the American context, "generally intimate publics ... [flourish] in proximity to the political because the political is deemed an elsewhere managed by elites who are interested in reproducing the conditions of their objective superiority, not in the well-being of ordinary people or life-worlds." Again parallels arise in Israel as protest leaders and participants foregrounded the concerns of "ordinary people" vis-à-vis the economic and political elite. Framed by the inclusion of Israel in the Organisation for Economic Co-operation and Development in 2010 (Ravid 2010), the resilience of the Israeli economy during the recent global economic downturn (Bassock 2011), and the continuing dominance of select Jewish Israeli business families (Ben-David and Wainer 2010), the Israeli intimate public targeted "tycoons" and politicians. Yet even as intimate publics seemingly produce division, thereby enabling their members to participate in a fantasy that displaces reality, these collectivities are contingent. Following Berlant, juxtapolitical cultures "thrive in *proximity* to the political, occasionally crossing over in political alliance, even more occasionally doing some politics, but most often not, acting as a critical chorus that sees the expression of emotional response and conceptual recalibration as achievement enough."[30]

Productive of both "emotional response" and "conceptual recalibration," as seen in the accounts throughout this chapter, success or "achievement" in the context of Israel's social protests can be read not solely in the attainment of goals outlined but also in their creation of a world of meaning, action, and influence. Here it is possible "to understand the flourishing of the social to one side of the political as something other than a failure to be politics" (Berlant 2008, 24–25), while at the same time asking what its thriving might do in political terms. At stake in Israel's intimate public were the material and affective possibilities created through a collective will and move to action, underwritten by the investment of so many participants who described "despair" and "disillusionment"—melancholia—as their primary political emotions. Born of disappointment from former days of activism and unrealized visions of "solutions" or futures, the bitterness of past political action was overcome as a new community, that elusive critical mass, arose under the banner of social justice. Here the adopted summarizing symbol held more than the promise of inclusive broad-based participation; rather, social justice promised to suture the fragmentation that has come to characterize Israeli society. As one former interview participant remarked in awe of the protests in late August, "It's really something for Israelis, who want so much always to *divide*."[31]

Imagined and manifested in the spaces of encampments, demonstrations, and rallies, this newly engendered solidarity was the potential price of failure, as protesters believed the carnivalesque promise of change, renewal, and becoming to be lasting rather than fleeting. Then, as formerly reticent citizens were moved to action, challenges posed to the new (or renewed) consensus took on a severity apart from the normalized ruptures that stabilize the small worlds depicted in chapter 3. When introduced to this juxtapolitical intimate public, politics—in meaning, rather than practice—elicited responses aimed at not repair but foreclosure. These protective social mechanisms were activated not by "outsiders" seeking membership in the protest body but by criticism and dissent expressed from within. While ushering in conflict, violence, and occupation in a manner similar to the participation of Palestinian citizens and Jewish settlers, this uninvited entrance of the political revealed seams of tension and division internal to the protests' intimate public. As protesters understood this particular mode of intrusion to be world-destroying rather than world-making (Berlant 2008, 269–70), appeals to gradualism and practices of self-exclusion came to act as the guardians of community, maintaining the protests' apolitical character in a context suffused by politics.

Gradualism

"Talking with you is different from talking to Israelis," Nili said during our meeting in Tel Aviv's port, her voice registering surprise and a hint of sadness. "If I was to say all of this to even my most activist Israeli friends they would become upset with me and tell me to 'be patient' with the protests."[32] She and I had become close friends during my fieldwork, and our occasional meetings provided an opportunity to express political views and contemplate the cost of these opinions when shared more widely. Openly describing her reasons for skepticism and non-participation in the popular social protests, Nili contexualized her criticism in the response that her hesitation evoked among her "most activist Israeli friends." As the summer progressed, this reaction to the search for politics within the protests—"be patient"—echoed widely as a means of quelling dissent and criticism.

Often articulated by individuals who considered themselves activists, whether former, current, or emergent, appeals to gradualism cast the omission of politics from protest discourses and agendas as a deliberately adopted strategy. Deemed a "long-term" vision or mode of "new resistance,"[33] gradualism pointed to the sense of continuity and community at stake in the summer's mass mobilization. By satisfying both critics and supporters of the protests' apolitical framing, reassurances that "We'll get there, it just takes time" sought to preserve cohesion and generate participation. Interestingly, these appeals were both expressed by and constraining of women's and feminist activist initiatives, groups historically at the forefront of Jewish Israeli anti-occupation activism, as described in chapter 4. Daphna, an interview participant from Tel Aviv who remains active with Machsom Watch, described the tension felt by many feminist anti-occupation activists when we met casually in late August. When I posed the question of whether the social protests had produced increased interest or participation in the activities of Machsom Watch, Daphna largely skirted the question. Instead, she replied that early in the protests the organization had held a meeting to decide whether or not to "pitch their tent" alongside the others on Rothschild Boulevard. According to Daphna, the group ultimately decided against "introducing their radical politics" in the interest of letting younger protesters determine the agenda, opting to support the protests as individuals rather than as a feminist, human rights, or anti-occupation organization. In this, they agreed to leave the politics of conflict at the door.[34]

Significantly, the appeasing phrases "It will get there" and "Let's see where this goes"[35] offered by anti-occupation activists mirrored the messages often directed at women and feminists participating in nationalist or liberation movements, including those specific to Israel-Palestine. Though as a category "women's equality" was enshrined in the 1948 Declaration of the Establishment of the State of Israel and the 1951 Law of Equal Rights for Women, as outlined in chapter 1, Jewish Israeli feminist activists have historically been told that their agendas are secondary to collective interests of "independence" or "nationhood," concerns often framed by security. Similarly, during the summer of 2011 many women and feminist activists chose to defer their anti-occupation and gender agendas to that of social justice, encouraging others to follow suit beneath a summarizing symbol inclusive of multiple and often contradictory meanings. "It's there, look in the subtext," seemed to be the word on the street among those participants critical of the occupation yet hesitant to withhold their participation from a social movement brewing among the once-quiescent public. Indeed, another Tel Aviv activist found conflict seemingly lurking beneath the surface of a late-July demonstration as she deemed the lack of settler participation "striking." In her estimation, the absence of settlers signaled the presence of the occupation at the event. Outwardly, her reasoning was that, as the government adequately supports the settlers and meets their needs, these parties had little material reason to join the protests. Yet she also argued that this specific absence could be read as a reaction to an implied leftist political platform underwriting the demonstrations—to her, the settlers' non-participation directly reflected the presence of political opposition among the majority of protest participants.[36] However, as described in the preceding section, Jewish right-wing, settler, and ultra-nationalist factions increasingly insisted on belonging in the protest movement, challenging the claim that leftist politics excluded these members of the national body. Settler leader Baruch Marzel couched his very demand for inclusion in the terms of "left" and "right," claiming, "when it comes to social issues, I'm more left than the left" (quoted in Mendel 2011).

Thus, by insisting that politics was simply waiting in the wings, anti-occupation activists attempted to quell criticism in the interest of a wider agenda that seemingly promised to include their own. Yet as this belief in the subtle presence of politics speaks to the persuasive influence of broadly engineered solidarity, it elides the extent to which a desire for normalcy—as if elsewhere—was woven deeply into the fabric of the protests. Walking amid the sea of humanity at the July 30 demonstration whose scene of raucous energy opened this chapter, Ilan traced connections between the protests, conflict, and normality, indicating how appeals to gradualism might maintain not only an intimate public but also the wider political reality: "People see that there's no solution to the conflict and they're tired of the issue. With these social issues there are solutions. Maybe after the social problems are fixed this will spill into the political sphere, but people are tired of hearing that security concerns come first. People just want some kind of *normalcy*. Once there is normalcy, after a few years maybe people will start to think about what that normalcy *is,* what it requires, and then they'll think about the occupation."[37]

Echoing Nili's earlier analysis, Ilan relays his sense that the occupation might be addressed once social issues are "solved," effectively securing "the most for me over here"—an admittedly shifting standard that sets a potentially unreachable goal.

Engaging (In)action

While appeals to gradualism sought to satisfy and pacify critics of the protests' apolitical platform and agenda, as the protests developed many of those who voiced wariness or dissent increasingly chose to withdraw their participation rather than jeopardize its intimate public. Here, exclusion takes shape not solely through enforcement by gatekeepers who guard against the intrusion of politics, but also as the product of individual choice or agreement, a kind of active disengagement that preserves solidarity.

Weighing the cost of rupture versus its potential benefit, critics of the social protests remained aware of how the newly engineered world of belonging displaced the fragmentation and alienation that overwhelmingly define individual experiences of politics among Jewish Israelis—this magnetizing core stood as both the prize of participation and the potential price of dissent. On an immediate level, the protests were certainly driven by a shared aspiration to "the good life," as participants and supporters outwardly sought to attain the European standard of living desired by the (Ashkenazi) middle class who catalyzed the protests. Yet on a deeper and subtler level, the stakes of success were those bonds that sutured together the critical mass and formed its intimate public. Despite the representation of Israeli society as largely unified beneath the banner of state and nation, the broad solidarities built by the protests were formerly inconceivable to many—a reality acknowledged by even the most ardent critics. Thus the protests' politics of belonging became central to securing and protecting its intimate public, preserving the guise of inclusivity by framing exclusion as an individual choice.

If read solely relative to the social protests, the expression of criticism seemingly presents a situation in which ordinarily avoidant individuals faced attack from those who were regularly politically active, this time paradoxically for their participation. However, throughout the summer of 2011 the protests and protesters enjoyed near-hegemonic status, as levels of support reached over 80 percent among the Israeli public (*Ha'aretz* 2011; Sheizaf 2011). As detailed above, this dominance generated and reproduced a range of marginal categories, among them political actors ordinarily considered "radical" in their opposition to Israeli state practices and policies. "What is it you said earlier, Guy? That maybe we're 'pissing in the cornflakes?'" I asked as we discussed the reception of our views among friends at a casual gathering. This elicited an eruption of laughter. "The original [phrase] is 'Don't piss in the well you drink from,'" a friend corrected. In its promise of solidarity, belonging, and renewed hope, the protests had achieved a sacred status, ostensibly beyond contempt or reproach.

As participation assumed a near-normative status, processes of self-imposed exclusion emerged in part through the degree to which individuals found their politics and worldviews reflected in the protests' discourses and practices. Recalling a radio interview with the popular Ashkenazi Jewish Israeli singer Aviv Geffen, Nili commented on the influence exerted and experienced in the drive to preserve consensus and define agendas within the protests. During a radio program previously aired by the army station Galatz, Margalit Tzan'ani—a well-known Mizrahi singer—had voiced criticism of the protests on the grounds that they primarily focused on the interests of Israel's Ashkenazi citizens and intentionally avoided politics (Lev 2011; Izikovitch 2011). According to Nili, Geffen responded to Tzan'ani's critique by declaring, "That's *so* 2010!" and summarily dismissed the interviewing journalist's provocation. Nili expressed her amazement at Geffen's suggestion, stating, "How incredible is it that the agenda and consensus—the community-building around these protests—can make all of those issues '*passé*'!"[38] In response to the public outcry generated by her comments Tzan'ani was quick to declare solidarity with the protesters and disavowed her earlier criticism, going so far as to perform at a later protest rally in Be'er Sheva. Appraised as a full narrative arc, Tzan'ani's words and actions notably demonstrate how positions "inside" or "outside" the protests seemingly became a matter of individual choice, rather than the product of external influence or imposition. As with the members of Machsom Watch, who decided against introducing their radical politics to the Rothschild Boulevard encampment, here exclusion was self-selected.

While this dynamic again troubles the distinction between action and inaction, it also makes visible the extent to which the protests evoked intimate connections to politics. As the summer of protests unfolded, conversations among friends and family increasingly focused on the collective will to action. For some this was a renewal of previous investment, for others a newfound site of identity and belonging, and for yet others an occasion for distrust. Yet in all instances, the promise of political action intersected with deeply personal experiences and sensations. At a friend's apartment in Baka, West Jerusalem, the depth of these intimate ties became clear as four Jewish Israeli men considered participation in the protests, discussing whether they might take part in that night's protest rally in (West) Jerusalem. Artists, filmmakers, and musicians, they had gathered to network and showcase their work; I attended as Guy's partner, though I was previously acquainted with the group through interviews and friendship. While we waited for the first film to load, conversation turned to whether my research would engage with the summer's events. Whereas until then my work "about the occupation" had been a tensely avoided topic, the apolitical protests now facilitated an expressly political discussion. As I recounted my visit to the Rothschild Boulevard encampment that morning, where I learned of Woodstock, Jim Morrison, and the Doors, Zohar asked, "Did anyone say anything interesting to you?" In answer, I described the protesters' clear separation of politics from "social issues," both in spoken word and in the signs adorning tent walls. Rather than causing the anticipated awkward silence, this time my observations generated further conversation. Zohar responded quickly, drawing on the first of many cigarettes: "It isn't about politics, I think, because to talk about politics brings in things like shame and family..." His words trailed away as the smoke curled above his head. Guy broke the silence, adding, "Politics brings up other things too, like responsibility—people don't want to take responsibility. A socioeconomic struggle is something that people can feel *good* about!" There seemed to be a quiet agreement in the room as Gil offered a final thought: "The participants and leaders might be keeping separate from the old Left because they [the old Left] are seen as part of the elite—the *Ashkenazi* elite."[39]

For Zohar, politics remains bound with family, as his mother helped to found Women in Black and his father practices various forms of "everyday resistance" in his employment as a university professor. Yet at the same time as Zohar expresses pride in his family's political actions, he links the meaning of politics to shame. In an earlier interview Zohar related that he feels estranged from his family, no longer considering himself an activist as his "passion disintegrated because the hope disintegrated"—among this family of activists, his relative inaction and hopelessness generate intimate experiences of shame.[40] Guy's statement also reflects personal understanding and lived experience, as he raises the possibility that the protests avoided politics due to the association of this term with personal responsibility. Having lived away from Israel-Palestine for twelve years and returning for the period of my fieldwork, Guy's coupling of politics and responsibility stems from his absence as a political actor in Israel. Throughout the course of the year when friends inquired what they, as Jewish Israelis, should do regarding the occupation, Guy's answer increasingly became, "Take responsibility." Admittedly, this attitude is perhaps more easily expressed from the distance of London than the proximity of Tel Aviv. Providing the final intimate texture, Gil suggests that popular understandings of politics relate closely to experiences of privilege. Here, his sense that the protest leaders and participants were actively attempting to distance themselves from the old guard invokes the dominance of Ashkenazim in Jewish Israeli society. Raised near Tel Aviv as the child of Iranian parents, Gil often found himself caught between ethnic identities due in part to his Ashkenazi physical appearance. Though assumed to be a member of the elite, Gil continues to understand himself as "other."

Rather than legitimizing the protests' apolitical platform and agenda, the accounts of Zohar, Guy, and Gil collectively reveal how intimate ties shape what it means to engage with politics in its fullest sense. Highlighting shame, family, responsibility, and privilege, these young Jewish Israeli men suggest an understanding of politics that extends to relational ties and understandings of self, giving depth to the relief promised by intimate publics. As argued throughout this chapter, these personal grounds lie at the core of the new "juxtapolitical" world; as Berlant (2008, 150) writes, "The history of its flourishing reveals individuals en masse hoarding a sense of belonging *against* what politics as usual seems to offer—a space of aversive intensities, increased risk, shame, vulnerability, exploitation, and, paradoxically, irrelevance."[41] Interestingly, within the connections traced by Zohar, Guy, and Gil, the political sphere and its dubious offer does not exist "out there" in a space beyond private life and personal experience—rather, here politics takes root in intimate dimensions that cannot be so easily escaped.

Shaped by, yet not limited to, the discourses and material realities that fuse the political in Israel-Palestine with security, violence, and conflict, the meanings ascribed to politics by these men straddle the boundary between private and public spheres, drawing together subject and state. As detailed throughout this book, the coupling of politics and intimacy overwhelmingly provides many Jewish Israelis with deeply personal reasons to avoid particular modes of political action. However, in the case of the social protests, this entanglement quickly became central to the crafting of a social movement that promised meaningful action without the intimate contingencies of politics—whether strategically or unintentionally, a personal offer of escape underwrote the ostensibly apolitical protests' appeal. Then rather than appraising Israel's heady summer of mass protests solely as a movement *toward* social and economic transformation, these actions must be understood relative to the desire of many Jewish Israelis to move *away* from politics and its purchase on the intimate dimensions of everyday life.

Yet, paradoxically, this collective attempt at distancing produced a significant effect at the macropolitical level of governance, identified by protesters as the site "where change happens." By targeting social and economic issues as if divorced from conflict, occupation, and violence, protest participants and their supporters not only left intact the key conditions that bind politics with intimacy in Israel-Palestine, but also reconfirmed the position of the state as the legitimate arbiter of politics. While the summer's social protests were cast as a "conflict" between a constitutive populace and its constituted sovereign, the former ultimately shored up the latter. Thus resistance and sanction are again held in tension, as protesters effectively parceled off politics to the state and cemented the belief that "that there" unfolds seemingly irrespective of "us here," beyond influence or control.

As the 2011 social protests provided formerly disillusioned or quiescent citizen-subjects with an opportunity to resist and take action, they simultaneously underlined the political authority of the state. Thus, the summer's events might be read not as the rupture or dissolution of widespread political apathy but as a process of world-making that allowed participants to inhabit a space suspended between action and inaction. Here individuals might engage and invest in ways and sites that did not evoke the personal dimensions of politics but promised transformation, belonging, escape, and the material comforts of normalcy. Constructed "next to" politics but seemingly free from its reach, this liminal world (re)produced and maintained political stasis. This is not to claim that individuals failed to care, see, feel, think, or act in ways that affected politics in its meaning or practice—rather, this chapter has detailed how protesters targeted and impacted both meaning and practice in their prioritization of "social" and "economic" concerns, if unintentionally so. Yet the summer of protests generated political apathy by largely affirming belief in, or perhaps more precisely the desire for, politics as a realm unto itself, which could be entered into selectively and barred from everyday life indefinitely. While this belief was contradicted by the experiences of marginal groups who sought inclusion and the deeply personal terms associated with politics, the protests' intimate public generated investment in a momentary fantasy that entrenched the wider political reality.

CONCLUSION

While creating a sensory and tangible world in the space between action and inaction, Israel's 2011 summer of protests sustained both conflict and stasis under the pretext of subverting the prevailing relations of power that subordinate domestic to international, social to political, and feminine to masculine. In practicing distinctly *political* disengagement, Jewish Israeli protesters not only confirmed the meaning of politics but also reaffirmed beliefs in and experiences of the state as the central political power. Underpinned by constructions of masculinity and femininity, framed by processes of inclusion and exclusion, and bound with intimate dimensions of everyday life, politics remained within the exclusive purview of the Israeli state.

In closing, this chapter provides an answer to a compelling query posed by Maya Mikdashi (2009): "When we surrender politics to the politicians, what are we doing?" As Israel's summer of protests makes clear, when politics is surrendered to the politicians, we consent to domination. As Jewish Israeli protesters fashioned and practiced an explicitly apolitical politics, they freed themselves from responsibility for conflict, violence, and occupation—even if some hoped to later shift focus to these very issues. Through selective disengagement and inaction, Jewish Israeli protesters pursued a course of action that sought transformation without challenging the key political condition that underlies economic and social life in Israel. Thus here "freedom from" colludes with "freedom to," as individuals and communities believed themselves to be absolved of political responsibility through participation in action.

Yet while separation from and avoidance of "the political" seemingly ensured the protests' appeal and efficacy, these very acts of division and suspension guaranteed its eventual demise. As the summer drew to a close, politics-as-conflict entered into the protests in no uncertain terms, making the refusal to articulate a political position increasingly untenable. September brought incidents of violence near Eilat, an impending Palestinian bid for statehood at the United Nations, and the specter of a future war with Iran, which confronted organizers, participants, and supporters with the wider realities that had previously been masked. Slowly but surely, energy waned, and friends and family increasingly returned unimpressed from visits to the once-robust Rothschild Boulevard encampment, voicing growing criticism along with concerns that the initiative was "losing steam."[42] Though a critic of the protests' apolitical politics, I felt conflicted about what this decline might mean as I began to understand the cost of world-loss. I wished urgently for something to be achieved so that the engendered solidarities might indeed fulfill the gradualist promise of "getting there eventually." On the day of the final march—a declared March of Millions, which would number 450,000 participants in total—we walked among what felt like drips, dribbles, and thin streams of protesters from Habima Square, this time to Kikar HaMedina (State Square), where massive scaffolding had been set up for a now regularized, normalized, and professionalized final rally. Making my way through the streets of Tel Aviv with friends once more, I remarked on the comparatively low energy and numbers, expressing my desire for some kind of actualization to buoy those participants who had surmounted despair in order to (re)invest in action. It seemed that "politics" was again taking center stage, supplanting the social issues, economic concerns, and fragile alliances that had temporarily been made visible and possible.

Passing Kikar Rabin (Rabin Square) we paused, scanning the procession in an attempt to grasp the size of the mass in which our small group was embedded. Surprisingly, though in streams and trickles, the body of protesters stretched far into the distance in either direction. The somber mood lifted, and in an instant my friend's face lit up with happy surprise as he proclaimed excitedly, "This is amazing, it has never happened like this in Israel before!" But, while the dribbles had now massed into an impressive larger body, a feeling of routine and finality remained, reflecting only a glimmer of the former energy and conviction that had electrified earlier protests.

And "this" *had* happened in Israel before, though in a historical moment profoundly political and politicized: the 1982 Sabra and Shatila massacres of the first Lebanon War. Then, over 400,000 Israeli citizens had protested against Israel's role in the massacre of Palestinian refugees at camps in Beirut (Davidi 2000; Kidron 2004); this had been the largest demonstration in the history of Israel, until that night in September 2011. Amid the mass we arrived calmly at the Gucci and Burberry storefronts of Kikar HaMedina, but we did not linger long—instead, we chose to depart before the emotive strains of the national anthem, *"HaTikva"* (The Hope), could confirm how politics had always underwritten this protest, even if elided. On that night we marched not only toward promises now recognized as fleeting, but also quietly past Sabra and Shatila, signaling a return to politics as usual.

Conclusion

TALL SHIP ON THE HORIZON. It is nearly one year to the day since I left Tel Aviv for the familiarity of London, trading sandals and sunscreen for an umbrella and a wool hat. We sit at Gilly's, the restaurant on the old port promenade that has somehow marked my experiences of Israel-Palestine—a first visit with the splendor of sea and savory "Israeli breakfast"; meetings and meals shared with family and friends; the memory of an omelet and a gunship, my first encounter with the banality of violence. Today we sit at the restaurant's wicker tables, beneath taut shades, preparing to leave once more. This five-day trip was the first since my year of fieldwork.

So little has changed, disappointingly and sadly reassuringly. The sun still scorches, the sea still sparkles, the air neglects to stir even as helicopters fly invariably south. Families parade the wooden seafront promenade, and the city's cafes and restaurants bustle into the early-morning hours, attesting to the social divisions that continue to shape lives and urban space. Road signs direct traffic to settlements in the West Bank as if they are legal; talk of "social justice" lingers, though fading with time; families sit in tense silence or talk about everything except politics (in the most political way). A city and its people continue to actively "get by" conflict, violence, and occupation, reaffirming the depth of normalcy's promise and with it the relevance of my research. These images and impressions cross my mind as I contemplate another omelet, ordered in the Hebrew which has not deserted me in those months away—this is my personal cycle within a larger national cycle, my own performance of normalcy. We three sit, passing the time, before a flight away from the dull lure of everydayness in Tel Aviv, its predictability, stability, and constancy. Glasses that held champagne drinks minutes earlier now stand empty. We wait.

With fork to mouth, I stop—what is that on the horizon at sea? Feeling impending *déjà vu,* I cannot make sense of the shape in the distance. I turn to Guy and find words for a question: "Is that a *pirate ship?*" Squinting, peering, and speculating ensue, though still we cannot decipher the form. We decide that it must be part of a new jetty at the marina, just far enough away to appear abstractly vessel-shaped. Back to eating and small talk. "No," I say after a few minutes' time, "it's moving. That *is* a pirate ship!" Slowly, the form has pulled away from what seemed to be its mooring at the marina, becoming distinguishable as an unattached vessel. Now the diners around us start to take notice; before, we were all engrossed in our separate breakfasts, cocktails, and conversations. Murmurs, pointing, the scraping of chairs across deck boards—signs of astonishment grow as smartphones attempt to capture what is most certainly a tall, four-masted ship sailing north along the coast. Strange and enchantingly anachronistic, the ship dazzles with its white sails billowing against blue skies and waters. Oohs and ahs rise from the promenade, and life grinds momentarily to a halt.[1]

In its simplicity, this scene recalls both the beauty of an unexpected moment and what fails to be remarkable in Israel-Palestine. I cannot help contrasting the curiosity and attention now greeting this sea-borne relic with the shrugs and nods that met my announcement of the gunship almost two years ago. Polished and smooth, this vessel sails into hearts and dreams, interrupting everyday life with its timeless beauty. In contrast, the blocky form of the gunship, gray and unmistakably utilitarian, melded seamlessly with the familiar, reaffirming threat and insecurity for those who took note. Yet if one peered hard enough into the bright horizon of September 2012, today's beautiful old ship travelled with company, escorted by a retinue of delicate sailboats and one small, blocky gunship.

This book has made visible what creates the conditions of possibility for the scene above—how the normality of everyday life happens, what kinds of bargains it entails and at what cost. Admittedly, this tale of omelets, tall ships, and impending departure exacts a small toll relative to its wider context. Yet the narrative above throws into relief how "events" are assessed for value and experienced as impactful or not, demarcating the commonplace and the extraordinary (Highmore 2002; Allen 2008; Berlant 2011). So too it highlights the extent to which emotions and reactions are not only subjective but also interpersonal and relational—how a single (re)action becomes multiplied and gains meaning through collective repetition (Butler 1993; Ahmed 2004; Berlant 2008). This scene also materializes the pervasive quality of militarization, illustrating how objects take on or repel charges relative to physical space and lived experience (Enloe 1989; Gonzalez 2007). So too it reveals how aspiration shapes awareness, demonstrating the ways in which desire might simultaneously displace and cement material realities (Berlant 2008; Wiegman 2012). At its widest scope, this tale of pirate ship and horizon implicates those present in the production and maintenance of domination—through what we choose to see and what is left invisible, what we choose to say and what remains in silence, what we know and what we knowingly do not know, as conflict resonates with comfort.

REVISITING NORMALCY

As the everyday becomes implicated in power, violence, conflict, and politics, the mundane, banal, ordinary, and "common-sense" must be evaluated explicitly for their effects (Mohanty 1988). With this guiding politics—a focus on costs and implications born of feminist critiques—a diagnostic of apathy has yielded an investigation into how everyday life produces and maintains domination. This book began with a single question: What can gender tell us about *Ma la'asot?* (What can we do?)—about what lies beneath this phrase and sustains its relevance in discussions of Israel's occupation? Through a process of unstitching and reweaving the threads of everyday life among Jewish Israelis in Tel Aviv and West Jerusalem, this book has begun to unpack apathy and with it the problem of normalcy in Israel-Palestine, considering what they conceal, rely on, and make possible. To grapple with apathy and normalcy among Jewish Israelis is to highlight a significant aspect of protracted conflict, one often elided through a focus on physical violence and spectacular events.

In the context of Israel-Palestine, existing critical scholarship deftly illuminates the ideological foundations, historical trajectory, political economy, material infrastructure, and macrostructural logics of Israel's occupation (Shafir 1989, 1999; Shlaim 2000, 2010; Lentin 2000, 2008; Abu El-Haj 2001; Shafir and Peled 2002; Masalha 2003; Ron 2003; Zertal 2005; Khalidi 2006; Massad 2006; Pappe 2006; Yiftachel 2006; Weizman 2007, 2013; Gordon 2008; Ghanem 2010; Hever 2010; Pappe and Hilal 2010; Abdo 2011; Allen 2013; Sa'di 2013). Together these approaches draw attention to the ways in which "the conflict," practices and policies of occupation, and existing relations of power are anything but temporary. Yet even as this body of scholarship makes visible the roots from which current political realities arise and the routes that they continue to shape and travel, these accounts lack a fine-tuned analysis of the micropolitical relations that produce and maintain domination. While scholars, activists, and observers might better understand the mechanics of why and how *things stay the same* on macropolitical scales, we know relatively little of how stasis takes shape on more intimate levels. If power is appraised solely as a top-down affair imposed by states and governments on citizens and subjects, we miss what has rendered the term "conflict" empty to the point of euphemism, what makes its material reality comfortable and particular lives livable, how it provides the foundation for normality and draws strength from its own resistance. In neglecting micropolitics we miss the complex and contradictory tensions that sustain domination, as related at length by Mira, a thirty-year-old Jerusalemite activist.

KN: Can you tell me more about what you meant when you said that it is easy to "disengage or detach" here? How so?

Mira: At the most basic sense, there's "Listen, I have to live my life." People get up, go to work in the morning, come home at night, veg in front of the television or meet friends. This happens in a very socially specific area—for example, in Rehavia. It was built by old rich Germans and now rich Americans and students live there, along with some of the Germans. They don't see it, what's going in the east of the city.

At the second level, it's easy to disengage ... it's a mess. It's difficult because the whole situation is difficult. There may be a dialogue between individuals on the Palestinian side and on the Israeli side, but there are very few real relationships being formed. Because what you have in fact is the Israeli left radical activists driven by what are basically liberal ideals or a sense of altruism. That's the Israeli side. On the Palestinian side of the interaction they have concrete, practical, particular problems—it's not ideologically driven, they just want their lives back! For example, the wells they dig up because they want their houses back. They're tired of being treated like shit. So you have two kinds of ... it's an interesting thing to see it coming together. They're [the Israelis are] coming from a place of being guilt-driven, they think they're not really coming to interact with a peer. They don't consider him [the Palestinian] equal if only because they don't know how to communicate in his own language, linguistically and culturally. This is awkward and it's easy to slip out of. I feel like it's like an Iggy Pop song: they [the Israelis] are "passengers," not really living their [the Palestinians'] lives.[2] I can go to the Sheikh Jarrah tent, sleep next to their homes—their former homes—and watch for the settlers to do something. But I'm still not living their reality. I can afford to go home and sleep in my bed at night. There's something not real about it, it's very artificial. So you can do one of two things: you can go, like the Sheikh Jarrah group, to all the trials—you can get "hoovered" into all the places, go to all the trials, get arrested three times a week. *Or* you can try to find balance.[3]

Normalcy in Israel takes work to produce, whether through the pursuit of balance, the material labor of "others," or in the acts of unseeing, "knowingly not knowing" (Cohen 2001), and rationalization that allow individuals to bargain with what underwrites the everyday—what is unpleasant or overwhelming about the world we live in (Berlant 2007, 291–92). The phrase *Ma la'asot?* used by Jewish Israeli leftists when grappling with the seeming intractability of conflict then signals an ambivalence about what underpins normalcy, what sustains and produces it. Conveying political emotions of despair, helplessness, and disappointment while posing a practical question of power, this phrase points to a collective practice of "getting by" or living out everyday life through particular types of compromise (Allen 2008; Kelly 2008; Richter-Devroe 2011). As stated in the introduction of this book, "getting by" does not imply equivalence between Palestinians and Jewish Israelis who aspire to live an ordinary life in conditions of occupation, conflict, and violence. Rather, while mechanisms might be shared or mirrored, among Jewish Israelis these practices, processes, ideals, and aspirations are "productive of" rather than "subject to" domination. As Michel de Certeau (1984) warns, power is at play not only between structures of practice but also within them. While drawing this distinction seemingly estranges "Israel" from "Palestine" and Jewish Israelis from Palestinians in perhaps unhelpful ways, it trains focus on power and the wider effects of normalcy produced and maintained. Not only framed by violent events, an interminably stalled peace process, and increasing social and political conservatism, the horizon of *what we can do* also takes shape through investment in everyday life. By revealing the logics that make conflict and domination possible at the levels of subjectivity and sociality, this book simultaneously offers a critique and a point of intervention.

In taking political apathy seriously, this analysis has deliberately defamiliarized normalcy and everyday life, estranging the ordinary to draw attention to the inconspicuous (Highmore 2002, 22). Framed by a historical legacy of and continuing commitment to "telling stories differently" (Hemmings 2011), feminist gender analysis presents an "interruptive strategy" particularly suited to the everyday (Brecht 1964, cited in Highmore 2002, 23). As an aspect of subjectivity, a relation of power, and a structure of states and societies, gender is integral to the practices of everyday life, though often elided. Gender shapes spaces and encounters, impacts understandings of selves and others, brings militaries into homes, informs experiences of political action, structures degrees of belonging, and influences our relationship to the politics that frames narratives, aspirations, and material realties. Indeed, following Cynthia Cockburn (1999 cited in Al-Ali and Pratt 2009, 8), gender "is seen to shape the dynamics of every site of human interaction, from the household to the international arena." To foreground gender as a political and analytical category, then, is potentially to make strange the ordinary, from its micropolitical base to its macropolitical logics.

Through this critical lens, normalcy emerges as a desire for the condition of stasis—in the words of Lauren Berlant (2007, 291), "of being able to be *somewhere* and make a life, exercising existence as a fact, not a project"—not merely surviving, but living. So too the pursuit of "ordinary life" among Jewish Israelis reflects a gap between experiences of what "is" and estimations of what "ought to be" (Kelly 2008), a tension between reality and ideals. Framed aspirationally, here the dependability, stability, and constancy of normalcy remain always out of reach, a destination made possible by the failure to arrive. Across diverse contexts, many of us settle for living "as if" (Wedeen 1999; Navaro-Yashin 2002; Allen 2013), for proximity to normalcy provided through narratives, relations, and desires—these bargains are consciously made and settled for. Yet in the context of Israel-Palestine, these negotiations and pursuits entrench violent conflict, maintain occupation, advance colonization, and reaffirm the seeming divisions separating "us here" from "them there" in ways that spell erasure, oppression, and dispossession.

By engaging with these tensions, this book has revealed how gender constitutes a central vector of normalization and regulation in Jewish Israeli society, providing structure to and rendering manageable lives that necessarily fail to attain an ideal. From the formation of subjectivities to the construction of family units and larger collectivities, patterns of gender lend familiarity and stability to a context shaped by narratives and experiences of constant precarity. Constructed in terms of masculinized defense and feminized vulnerability, dominant roles and codes ensure the perceived sanctity of home and the domestic seen to underwrite small worlds and simple lives. So too prevailing norms and relations maintain the hierarchies of power and privilege that demarcate the realm of politics, creating alternative sites of stability and transformative potential in which women and men might find relief or escape. Intersecting with vectors of race, class, sexuality, religion, and geopolitical location, this book has demonstrated how gender provides a thread of meaning and constancy within the everyday, buffering the at times uncomfortable bargains made with power. Thus as Jewish Israeli women and men live out normalcy as best they can in the urban spaces of Tel Aviv and West Jerusalem, a particular kind of material reality emerges: one that promises security while simultaneously sustaining conflict, occupation, and domination.

Of Threads and Tapestries

As this book has depicted and troubled a tapestry of the ordinary among Jewish Israelis, gender emerges as a structural thread that sews conflict deep into everyday life and shapes political action. In the context of Jewish Israeli society, gender assumes its normative form and function largely through the hegemonic narrative of Zionism, whose arc recalls threat, persecution, and transcendence (Zertal 2005, 2; Lentin 2000, 188). From historical roots to its current incarnation, the framework of Zionism provides a template for practice and belief that both shapes and arises from the relationships between state, society, and subject. Grounded in the historical experiences of European Jewry, Zionist ideology and practices have yielded the patriarchal gender relations that situate men—largely heterosexual, middle- or upper-class, and Ashkenazi—in public and political spheres, while relegating women to the ostensibly depoliticized private and domestic. While these positions are complicated by looking at how the relative locations of women and men intersect with race, ethnicity, and projects of modernization, the logics and norms of Zionism-as-patriarchal-nationalism continue to entrench male privilege. At the same time as prevailing narratives shape the political realm in terms of access to political voice and power, they also inform the domestic, connecting public and private while at the same time constructing these spheres as separate and unequal.

Through this connective thread, nationalism, militarism, and increasingly neoliberalism gain purchase in everyday lives, bearing with them the central social pillars of fraternity, security, and modernity. Here, gender regularizes and normalizes as dominant roles, norms, codes, and relations produce a hegemonic "gender order," which constitutes a significant social structure (Connell 1987, 134–139, 2002, 3). In the context of Jewish Israeli society, this order privileges heterosexuality, reinforces the role of women as biological and cultural reproducers, and divides "us" from "them" as modern subjects.

Critically, these patterns hold implications for political participation among leftist Jewish Israelis, fostering the prevailing sense of disillusionment, despair, and fatigue with a politics that underwrites disengagement and inaction.

As patterns of gender shape political emotion and engagement, so too they impact wider social relations, shoring up borders and boundaries while at the same time facilitating their collapse. Here, a society divides itself in ways that create and reflect hierarchies of power and privilege, demarcating "us" and "here" as separate from "them" and "there." Read on bodies, in space and through encounter, gender plays a significant role in maintaining the relations of belonging and exclusion so central to the formation of collectivity. However, while fostering division and cementing separation, patterns of gender also enmesh Jewish Israelis with Palestinians at the level of everyday life. As made evident through the range of labor practices that raise, feed, and nourish Israel, this entanglement ensures that the processes of political disengagement are necessarily *active*, as individuals are confronted with the social, economic, and political conditions that underwrite normalcy.

Yet rather than forcing acknowledgement or catalyzing political action, awareness of what makes ordinary life livable prompts many Jewish Israelis to retreat into intimate constellations of community. Contrary to the wider reality of conflict, occupation, and violence, these sites promise belonging, stability, meaning, and substantive return on the investment of action. Here, politics is seemingly kept at bay through social mechanisms that maintain and repair a sense of normalcy, as joking, bypassing, unseeing, and silencing give rise to "small worlds," "elsewheres," and "simple lives" that hold the promise of security, influence, and moral consistency. As gender shapes mechanisms and enclaves, it also gives texture to the particular kinds of activity that underpin disengagement, revealing how apparent passivity is produced through knowing, caring, seeing, investing, engaging, and doing, in sites and manners deemed meaningful and effective.

Yet, some Jewish Israelis *do* acknowledge the political, economic, and social conditions that make normalcy possible, and take action on broader levels in ways that aim to resist or contest conflict, occupation, and violence. From "everyday" forms of resistance at home and through labor, to participation in a range of organized activist initiatives, these individuals act politically, sometimes at great personal and professional cost. However, gender analysis reveals how resistance risks becoming caught up in power, as contestation at one level might fail to challenge wider relations and realities. Here gender informs both organizational conduct and personal experiences of resistance, revealing how particular modes of protest become normalized or routinized and in turn shape "rules of the game," which are explicitly contested by new generations of activists. As oppositional action remains embedded in past experiences and understandings, individuals come face to face with the limits of resistance, whether in the apparent inadequacy of an agenda or in the specter of enforced conformity. Then political participation might beget disengagement by generating "resistance to resistance"—as such, action and inaction indeed cannot be so easily separated.

Emerging as points along a shared spectrum, action and inaction do not simply collude to reaffirm the status quo or reproduce existing relations of power; rather, these practices may be oriented toward the construction of new social worlds. As Israel's 2011 summer of social protests revealed, political apathy might be productive in unanticipated ways, creating a space between action and inaction wherein individuals and communities invest in particular kinds of transformation. As participants and their supporters sought "social justice" in the form of improved material conditions, patterns of gender structured the protests' body, discourses, practices, and agendas. Paradoxically, in disavowing "politics" these actions left intact the key political conditions underwriting social and economic life in Israel. In this, the protest bolstered existing relations of power, reaffirming beliefs in and experiences of the state as the central political authority. However, in their very apolitical framing, the summer of social protests succeeded in creating a world of belonging and hope made anew, mobilizing and galvanizing a formerly disillusioned and quiescent public. The scope of action, then, was not *world-changing* but *world-making*, exposing the intimate stakes of failure and how political apathy may be profoundly productive.

RETHINKING APATHY AND DOMINATION

Thus, gender analysis reveals how normative narratives, intimate relations, social mechanisms, and sites of investment generate political apathy among leftist Jewish Israelis and sustain conflict in Israel-Palestine. Through the lens of gender, scholars, activists, and observers might see more clearly the micropolitics of domination, particularly how consent is secured at the level of society through both passivity and action (Gramsci 1971). Here, seeming inaction emerges as underwritten by diverse modes of activity, produced through seeing, knowing, hoping, caring, engaging, and doing. Not solely a matter of coercion or the imposition of power, domination takes shape and gains purchase through the mundane, ordinary, or everyday—through quotidian investments, pursuits, and desires. Regularized and normalized through the familiarity of gendered roles, codes, norms, and relations, power does not merely become "tolerable only on the condition that it mask a substantial part of itself," as suggested by Michel Foucault (1998 [1978], 86), but makes particular lives livable, as this book has illustrated.

During interviews in Tel Aviv and West Jerusalem I often heard the desire for normalcy expressed in plaintive or wistful tones, a wish identified by its speaker as fleeting at the moment of articulation. It struck me then that this practice of living in pursuit, or "as if," might be *sof ha derech*, "the end of the road" or "the best of the best" for Zionism and Jewish Israelis living in Israel. Resonant with dominant narratives, daily life lived as constant aspiration seemed to be the ultimate triumph of Zionist ideology—the Israeli state and its people must never arrive at their destination. Understood thus, striving assumes an eternal quality, despite the creation of a "homeland" and the provision of security, the stated goals of early political Zionism. Yet this book has argued that some Jewish Israelis see normality for what it is—they experience and understand the dependency of everyday life on conflict, just as they recognize their implication in power. The query posed here is how this awareness produces disillusionment, despair, hopelessness, silence, disengagement, and inaction, and what it might reveal about a wider political reality. What can resistance and action desired, yet not pursued, tell us about power in Israel-Palestine?

In taking political apathy seriously, this book has made visible how micropolitical dynamics draw resistance and power together, as degrees of division and entanglement, modes of avoidance and action, and sites of investment and withdrawal collude to sustain conflict, occupation, and violence. Then here normalcy becomes a meeting point, the site in which everyday life becomes directly implicated in domination. Not only a tension (Kelly 2008) or desire (Berlant 2007, 2008), normalcy critically provides the fabric through which power circulates and gains purchase. Suffused with hierarchies of privilege and power, normality exists not as a neutral state of passivity or a "default" setting, but as a practice of living politically charged by aspiration and action.

Ultimately, the question of whether apathy exists among Jewish Israelis in Tel Aviv and West Jerusalem cannot be answered simply with yes or no. As related in this book and indeed evident in the recent 2015 elections, Jewish Israelis vote in high numbers, readily demonstrate their politics in streets and conversations, and care deeply about the worlds they live in. This is not the apathy of total disconnection, even as individuals articulate despair, disenchantment, and hopelessness. Instead, what emerges is active disengagement, a kind of hoping, trying, building, believing, knowing, relating, engaging, and acting oriented toward self-preservation. In wanting intensely to hold fast to the promise of constancy and familiarity, individuals and communities knowingly enter into bargains whose terms are increasingly costly, whose politics may grate against their own. Apathy, then, is not solely a matter of political practice or participation (Rosenberg 1954; Sevy 1983; Boyer 1984; Herzfeld 1992; Eliasoph 1997, 1998; Dolan and Holbrook 2001; Hay 2007; Greenberg 2010) but emerges from the accord between conflict and normalcy, politics and intimacy, action and inaction. Importantly, this conceptualization problematizes apathy as a position of victimhood, even as many Jewish Israelis claim paralysis, impotence, and fatigue in the face of politics and conflict—like resistance and normalcy, apathy takes work to produce.

However, the labor required to produce and maintain apathy is different from the types of engagement and action that underpin resistance and normalcy among Jewish Israelis. As twenty-nine-year-old Sarit related in the kitchen of her Jaffa flat:

> There is a part in everyone that wants to live a normal life—this isn't to say that being an activist isn't "normal." Also you're part of the occupation, you're a part of the tension here if you like it or not. People say we're *adish*—indifferent or apathetic. OK, apathetic, I guess. They say that we're a generation of indifference, that no one is doing anything, we're all just talking and venting, no one is going to the streets. Life is not easy here. There's work, you have to pay rent, I'm sure it has some effect. There's also some kind of normalization—you grow up with it as a part of life. It sounds odd, but people also have had to sacrifice. There's time given in the army and it's probably not a conscious thing, but at some point it's like, "Enough—I want to live my life, go to work, to the coffee house after, have a beer with friends. Enough."
>
> It's not that there is antagonism toward the occupation—well, yes, maybe there is. People just say "enough." How many layers of it will affect my life, my identity? How much do I allow it to take over my identity? Some people use it as a building part in their identities, but for others, *maspik* [enough]. It makes people face issues which are hard to emotionally face: ethics, empathy, human rights versus nationalism, the emotions for the experiences they've gone through. These are internal clashes that people don't want to face, they don't want to deal with them.[4]

Although normalcy, resistance, and apathy all require intentional action, political apathy uniquely takes hold when deep-seated beliefs that the surrounding world *could* and *should* be transformed are somehow met with disavowal. Apathy does not reconcile resistance and normalcy, or subsume one to the other, but holds them in tension. As Sarit's narrative highlights, the limits of "enough" signal a personal and political breaking point, where knowledge of what occurs directly generates effacement or seeming indifference among those who would take action. Concluding our interview in his Tel Aviv living room, Dov likewise revealed how limits are produced by a state of suspension. "I believe both sides are assholes," he said, as he crushed a final cigarette and we finished our glasses of Coca-Cola. "That's why I want peace. But what is peace? I want my life to be good, and theirs too. I want to consider them like Sweden or New Zealand. There are so many countries that have problems that I don't care or think about, I don't stay awake at night over them. Shitty things happen all the time. But this is our life here."[5] As Sarit and Dov make clear, apathy is unique in both caring deeply and wanting to not care—acknowledging that the world needs changing, but failing to meet the challenge of mobilization and transformation. In the context of Israel-Palestine, and indeed beyond its borders, this tension maintains domination.

Yet it is tempting to argue that political apathy might indicate a critical tipping point, that disengagement and inaction in one context might point to a radical new politics taking shape on a broader horizon. Like Dov, many Jewish Israelis have grown tired of "triumphing over difficulties" as the normative narrative prescribes—perhaps their adherence to normalcy signals the *failure* of Zionism rather than its success. In order for Zionism to persist as an ideology, practice, and politics it requires constant threat; yet this book has detailed precisely how this relation has grown increasingly unsustainable, requiring ever more labor and disavowal. People are tired, exhausted from living life as a project rather than a fact, wearied by surviving rather than living (Berlant 2007, 291). Then the continuing "success" of Zionism may be its very demise—if Zionism cannot be separated from its journey and cycles of repetition, fatigue and arrival might spell destruction.

Following this argument, *"Ma la'asot?"* may indicate a growing fracture even as it makes visible how apathy takes shape as active disengagement. Indeed, those who expressed this sentiment did so precisely in an attempt to convey their lack of apathy, how they continue to care despite hopelessness and feel that they should act despite inefficacy, how they remain aware and opposed to what happens around them. These individuals would be or could be moved to act, they want to act, used to act, feel the need to act, or claim scant knowledge of how to act—in its kinetic and potential energy, action lies at the heart of their tension.

Therein lies a radical possibility: that the action of disengagement from the immediate context might engender new modes and sites of re-engagement. Irit, an activist with Gisha, Zochrot, and B'Tselem,[6] first raised this prospect during our exchange at a Tel Aviv cafe:

> [People are not interested in being involved] because there is a big personal price. I felt that I paid a big price at the time of the [first] *intifada*. [Involvement] requires you to disconnect from society, you have to deal with things which are unpleasant, you have to take responsibility for things. To sympathize and to do something—they are something else.... People live small lives. It's disturbing to get out of these lives and deal with things here—it's all so loaded.[7]

Irit does not wax poetic about the potentials of radical or transnational activism but highlights how "involvement" in resistance to conflict, violence, and occupation necessitates an intentional move to "disconnect" from Jewish Israeli society. Interestingly, she posits that oppositional political action *requires* this kind of disengagement, naming the assumption of responsibility as what catalyzes this process. Then disconnection or disengagement from Jewish Israeli society might lay the foundation for action in alternative sites and on broader scales. Through acknowledging implication in conflict and domination without falling back on claims of victimhood, indoctrination, or powerlessness, doors may open to new political alliances, new movements and partners, even as participation exacts potentially heavy tolls. Those willing to assume responsibility and disconnect from the very society that they care deeply about might translate active disengagement into new forms of political relationality, building alternative constellations of community.

However, as promising as this radical possibility is, this book has consistently drawn attention to what sutures most Jewish Israelis to their wider society rather than what motivates them to break ties. The project at hand is not to posit a "solution" to conflict, occupation, and domination in Israel-Palestine but rather to illuminate the micropolitical logics and social mechanisms that presently sustain these conditions. As such, while Jewish Israelis who define themselves as "radical" activists might share Irit's willingness to assume responsibility, for many leftists the imperative of responsibility reflects back on the Jewish Israeli collective—not on the wider political realities of Israel-Palestine or how domination impacts Palestinian populations and territories. The radical transitivity of disconnection then swings away from the broader context and toward familiar communities and sites of belonging, whether national or familial. Indeed, as NGO worker Noa related earlier, "I feel the whole country, the whole world, is concentrated on the conflict. 'God damn it!' I said, 'We need to do something also for ourselves.'"[8]

Thus, while fatigue with the politics of conflict, occupation, and violence potentially signals an unanticipated and transformative kind of disengagement, for most it produces and maintains apathy. As detailed throughout this book, political apathy among leftist Jewish Israelis is complex and often contradictory, at times unsettlingly understandable in its intimate roots and relations. Yet it sustains the very conditions that would-be, could-be, and should-be actors oppose, further distancing them from the plight of Palestine and deepening the hold of conflict in everyday life. Apathy does not just abstractly maintain power, privilege, and domination in Israel-Palestine but concretely secures what I have called at various points throughout this book "the status quo." With respect to broader Israeli society—inclusive of Palestinian citizens and a range of non-national subjects—political apathy maintains tiered systems of education and patterns of labor, which hierarchically order individuals and communities according to race and religion, entrench existing class-based divisions, and constrain collective futures (Ghanem 2001; Kanaaneh and Nusair 2010; Abdo 2011; Jamal 2011). So too apathy permits the partition of geographical space, creating bounded regions and zones of segregation that underline the privilege (differently) afforded to Israel's Jewish citizens and denied to "others" (Yiftachel 2006). Political apathy also enables legislation to become increasingly insular and aggressively exclusive, as evident in the passage of laws that distinguish and discriminate among categories of citizens, and attempt to silence and penalize those who speak or act against prevailing political sentiments (see e.g. Hovel and Khoury 2014; Lis 2013b).

Beyond the recognized borders of the Israeli state, apathy among leftist Jewish Israelis perpetuates and accelerates processes of de-development in the Gaza Strip and West Bank (Roy 1995, 1999; Hever 2010), securing captive markets for Israeli goods, locking communities in conditions of relative poverty, and effectively isolating Palestine and Palestinians from the Middle East and the wider world. So too political apathy allows the increasing annexation and bantustanization of Palestinian lands to proceed unchecked (Weizman

2007; Khan 2008), barring heirs and owners from their property while allowing Israel haShlema (Greater Israel) to take shape not as an effect of ideology but as a matter of political practice. Apathy among leftist Jewish Israelis also impacts political engagement and action among ordinary Palestinians—as scholars, activists, and regional commentators increasingly detail, rates of disengagement and inaction are rising among Palestinian populations faced with the prospect of deepening stasis (Allen 2013; Deger 2014).

Yet on the level of everyday life, for most Palestinians living in the West Bank, Gaza Strip, and annexed East Jerusalem, political apathy among leftist Jewish Israelis spells the continuation of decades-long histories of displacement and dispossession, as Israel's practices of colonization produce conditions of apartheid and sustain practices of ethnic cleansing that aim at total segregation, if not erasure. Certainly, the apathy expressed and practiced by leftist Jewish Israelis is not the sole cause of the realities depicted above; overwhelming public sanction, complicity among the international community, regional political maneuvering, and historical legacies of violence all play significant parts in producing the political and material conditions that prevail today. However, as argued throughout this book, active disengagement colludes with active support in ways that directly sustain conflict and maintain domination, shaping lives and futures across the breadth of Israel-Palestine.

THE ROAD'S END

Rather than perpetuating the present stalemate, this book has attempted to clarify the micropolitical logics that sustain conflict and domination in Israel-Palestine, troubling the boundaries between action and inaction in the hopes of providing a critical point of intervention. In keeping with feminist politics and methodology, an exercise in mapping the mechanisms that secure the status quo illuminates an unexpected avenue to transformation—by illustrating how "narratives are meaning-making structures," which produce not only political and material realities but also counter-narratives (Lentin 2000, 2, 21, 24), this book invites scholars, activists, and observers to envision the future differently. Together, we might think and work with those living in Israel-Palestine to bring about a new political future, perhaps one made possible through surprising processes of disengagement and re-engagement, as suggested above.

However, at their core the accounts and analyses in these pages detail deeply rooted obstacles to transformation, a process of change made even more unlikely by the results of the 2015 elections. Rather than catalyzing transitive breaks, the rise and consolidation of power of the political Right in Israel provides greater impetus for leftist Jewish Israelis to move into the intimate realms and relations that promise security, stability, and belonging. In highlighting the mechanisms and logics that actively underpin political stasis, this book has revealed how richly textured apathy materializes at the intersection of history, ideology, and encounter, through the entanglement of self, family, and community, in the assumed interstice between politics and society. So too it has illustrated how the material and political realities of domination arise through the combination of discursive, psychosocial, and relational dynamics. Yet, the situation is not intractable.

Then this book concludes in a flurry of tensions old and new: the yes-no matter of whether apathy exists among Jewish Israelis has gained complexity rather than clarity, and a potential path to transformation takes shape explicitly through its impediments. Yet with focus trained on the centrality of gender to conflict, apathy, and domination, new means and modes become clear, even as new tensions present shifting limits and challenges. Motivated by belief in the merit of diagnosing power, this analysis takes heart in the observation of Michel Foucault (1998 [1978], 86), who argued that power's success "is proportional to its ability to hide its own mechanisms." In traveling the road from Birzeit through Jerusalem and on to Tel Aviv, this book deepens understanding of *how things stay the same* in Israel-Palestine with the intention of helping shape a future in they are markedly different.

May one road's end be another's beginning.

NOTES

PREFACE

1. On May 7, 2015, Likud announced the formation of a new government, which holds a narrow majority of 61 seats in the 120-seat Parliament. Until May 4, nationalist party Yisrael Beitenu (Israel Is Our Home) was also expected to join the coalition, adding six more seats to the majority; however, leader Avidgor Liberman withdrew and signaled that his party would join the opposition (*Guardian* 2015).

2. Netanyahu has since apologized to Israel's Arab (Palestinian) citizens, and also retreated from his vow to block the formation of an independent Palestinian state. While these subsequent moves demonstrate how Likud instrumentalized security concerns during the 2015 campaign, many observers—including US president Barack Obama—"took him at his word" (as quoted in Bryant 2015) and understood Netanyahu's comments as a rare moment of political transparency.

INTRODUCTION

1. Israel issues different identification documents to Palestinian citizens of Israel, Palestinian noncitizens in East Jerusalem, and Palestinians in the West Bank and Gaza. See the work by Helga Tawil-Souri (2012), which illustrates how the color-coded and biometric identification cards constitute an important nexus of power in Israel-Palestine, "produc[ing] distinct people and bind[ing] them to specific territories."

2. Field notes, April 13, 2011. Throughout this book ethnographic material is cited in footnotes that indicate the date on which the relevant event took place. I employ this referencing in order to render conversations and details as closely as possible, which is particularly important to studies of conflict and contentious politics.

3. By engaging with Jewish Israeli society and the urban spaces of Tel Aviv and West Jerusalem this book departs from critical analyses by Tobias Kelly (2006, 2008) and Avram Bornstein (2002). While these authors focus on movement and

encounters in Israel-Palestine, their accounts "cross checkpoints" to reveal how structures and systems of control sustain domination at the level of everyday life among Palestinians in the West Bank.

4. I employ the frame of "conflict" deliberately throughout this analysis, though I recognize that the term is politically problematic and often imprecise. Rather than subscribing to the view that continuing violence in Israel-Palestine is the result of a struggle between two parties with equal strength, I understand "conflict" to be the language through which settler colonialism masks itself in this context. However, analyses and interventions must take up this very terminology as a means of challenging its logics.

5. In bringing together scholarship on the pursuit of normalcy among Palestinian and Israeli populations I do not mean to imply parity between these groups. Instead, this book consistently draws attention to how domination and conflict in Israel-Palestine sustain—and are sustained by—unequal power relations.

6. The left-to-right political spectrum is specific to Jewish Israeli society and Israel-Palestine; as detailed in the following chapters, in this context categories of political left and right are defined largely in relation to matters of conflict and security.

7. Thanks to Professor Laleh Khalili for this concise working definition.

8. The term *disengagement* holds particular political relevance in Jewish Israeli society, as the 2006 withdrawal of Jewish settlers from the Gaza Strip was officially conducted according to a Disengagement Plan. As such, it carries a specific charge in public and political discourses.

9. Engaging with political apathy in the United States, Nina Eliasoph's (1997, 1998) work likewise reflects on how a position of seeming political passivity or depression reflects an important critique of democracy. However, while Greenberg (2010) considers the tension between political participation and democratization, Eliasoph shifts focus to actions taken elsewhere, arguing that investment in volunteer, recreation, and activist spheres reveals how citizens uphold democratic ideals in unexpected places and manners.

10. Interview in Jerusalem, June 14, 2011.

11. Interview in Jerusalem, June 13, 2011.

12. Interview in Tel Aviv, January 19, 2011.

13. This imperative follows on Bertolt Brecht's theory of estrangement, as delineated in work by Frederick Jameson (1991, cited in Highmore 2002, 22–24).

14. Thanks to Professor Kimberlé Crenshaw for her valuable feedback on this project and its contribution to intersectional theory.

15. According to a 2012 opinion poll conducted by the Yisraela Goldblum Fund, 58 percent of Jewish Israelis believe that there is already some form of apartheid in Israel, 74 percent believe in segregated roads for Israelis and Palestinians in the West Bank, 47 percent support the transfer of some Palestinian citizens to the Palestinian National Authority, and 69 percent object to giving Palestinians the right to vote if Israel were to annex the West Bank (Levy 2012; Sherwood 2012). On an everyday level, the poll reflected that nearly 60 percent of Jewish Israelis expressed a desire for

hiring practices that give preference to Jews over Palestinians in government ministries, 49 percent believe that Jewish citizens should be treated better than Arabs, 42 percent would object to living in the same building as Arabs, and 42 percent do not want their children going to school with Arabs. In 2014, an approval poll reflected that the breakdown of a recent round of peace talks resulted in increased support for the Israeli right wing, with sustained highly positive opinions of the acting chief of the Israel Defense Force and the defense minister, and a rise in popularity for prime minister Benjamin Netanyahu (Verter 2014). This trend was mirrored in the results of the 2015 national elections, which saw Likud and Netanyahu re-elected to form a coalition government.

16. Personal communication with Lisa Hajjar, January 15, 2013.

17. Though specific to Jews of Eastern European origin, within Jewish Israeli society the term Ashkenazi has been extended to include those Jews immigrating to Israel from Europe and America; this book employs the latter inclusive understanding unless otherwise stated. Recent critical scholarship by Orna Sasson-Levy (2013) details how this ethnic group has been constructed as Israel's "white" Jews, enjoying relative privilege within Israeli society and sharing common characteristics with whiteness in the United States.

18. Mizrahi refers to Jews of North African or Middle Eastern origin.

19. This distinction mirrors the categories officially identified and recorded by the Israeli state, which falsely distinguishes between "Palestinian," "Druze," and "Bedouin" as a means of fragmenting the Palestinian population in Israel (Kanaaneh 2008; Kanaaneh and Nusair 2010).

20. Though I am neither Jewish nor Israeli, marriage-based family ties brought me "inside" Jewish Israeli society to a degree and facilitated formation of the social networks which would become key to my research.

21. Negotiations in 1949 resulted in agreed borders between Israel and Egypt, Lebanon, Jordan, and Syria, successively; according to these agreements, the bounded area of the Israeli state does not include the West Bank, Gaza Strip, Golan Heights, Sinai Peninsula, or the entirety of Jerusalem.

22. *Kibbutzim* and *moshavim* are two forms of rural collective organization in Israel. While both emphasize community labor and agriculture, *kibbutzim* are often characterized by an ideological (socialist) subscription to shared wealth among members, whereas *moshavim* permit individual ownership and are rooted in "the ideology of the family" (Nevo 1991, 276).

23. While I conducted nearly sixty interviews over the course of twelve months, not all are reproduced in the pages of this book. Rather, my approach has been to take as a baseline the participants' commonality in expressing a feeling of political despair, and engage with those narratives that specifically elucidate mechanisms or raise compelling tensions in relation to this phenomenon.

All interviews were conducted in English, as the researcher and all participants were comfortable, if not fluent, in this language. During interview exchanges, discussion centered on five topic areas, assembled through a process of refinement in response to early interviews: (1) personal background, including military service; (2)

relationship to and experiences of political activism; (3) understanding of Israel's occupation and experiences of conflict; (4) politics and family relations; and (5) perception of ability to influence or transform the status quo. After securing verbal consent, the interviews took place in public cafes or private homes and lasted between 60 and 120 minutes, during which time I recorded accounts and responses in hand-written notes. While these notes may not convey the subtleties of hesitation and intonation in the same manner as recorded audio data, this mode of recording set participants at ease and granted silences the space in which to become intimate reflections. After each session, interview notes were supplemented with descriptions of the surrounding environment, the atmosphere of exchange, and any additional observations relevant to the data. At this time, notes regarding pauses, silences, and changes in bodily comportment or vocal intonation were inserted into the written account, which was transcribed within two days of the interview session.

CHAPTER ONE

1. Field notes, October 7, 2010.
2. The Arabic term *naksa* (setback) is used by Palestinians to mark the 1967 or Six Day War in which the West Bank, Gaza Strip, East Jerusalem, Golan Heights, and Sinai Peninsula were captured by the Israeli military, resulting in ongoing occupation and annexation.
3. Field notes, June 5, 2011.
4. In addition to mandating the conscription of Jewish Israeli women and men living in Israel, the IDF provides opportunities for non-Israeli Jews and Jewish Israelis living abroad to volunteer for service in the Israeli military (www.mahal-idf-volunteers.org).
5. Interview in Jerusalem, June 27, 2011.
6. Interview in Tel Aviv, April 11, 2011.
7. Interview in Tel Aviv, April 11, 2011.
8. Interview in Jerusalem, July 3, 2011.
9. Though all citizens are legally required to complete military service whether women or men, in practice Palestinian citizens of Israel are largely precluded from doing so by virtue of their association with threat to national (Jewish) security (Shafir and Peled 2002, 126–27).
10. Similarly, Laleh Khalili (2011) points to the ways in which the participation of women in the formulation of counterinsurgency strategies and policies in the United States constructs new modes of "colonial feminism," aligned with American military interests. Mirroring the tense and at times seemingly contradictory position of women in Israel—simultaneously combat fighters and mothers of the nation—Khalili writes of the American context, "The images of the counterinsurgent women shows them as feminine, dressed in ball gowns, kissing their counterinsurgent officers, all the while flaunting their warrior credentials (one counterinsurgent woman has been a former air force pilot, the other a professor at the US

Marine Corps University). Others work in the Pentagon in various—and often influential—positions" (1489).

11. Interview in Tel Aviv, February 16, 2011.

12. Interview in Jerusalem, May 3, 2011.

13. A recent ad campaign by BlueStar—a San Francisco-based "organization dedicated to empowering the next generation of Israel advocates and leaders"— highlights this critical relationship: "Where in the Middle East can gay officers serve their country? Only in Israel. In a democracy positions of leadership and political office are open to all citizens, no matter their race, religion, or sexual orientation. Support democracy. Support Israel" (http://www.bluestarpr.com/wp-content/uploads/2014/09/wp_gay-rights.pdf).

14. Interview in Tel Aviv, January 21, 2011.

15. The "Holocaust generation" is popularly understood as those Jewish Israelis who directly experienced World War II in Europe and immigrated to Israel. As Ronit Lentin (2000, 4–5) writes, "Equally complex is the definition of Israeli 'children of *Shoah* survivors,' termed both in the literature and popularly 'the second-generation.' This is a contested term, since some ... believe either that children of survivors have no characteristics distinguishing them from other Israelis, or that they do not have the same entitlements as do their survivor-parents." Importantly, Lentin (2000, 163–64) corroborates Matan's claim of an ease of communication between the third generation and survivors of the Holocaust or *Shoah,* in contrast to the tension that often characterizes the relationship between parents and their second-generation children.

16. Interview in Jerusalem, June 21, 2011.

17. Sheikh Jarrah is a Palestinian neighborhood in East Jerusalem which has become a prominent site of solidarity activism in Israel-Palestine. Once populated by a small Jewish community, which left before 1948, the neighborhood has been home to Palestinian families who were made refugees by the war and resettled in 1956. Recently, Jewish Israeli settlers acting on legal claims made by Jewish organizations are increasingly displacing these families. Since 2009, Jewish Israeli, Palestinian, and international activists have staged weekly joint protests against the evictions (http://972mag.com/sheikh-jarrah; http://www.en.justjlm.org). Throughout the course of my research, Sheikh Jarrah emerged as the most popular protest site and initiative among leftist Jewish Israeli women and men who consider themselves in some way "activist," whether mainstream or radical.

18. Emphasis added.

19. Interview in Jerusalem, June 13, 2011.

20. Interview in Tel Aviv, February 6, 2011.

21. This argument primarily relates to secular Jewish Israeli schools. With many students able to claim exemption from mandatory military service, Jewish Israeli Orthodox religious schools would present a different mode of hierarchical organization; so too schools serving Israel's Palestinian citizens will be characterized by different modes of stratification (Abdo 2011).

22. Interview in Tel Aviv, February 6, 2011.

23. Interview in Tel Aviv, February 6, 2011.

24. Pesach or Passover is an annual Jewish holiday commemorating the emancipation of the Israelites from slavery after exodus from Egypt (www.jewishvirtuallibrary.org/jsource/Judaism/holidaya.html).

25. While these Jewish Israeli holidays follow the Hebrew calendar, Palestinians annually observe May 15 as Nakba Day, the day of "catastrophe" on which the Israeli state gained international recognition, one day after Ben-Gurion's proclamation of the Declaration of the Establishment of the State of Israel. This proximity means that Memorial Day, Independence Day, and Nakba Day commonly fall within the same week.

26. Interview in Jerusalem, June 21, 2011.

27. Interview in Jerusalem, June 21, 2011.

28. In *Marxism and Literature,* Raymond Williams (1977, 132) describes "structures of feeling" as "thought as felt and feeling as thought: practical consciousness of a present kind, in a living and inter-relating continuity . . . a social experience still in process, often indeed not yet recognized as social but taken to be private, idiosyncratic, and even isolating, but which in analysis (through rarely otherwise) has its emergent, connecting, and dominant characteristics, indeed its specific hierarchies."

29. Interview in Tel Aviv, April 7, 2011.

30. Interview in Jerusalem, May 5, 2011.

31. Interview in Jerusalem, May 12, 2011.

32. Interview in Tel Aviv, April 7, 2011.

33. At the time of our interview, former prime minister Ariel Sharon was in a permanent coma due to a stroke in 2006. In this passage the speaker misidentifies his condition as "dead," indicating the abruptness and finality of his departure from politics. Sharon passed away on January 11, 2014.

34. Interview in Tel Aviv, January 17, 2012.

35. Interview in Tel Aviv, January 21, 2011.

36. Interview in Tel Aviv, April 11, 2011.

37. However, this is not to imply parity between these categories or their degrees of exclusion.

38. Sheikh Jarrah Solidarity is a Jewish Israeli activist initiative supporting Palestinian families forcibly expelled from East Jerusalem's Sheikh Jarrah neighborhood by settlers; for historical context see note 17.

39. Interview in Jerusalem, June 28, 2011.

40. Interview in Jerusalem, May 5, 2011.

41. This accord between seeming contradictions in political emotion bears striking similarity to Palestinian contexts. As Lori Allen (2013, 26) writes, "In Palestine cynicism is an emotion tied to political stasis, apathy, and hope, all uncomfortably combined and anchored in a political phase of perceived limbo."

42. Interview in Jerusalem, June 27, 2011.

43. Interview in Jerusalem, May 12, 2011.

44. Importantly, Ronit Lentin (2000, 219) points to tensions around the simultaneous embrace of a triumphal Holocaust narrative and the social rejection of its

survivors in Israel: "By nationalizing the memory of the Shoah, deemed necessary in the process of establishing the state of Israel, and by centring its commemoration machinery around the un-written principle of an Israeli 'victory over the Shoah,' Israel erased the very memory of the Shoah itself."

45. Interview in Jerusalem, June 21, 2011.

46. Emphasis in original text.

47. However, this ability to choose is necessarily constrained by relative positioning with hierarchies of power and privilege, as illustrated by the case of Palestinian citizens of Israel (Rouhana 1998; Ghanem 2001; Ghanim 2009b; Nusair 2010; Abdo 2011; Jamal 2011; Dallasheh 2013).

CHAPTER TWO

1. *The Promise,* aired by Channel Four in 2011.

2. Field notes, March 19, 2011.

3. Maintained through regulation by both state and society—the guard and the groups of hikers—the position of Palestinians on the "periphery" or "margins" is more a matter of force than the choice enjoyed by Jewish Israelis when faced with a view of the Roman ruins or Jisr-az-Zarka.

4. The Alternative Information Centre is a Jerusalem-based Palestinian-Israeli joint activist organization "engaged in dissemination of information, political advocacy, grassroots activism and critical analysis of the Palestinian and Israeli societies as well as the Palestinian-Israeli conflict" (www.alternativenews.org/english/index.php/about-the-aic).

5. Deemed fascist and McCarthyist by *Ha'aretz* journalist Gideon Levy (2010), Im Tirtzu is a right-wing extraparliamentary organization which "works to strengthen and advance the values of Zionism in Israel" (http://en.imti.org.il); it does so in part through targeting academics, institutions, and organizations deemed "anti-Zionist" by its own estimation. In Hebrew the name means "if you will it" and is derived from Theodore Herzl's dictum pertaining to the creation of the state of Israel: *Im tirtzu, ein zo agada*—"If you will it, it is no dream."

6. Interview in Jerusalem, May 3, 2011.

7. Like the label Mizrahi, Sephardi/Sephardic refers to Jews of Middle Eastern and North African origin.

8. Interview in Jerusalem, July 3, 2011.

9. Interview in Mevasseret-Zion, May 20, 2011.

10. Field notes, May 5, 2011.

11. Emphasis in original.

12. Sexuality additionally intersects with race and gender as markers of difference or "otherness" in this context, as detailed throughout this book. In this, gendered processes of telling and othering in Israel-Palestine are also characterized by a hypersexualization of the racially marked "other," as highlighted in postcolonial perspectives on sexuality and gender (see e.g. McClintock 1995; Stoler 2002). Many

thanks to Professor Clare Hemmings for emphasizing the significance of this dynamic.

13. The adoption of this label is uncommon among Jewish Israelis of Middle Eastern origin, as "Jewishness" and "Arabness" have been popularly and politically constructed in antithetical terms (Shohat 1988; Massad 1996; Pappe 2010, 160); as such, Yoni's self-identification as an "Arab Jew" may be read as overtly political.

14. Interview in Jerusalem, July 3, 2011.

15. Lentin (2000, 3) intentionally uses the term *Shoah* rather than Holocaust, stating, "'Holocaust' derives from the Greek *holocauston,* meaning 'whole burnt,' referring in Septuagint to sacrifice by fire as distinct from the Hebrew term for sacrificial offering, *olah*. Many Jews, aware of the Christian notion of a Jewish calvary and sacrifice, reject the term."

16. Jasbir Puar (2013, 336) writes, "In my 2007 monograph *Terrorist Assemblages: Homonationalism in Queer Times* . . . I develop the conceptual frame of 'homonationalism' for understanding the complexities of how 'acceptance' and 'tolerance' for gay and lesbian subjects have become a barometer by which the right to and capacity for national sovereignty is evaluated." This concept is further discussed with respect to Israeli state and society in chapter 3.

17. Due to security concerns Palestinian citizens of Israel are in effect deemed ineligible for service in the IDF; until 2012 ultra-Orthodox or Haredi Jewish Israeli men were able to claim legal exemption from mandatory conscription based on the Tal Law, which permitted deferral of service for students at *yeshiva,* an education institution focused on the study of religious texts (Shafir and Peled 2002, 126–27, 143–44; Harel 2012).

18. Interview in Jerusalem, May 4, 2011.

19. In Jewish Israeli society, popular discourse reflects a perceived distinction between "ideological" and "economic" settlers; the latter are seen as residing in occupied territory due to the lack of available housing within Israel's borders. As an acquaintance claimed of Har Adar, a de facto illegal settlement, "It isn't really a settlement because it isn't ideological—people go there to build houses, big houses! When people want to move out of the city, to have open space, this is where they go" (field notes, May 2, 2011).

20. While in his theorization of "telling" Feldman (1991, 69–70) briefly highlights gender—describing processes of discursive feminization and posthumous masculinization that accompanied violent encounter in Northern Ireland—Yuval-Davis moves to centralize the role of gender in practices of boundary maintenance, drawing attention to the cultural, symbolic, biological, and discursive modes of reproduction which consolidate and mark communities.

21. The Israeli Parliament.

22. As many of the passages in this chapter are clearly Orientalist or racist, it can be difficult to understand their articulation by self-professed leftists. However discomfiting, these sentiments reveal the complexity of political opinion and identification among Jewish Israelis, potentially challenging readers' conceptions of political "left" and "right."

23. Interview in Jerusalem, May 5, 2011.

24. Interview in Tel Aviv, November 25, 2010.

25. In his work Gershon Shafir (1999, 83–90) outlines Israel's transition from pure settlement colony to ethnic plantation colony, problematizing analyses of Israeli society that divide its history into pre- and post-1967 eras. While Shafir explicitly states that "no preconceived notions but trial and error led the Zionist institutions to develop their method of colonization" (83) prior to the First World War, he critically traces colonialism to the earliest Zionist immigrants who arrived in Palestine in the First Aliya beginning in 1882.

26. As Shir Hever (2012, 126) notes, "Prior to the outbreak of the first Intifada, 32% of the West Bank workforce and 57% of the Gaza workforce were employed by Israeli employers, and work in Israel was the biggest source of income in the Palestinian economy. Currently 0% of the Gaza workforce is employed by Israeli employers, and 12.6% of the West Bank workforce is employed by Israeli employers (3.2% in the colonies)."

27. From 1948 through 1966 Palestinian citizens of Israel were subject to rule by "military government," during which time their rights were largely suspended through the imposition of restrictions on freedom of movement, blocked entry to the Jewish labor market, and placement under surveillance and military law (Shafir and Peled 2002, 89, 111–12).

28. Interview in Jerusalem, May 4, 2010.

29. Interview in Jerusalem, May 4, 2010.

30. As made evident in interview narratives and events during the time of my fieldwork, this phenomenon continues to be relevant today. For example, the December 2010 "Rabbis' Wives Letter" explicitly activated these tropes of race, gender, and security (Altman 2010):

> As soon as they have in you in their grasp, in their village, under their complete control—everything becomes different. Your life will never be the same, and the attention you sought will be replaced with curses, physical abuse and humiliation.... Your grandmothers never dreamed that one of their descendants would, by one act, remove future generations from the Jewish people. For you, for future generations, and so that you will never have to endure the terrible suffering, we appeal to you, begging, pleading, praying: Don't date them, don't work where they work and don't perform National Service with them.

Backed by the anti-intermarriage organization Lehava, this letter followed on the heels of the official "Rabbis' Letter," which moved to forbid the rental of property to non-Jews, popularly understood as "Arabs" (Levinson 2010). The rhetoric of sexualized and racialized threat also extends to the African migrant population in Israel, many of whom hope to gain refugee or asylum status (Zitun 2010; Derfner 2010; Dana 2011).

31. Interview in Jerusalem, May 2, 2011.

32. Interview in Tel Aviv, January 31, 2011.

33. As Sonya recalled during our interview, after 1967 "we heard that they were earning more money than before, that it was good for them. It was called 'the

enlightened occupation,' as I'm sure you've heard it called. Everyone talked about 'the enlightened occupation.' We were perfectly satisfied with it—it seemed like a good thing" (interview in Tel Aviv, January 31, 2011).

34. Though many are barred from legal entry, Palestinian women living in the West Bank may steal across the border and separation wall to work illegally as cleaners inside Israel; a 2012 documentary, *White Night* (directed by Irit Gal), portrays these acts of border crossing, along with their attendant rewards and risks.

35. *Matza* (plural: *matzot*) is an unleavened bread traditionally eaten during the holiday period of Passover, or Pesach.

36. Celebrated with costumes and parties in a manner similar to Halloween, Purim is a Jewish holiday commemorating the deliverance of the Jews in ancient Persia.

37. Interview in Jerusalem, May 2, 2011.

38. As evident in chapter 4, the range of titles applied to Palestinians significantly denotes different—and dynamic—relations of belonging and threat vis-à-vis the Israeli state and Jewish Israeli society.

39. Field notes, April 6, 2011.

40. Interview in Jerusalem, May 2, 2011.

41. Interview in Tel Aviv, April 28, 2011.

42. While some "Arab" or "Middle Eastern" cuisine may have arrived in Israel through emigration from diverse Jewish communities in the region, the incorporation of distinctly Palestinian dishes into "Israeli" cuisine constitutes an act of colonial appropriation. Many thanks to Ronit Lentin for emphasizing this dynamic.

43. The Palmach was the elite fighting unit of the Haganah, the Zionist pre-state paramilitary organization that would later become the Israel Defense Force (Shlaim 2000, 22, 34).

44. Neve Shalom is a binational village in Israel which has frequently been the site of Israeli-Palestinian dialogue initiatives.

45. Field notes, May 10, 2011.

CHAPTER THREE

1. Field notes, June 10, 2011.

2. This is not to say that the meaning of the Pride Parade should be read solely through the lens of conflict in Israel-Palestine; rather, this reading draws attention to how homonationalism, or the selective inclusion of particular non-normative sexual identities for purposes of producing and solidifying national consensus (Puar 2008, 47), catalyzes processes that reveal precisely how relations of power intersect and interact.

3. Interview in Tel Aviv, April 7, 2011.

4. This observation owes much to Charles Tilly's (1982) conceptualization of "protection rackets," through which a state directly or indirectly manufactures the very threats from which it purports to protect its citizenry; see also Peterson (1992).

5. The city was characterized as a "bubble" or as *medinat Tel Aviv* (the state of Tel Aviv) in various interviews; this prevailing discourse is also echoed in scholarship and popular media (Konopinski 2009; Mendel 2009; Vick 2010; Simon 2012; Deger 2012).

6. Interview in Mevasseret-Zion, May 20, 2011.

7. Importantly, normalization and routinization are distinct phenomena. While normalization avoids the abnormal or absorbs and renders it seemingly ordinary, routinization implies the production of habit without the guise of normality—through the latter process an abnormal event or situation remains so even as it becomes marked as quotidian (Allen 2008).

8. Assessed primarily in terms of ethnicity, class, and gender, studies of social stratification in Israel locate Ashkenazi Jews at the highest social level and Mizrahi Jews at a secondary level, followed by Palestinians living in Israel, and finally labor migrants—many non-Jewish—at the lowest social position (Semyonov and Lewin-Epstein 2004, 4). Oren Yiftachel (2006) complicates this prevailing model by looking at the total area of Israel's effective sovereign rule, including Palestinian residents of the Occupied Territories.

9. Peace Now or Shalom Achshav (http://peacenow.org.il/eng) is a long-time Jewish Israeli activist organization that promotes the creation of two states in Israel-Palestine.

10. Machsom Watch (www.machsomwatch.org/en) is a Jewish Israeli feminist anti-occupation organization, whose work aims at influencing public opinion through conducting and documenting "daily observations of IDF checkpoints in the West Bank, along the separation fence and in the seamline zone, on the main roads and on out-of-the-way dirt roads, as well as in the offices of the Civil Administration (DCOs) and in military courts."

11. Interview in Tel Aviv, January 31, 2010.

12. Throughout the course of interviews and fieldwork, a wide spectrum of political orientation and religious belief emerged as characteristic of many Jewish Israeli families. Bound by blood relation and value systems that at some level remain shared, family units often bring together a tense amalgamation of politics and perspectives.

13. Field notes, June 23–25, 2011.

14. Machsom Watch, Women in Black, and the Coalition of Women for Peace are among the most visible feminist anti-occupation organizations in Israel. They employ different strategies for mobilization and action. While Machsom Watch (www.machsomwatch.org/en) focuses on reporting human rights violations at Israeli military checkpoints, as an international anti-militarist network Women in Black (www.womeninblack.org/old/en/about) raises consciousness through weekly vigils. The Coalition of Women for Peace (www.coalitionofwomen.org/?page_id=340&lang=en) "initiates public campaigns and education and outreach programs" and is responsible for the Who Profits? campaign, which exposes corporate involvement in Israel's occupation.

15. Interestingly, Orna Sasson-Levy, Yagil Levy, and Edna Lomsky-Feder (2011, 757) look to the exercise of women's political voice within and subsequent to

military service via the activist initiative Women Breaking the Silence (WBS). Here the authors highlight how military service potentially grants legitimacy to women's antiwar discourses, though not without tension: "The case of WBS reveals that military service can be a new source for women's symbolic power in the political field. Hence, the same legitimating system that was hitherto deployed to marginalize women can also be leveraged to justify a political voice. However, employing military service as leverage to justify a political voice is also the source of its weakness."

16. Interview in Jerusalem, June 14, 2011.
17. Interview in Jerusalem, May 12, 2011.
18. Field notes, August 31, 2011.
19. Field notes, February 4, 2011.
20. Lauren Berlant's chapter "Cruel Optimism" (2011, 23–49) gives an excellent account of the fatigue produced by world-maintenance in the American (US) context.
21. Clare Hemmings (2005, 550, 557–58) critiques the recent "affective turn" in cultural theory, as its purported epistemological freedom and "capacity to transform" largely overlook both postcolonial and feminist theory, which "value continuity of difference over time" in questions of social meaning. Critically, this "myopia" allows affect theory to posit itself as "the way forward" in contemporary cultural theory.
22. Interview in Jerusalem, May 5, 2011.
23. In her work on transnational techno-science and cultural studies, Haraway (1992, 297) writes: "Nature for us is *made,* as both fiction and fact. If organisms are natural objects, it is crucial to remember that organisms are not born; they are made in world-changing techno-scientific practices by particular collective actors in particular times and places." Through these claims Haraway argues that worlds, realities, identities, and even individuals are produced and manufactured—by specific communities whose interests are framed by particular historical moments and locations. Yet Haraway remains wary of broadly deterministic constructivist theories and posits an alternative to what she deems "hyper-productionism," or the postmodern narrative that "'man makes everything, including himself, out of the world that can only be resource and potency to his project and active agency.'"
24. Interview in Mevasseret-Zion, May 20, 2011.
25. Interview in Mevasseret-Zion, May 20, 2011.
26. Interview in Jerusalem, May 12, 2011.
27. Precipitated by the October 1973 or Yom Kippur War, Gush Emunim (Bloc of the Faithful) was a political religious nationalist movement which encouraged Jewish Israeli settlement of the Gaza Strip, West Bank, and Golan Heights (Shafir and Peled 2002, 159–83; Shlaim 2010, 25–36).
28. Interview in Jerusalem, May 15, 2011.
29. As described in chapter 1, while Memorial Day and Independence Day are Jewish Israeli holidays marking the deaths of citizens (military and civilian) in conflict and the 1948 establishment of the State of Israel, respectively, Nakba Day is

observed by Palestinians as the day of the "catastrophe" when the Israeli state gained international recognition. Memorial Day and Independence Day follow the Hebrew calendar, while Nakba Day is commemorated annually on May 15; Memorial Day, Independence Day and Nakba Day commonly fall within the same week, only one week after Israeli commemoration of the Holocaust.

30. Interview in Jerusalem, May 15, 2011.

31. Joseph Massad (2006, 19) notes that the official document marking the foundation of Israel is the Declaration of the Establishment of the State of Israel; it was renamed the Declaration of Independence in popular discourse. Massad pointedly argues that as Zionist settlers achieved statehood with the backing of imperial powers, their declaration of "independence" stands as an attempt to recast the colonial establishment of the Israeli state as an anticolonial struggle, ostensibly heralding a postcolonial era in Israel-Palestine. So too Ronit Lentin (2000, 6) casts critical light on the claim to postcoloniality, if differently so: "Zionism can ... be seen as both a de-colonisation process (Jews freeing themselves from the Euro-Aryan yoke) and a re-colonisation process (in relation to the land of Israel and the indigenous Palestinians). However, this call on post-coloniality does not sit comfortably with theories of diaspora: we must ask, in relation to the negation of the Jewish diaspora implied in narratives of the newly constructed Israeli nation, where does homeland begin and diaspora end."

CHAPTER FOUR

1. Field notes, November 4–5, 2010.
2. The categories listed here emerged throughout the process of interviews in Tel Aviv and West Jerusalem, as participants constructed these labels in describing their degrees and modes of political action.
3. Interview in Jerusalem, April 17, 2011.
4. Interview in Mevasseret-Zion, May 20, 2011.
5. Interview in Tel Aviv, January 17, 2010.
6. Interview in Jerusalem, June 13, 2011.
7. SOS (www.sospets.co.il) is an animal rescue organization.
8. Interview in Tel Aviv, January 17, 2011.
9. In numerous interviews individuals expressed their sense that the political Right is able to mobilize more effectively than the Left, noting that these parties and organizations are better versed in the politics of protest and popular appeal.
10. For footage of this February 1, 2011, protest near the Egyptian embassy, see http://vimeo.com/21132162.
11. Field notes, February 1, 2011.
12. For footage of the December 10, 2010, Human Rights Day march, see http://democracy-project.org.il/en/2010/12/highlights-from-the-march-part-2-the-refugees. The solidarity demonstration against the Holot detention center was held on December 24, 2010 (Lior 2010).

13. Interview in Tel Aviv, January 5, 2011.

14. In September 2014, the Israeli High Court of Justice ruled that the Holot detention facility for asylum seekers should close within ninety days (Lior 2014); however, as this book is being prepared for publication (July 2015) the facility continues to operate.

15. During the time of my fieldwork, public racism and violence against African migrants—often refugees and asylum seekers—increased dramatically, reflecting the discrimination and prejudice directed at Palestinians while at the same time supplanting this group at the lowest level of Israeli society (Ettinger, Hasson, and Lior 2010; Sheen 2011a). However, Jewish Israeli attitudes and behaviors toward this community often exposed significant tensions. While largely reviled and demonized in public discourse, within individual exchanges black African migrants were regarded with a degree of pity and empathy not extended to Palestinians. For example, during an *ulpan* lesson our instructor related her understanding that where many African migrants lived, in (south) Tel Aviv, tended to be "violent and dirty, with drugs and homelessness." Shaking her head sadly, our instructor told the class, "These conditions bring out the worst in them and this brings out the worst in us [Israelis], and people then take advantage of them" (field notes, December 28, 2010).

16. Field notes, March 26, 2011, and interview in Tel Aviv, March 27, 2011.

17. Each of the organizations listed may be considered part of a wider "anti-occupation movement" in Israel; see the end of the bibliography for links to organization websites.

18. As related in chapter 1, Naksa Day marks the Palestinian commemoration of the 1967 War, which resulted in further dispossession and displacement of Palestinians along with the military occupation of the West Bank, Gaza Strip, East Jerusalem, Golan Heights, and Sinai Peninsula. The 2011 anniversary was marked by protests and the killing of unarmed Palestinian civilians by the IDF as individuals attempted to cross the border fence from Syria into Israel (Khoury, Ashkenazi, and Harel 2011).

19. Interview in Jerusalem, June 5, 2011.

20. Interview in Jerusalem, May 5, 2011.

21. Interviews in Jerusalem, May 11 and June 20, 2011. While Kotef and Amir (2007) contest this claim with accounts of younger women's sexualization in Machsom Watch, both strategic and unsolicited, no corroborating narratives emerged during multiple interviews involving Machsom Watch volunteers across a range of ages.

22. See www.machsomwatch.org/en; Kotef and Amir (2007).

23. As Professor Yagil Levy (2011) argues: "Even if the leftist groups' intention is to ensure upholding Palestinian rights ... the unintentional result of their activity is preserving the occupation. Moderating and restraining the army's activity gives it a more human and legal facade. Reducing the pressure of international organizations, alongside moderating the Palestinian population's resistance potential, enables the army to continue to maintain this control model over a prolonged period of time." Many Machsom Watch volunteers are aware of this tension in their work (interviews in Tel Aviv, January 31, 2011, and Jerusalem, April 17 and 14 June, 2011).

24. Many interview participants attested to the increasing appeal of "human rights" work; at the same time, a small number of participants drew attention to the potentially neutralizing or depoliticizing aspects of this discourse and practice (see also Einhorn 2010, 180–82; Allen 2013, 90). Importantly, this depoliticization remains associated with feminization, again bringing valuations of gender squarely into resistance.

25. While Sheikh Jarrah Solidarity protests take place in East Jerusalem, organized actions in Bil'in, Na'alin, and Nabi Saleh are located within these respective Palestinian West Bank villages; the latter sites are associated with the Popular Struggle Coordination Committee (https://popularstruggle.org).

26. These demonstrations began in response to the annexation of Bil'in lands by the Jewish Israeli settlement Modi'in, made possible by the construction of the Wall through village territory (http://palsolidarity.org/tag/bilin). The Israeli High Court ordered the Wall to be rerouted in 2007, and the structure was finally moved in 2011; however, 150,000 square meters of village land presently remain annexed (*Ha'aretz* 2010a), and protests continue.

27. Weekly actions are also held on Fridays in the West Bank village of Ma'asra.

28. Interview in Tel Aviv, April 20, 2011. For excellent analyses of the ways tourism intersects with conflict and security practices in Israel-Palestine, see Stein (2008) and Ochs (2011, 138–160).

29. Located in the Negev Desert of south Israel, the Arava Institute for Environmental Studies (www.arava.org) "prepar[es] future Arab and Jewish leaders to cooperatively solve the region's environmental challenges."

30. In Chuck Palahniuk's 1996 novel, the wording is: "After a night in fight club, everything in the real world gets the volume turned down. Nothing can piss you off. Your word is law, and if other people break that law or question you, even that doesn't piss you off."

31. Made by Jewish Israeli activist and documentarist Shai Carmeli-Pollak in 2006, the film *Bil'in Habibti* (*Bil'in My Love*) focuses on the popular struggle in Bil'in.

32. Anarchists Against the Wall is a Jewish Israeli group "supporting the popular Palestinian resistance to the Israeli separation wall" (www.awalls.org).

33. The makeshift coffin present that day signified the disunity and factionalism that were meant to end with the then-recent Hamas–Fatah reconciliation.

34. Rani, a young Palestinian man partially paralyzed in 2000 during the start of the second or *al-Aqsa intifada,* is now an iconic figure in the Bil'in protest. Interestingly, the mythology of the protest among Jewish Israelis contends that Rani was injured at Bil'in rather than in Jerusalem, though the latter site is named in the documentary *Bil'in Habibti.*

35. Field notes, May 6, 2011.

36. Interview in Tel Aviv, January 28, 2011.

37. Field notes, May 6, 2011.

38. The scholarship highlighted here pays particular attention to the ways in which Israeli militarism creates and emerges through particular valuations of

gender, race, class, and sexuality, contributing an intersectional approach to the study of militarism and militarization.

39. Interview in Tel Aviv, April 11, 2011.
40. Interview in Tel Aviv, April 11, 2011.
41. Interview in Tel Aviv, March 21, 2011.
42. Interview in Tel Aviv, March 31, 2011.

CHAPTER FIVE

1. Field notes, July 30, 2011.
2. The ethno-national contours of this earlier protest became visible on a popular Israeli late-night comedy program, as when asked about his views regarding the cottage cheese protest Palestinian MK Ahmed Tibi shrugged and replied, "We don't eat cottage [cheese] for breakfast—we eat *labneh*."
3. Field notes, August 1 and 6, 2011.
4. For an analysis of the protests' relative disorder, particularly at the Rothschild Boulevard site, see Thom (2011). Also see Livio and Katriel (2014) for a discussion of the spatial aspects of order and chaos in the protests.
5. Following the 2011 protests against the cost of living in Israel, protest leaders Stav Shaffir and Daphne Leef became involved with the Israeli government, though differently so. Shaffir was elected to the Knesset as a member of the Labor Party in 2013 (Lior 2011; Lis 2013a); a number of Leef's activities and engagements abroad were coordinated with the government's *hasbara* or "information" program (Lis 2013a; Glaser 2012).
6. Different from "elaborating symbols," which order experience (Ortner 1973, 1340), summarizing symbols draw together a complex system of ideas under a unitary mode of representation, streamlining difference in the interest of cohesion.
7. In their research with Women in Black, Sara Helman and Tamar Rapoport (1997, 688–89) additionally cite the group's lack of "ideological deliberation" as key to "maximiz[ing] enlistment" and crystallizing the "distinction between those within the demonstration and those outside it."
8. Jewish Israeli soldier Gilad Shalit was captured in 2006 on the border with the Gaza Strip and held captive for five years. During this time a media campaign galvanized public support for efforts to pressure the government into securing his release, and Shalit became a national symbol (Cohen 2011). He was released in 2011.
9. Field notes, August 1, 2011.
10. Emphasis added.
11. Yehouda Shenhav (2013) likewise approaches the 2011 social protests in Israel through the lens of the *carnivalesque,* highlighting how dynamics of temporary suspension served to entrench the "antidemocratic" status quo. However, while Shenhav focuses on this phenomenon in relation to postmodern neoliberalism, this chapter appraises the gendered micropolitics that ordered and underwrote the process of inversion and reversion.

12. Field notes, August 1, 2011.

13. As argued by Sasson-Levy, Levy, and Lomsky-Feder (2011, 749–50), the accusation of being politically "leftist" in Jewish Israeli society produces a silencing effect, described by the authors in the context of military service: "The women soldiers, combatants and non-combatants alike, stated that they did not speak up during their service because of the very real fear of being socially ostracized, labeled, identified as one-sided, as well as due to a sense of weakness and being in the minority.... The few who dared raise even the most measured criticism were marked as leftists and informers, were socially ostracized, and had to pass more initiation rites than others to prove their loyalty to the army and the state."

14. Conversely, Hanna Herzog (2013) views the 2011 protests as an assimilation of the feminist struggle in Israel, highlighting their centralization of a marginal "politics from below."

15. As Livio & Katriel (2014, 155) interestingly highlight, these practices are also linked to the conduct of early Zionist organizing.

16. For a discussion of the *freier* figure in Israeli politics, see Ilan (2007).

17. Field notes, September 3, 2011.

18. Field notes, August 1, 2011.

19. Field notes, July 30, 2011.

20. Field notes, August 12, 2011.

21. Field notes, August 30, 2011.

22. Field notes, August 2, 2011.

23. Likud is the right-of-center political party to which current prime minister Benjamin Netanyahu belongs; both Israel Beitenu and National Front are far-right parties presently gaining power in Israeli politics. Kadima is a centrist political party that once led a coalition government under Ehud Olmert, but has since lost much of its political influence.

24. Max Blumenthal and Joseph Dana (2011) cite Kopty in their compelling article, "J14: The Exclusive Revolution," written for +972 *Magazine* during the protests: "'The injustice will continue,' Kopty declared flatly. 'And I don't believe J14 will create changes that are socio-political. But our struggle is completely political. So when J14 finally explodes because the different internal groups have contradicting interests—and they can't remain apolitical forever—our struggle will go on.'"

25. Kahanists follow the teaching of Rabbi Meir Kahane, whose political party Kach "called for the 'transfer' of all Palestinians, citizens and non-citizens alike, out of the Land of Israel." In 1988 Kach was disqualified from participation in Knesset elections (Shafir and Peled 2002, 127).

26. Shortly after Marzel's suggestion that the housing crisis could be solved by the expansion of building in Jerusalem, primarily possible in the city's illegally occupied Eastern Sector, Prime Minister Netanyahu's government approved the construction of 227 new units in Ariel, a Jewish settlement in the West Bank (Levinson and Associated Press 2011).

27. Also, the continuing presence of Ayalim (http://ayalim.org.il/en)—an organization that advocates building expansion in the Negev and Galilee

regions—remained largely uncontested despite their adoption of settlement rhetoric and clear designs on "Judaizing" these majority Bedouin and Palestinian areas. During a later visit to the Rothschild encampment, a representative related that the organization aimed to increase Jewish settlement "in all of the area given to the Jews" through the establishment of "youth villages." As evidence, he described how members had recently adopted a "new" strategy to counter the bureaucratic delays which commonly slowed development: "Yesterday we did something amazing, really amazing. For the first time we just went to a place and starting building! We built an outpost and put an Israeli flag on it!" (field notes, August 1, 2011).

28. This is not to imply parity between Palestinian and settler initiatives as both sought inclusion within the protests, however. Rather, the comparison primarily reflects on how the protests adhered to the contours of the (Jewish) national body.

29. Field notes, August 2, 2012. Yonathan Mendel (2013) writes similarly of the connection between the protests' politics of comfort in 2011 and the 2013 elections in Israel, which saw former television presenter Yair Lapid and his party Yesh Atid (There is a Future) gain a surprising nineteen seats in the Knesset: "I remembered the reaction of my friend Abigail, who lives in Oxford and who came to visit during the 'social justice protests' in the summer of 2011. 'Why do people here keep speaking about a social protest?' she asked after a trip to Rothschild Avenue. 'This is a consumer protest.' . . . The reason Lapid has been so successful is that he knows that in a consumerist society the candidate who promises to make the most of our money is the star; that it would be a waste of his time to talk about the Palestinians."

30. Emphasis in original text.
31. Field notes, August 31, 2011.
32. Field notes, August 2, 2011.
33. Field notes, August 31 and July 30, 2011, respectively.
34. Field notes, August 30, 2011.
35. Field notes, July 30, 2011.
36. Field notes, July 30, 2011.
37. Field notes, July 30, 2011.
38. Field notes, August 6, 2011.
39. Field notes, August 1, 2011.
40. Interview in Jerusalem, July 2, 2011.
41. Emphasis in original text.
42. Field notes, August 19, 2011.

CONCLUSION

1. Personal diary, September 24, 2012.
2. Reference to "The Passenger," by Iggy and the Stooges, 1977.
3. Interview in Jerusalem, May 30, 2011.
4. Interview in Jaffa, March 27, 2011.
5. Interview in Tel Aviv, March 21, 2011.

6. Gisha—Legal Center for Freedom of Movement is a Jewish Israeli activist organization which uses legal assistance and public advocacy "to protect the freedom of movement of Palestinians, especially Gaza residents" (www.gisha.org/content.asp?lang_id=en&p_id=5). Zochrot carries out actions including organized tours, cinematic events, demonstrations, and preservation initiatives to "challenge the Israeli Jewish public's preconceptions and promote awareness, political and cultural change within it to create the conditions for the Return of Palestinian Refugees" (http://zochrot.org/en). B'Tselem—The Israeli Information Centre for Human Rights in the Occupied Territories focuses on documentation and aims to "educate the Israeli public and policymakers about human rights violations in the Occupied Territories, combat the phenomenon of denial prevalent among the Israeli public, and help create a human rights culture in Israel" (www.btselem.org/about_btselem).

7. Interview in Tel Aviv, March 13, 2011.

8. Interview in Tel Aviv, March 31, 2011.

BIBLIOGRAPHY

Abdo, N. 2011. *Women in Israel: Race, Gender and Citizenship.* London: Zed.

Abdo, N., and Lentin, R., eds. 2002. *Women and the Politics of Military Confrontation: Palestinian and Israeli Gendered Narratives of Dislocation.* Oxford: Berghahn.

Abdo, N., and Yuval-Davis, N. 1995. "Palestine, Israel, and the Zionist Settler Project." In *Unsettling Settler Societies: Articulations of Gender, Race, Ethnicity and Class,* ed. D. Stasiulis and N. Yuval-Davis, 291–322. London: Sage.

Abu El-Haj, N. 2001. *Facts on the Ground: Archaeological Practice and Territorial Self-Fashioning in Israeli Society.* Chicago, IL: University of Chicago Press.

Abu-Lughod, L. 1990. "The Romance of Resistance: Tracing Transformations of Power through Bedouin Women." *American Ethnologist* 17(1):41–55.

ACRI. 2011a. "'Slavery Law' Passes Final Vote," May 18. Association for Civil Rights in Israel. www.acri.org.il/en/2011/05/18/slavery-law-passes-final-vote.

———. 2011b. "ACRI Condemns Efforts to Suppress Tent City Protestors," July 26. Association for Civil Rights in Israel. www.acri.org.il/en/2011/07/26/acri-condemns-efforts-to-suppress-tent-city-protesters.

Ahmed, S. 2000. *Strange Encounters: Embodied Others in Post-Coloniality.* London: Routledge.

———. 2004. *The Cultural Politics of Emotion.* Edinburgh: Edinburgh University Press.

Ahronovitz, E. 2011. "Panther & Son." *Ha'aretz,* August 19. www.haaretz.com/weekend/magazine/panther-son-1.379557.

Al-Ali, N., and Pratt, N., eds. 2009. *Women and War in the Middle East: Transnational Perspectives.* London: Zed.

Al-Werfalli, M. 2011. *Political Alienation in Libya: Assessing Citizens' Political Attitude and Behaviour.* Reading: Ithaca.

Allen, L. 2005. *Suffering through a National Uprising: The Cultural Politics of Violence, Victimization, and Human Rights in Palestine.* PhD dissertation, University of Chicago.

———. 2008. "Getting by the Occupation: How Violence Became Normal during the Second Palestinian Intifada." *Cultural Anthropology* 23(3):453–87.

———. 2013. *The Rise and Fall of Human Rights: Cynicism and Politics in Occupied Palestine*. Stanford, CA: Stanford University Press.

Althusser, L. 1971. *Essays on Ideology*. London: Verso.

Altman, Y. 2010. "Rabbi's Wives: Don't Date Arabs." *YNet News,* December 28, 2010. www.ynetnews.com/articles/0,7340,L-4005896,00.html

Anthias, F., and Yuval-Davis, N. 1992. *Racialised Boundaries: Race, Nation, Gender, Colour and Class and the Anti-Racist Struggle*. London: Routledge.

Arendt, H. 1998 [1958]. *The Human Condition*. Chicago, IL: University of Chicago Press.

Asberg, M.J. 2008. *Go On, Give Up: Cynical Aporias*. PhD thesis, University of Western Ontario.

Auyero, J. 2007. *Routine Politics and Violence in Argentina: The Gray Zone of State Power*. Cambridge: Cambridge University Press.

BBC. 2011. "Jerusalem on a Plate," December 20, 2011. www.bbc.co.uk/programmes/b017znj9.

———. 2015. "Netanyahu Apologises to Israeli-Arabs over Election Remarks," March 23, 2015. www.bbc.co.uk/news/world-middle-east-32026995.

Bakhtin, M. 1984 [1968]. *Rabelais and His World*. Bloomington: Indiana University Press.

Bardenstein, C. 1998. "Threads of Memory and Discourses of Rootedness: Of Trees, Oranges and the Prickly-Pear Cactus in Israel/Palestine." *Edibeyat* 8:1–36.

Bassock, M. 2011. "Israeli GDP Surges up OECD Ranks in 2010." *Ha'aretz,* February 17. www.haaretz.com/print-edition/news/israeli-gdp-surges-up-oecd-ranks-in-2010-1.343832.

Bayat, A. 1997. *Street Politics: Poor People's Movements in Iran*. New York: Columbia University Press.

———. 2010. *Life as Politics: How Ordinary People Change the Middle East*. Stanford, CA: Stanford University Press.

Belkind, N. 2013. "Israel's J14 Social Protest Movement and Its Imaginings of 'Home': On Music, Politics and Social Justice." *Middle East Journal of Culture and Communication* 6:329–53.

Ben-David, C., and Wainer, D. 2010. "The Controversy over Israel's Business Elite." *Bloomberg Businessweek,* October 7. www.businessweek.com/magazine/content/10_42/b4199010761878.htm.

Berlant, L. 1993. "The Queen of America Goes to Washington City: Harriet Jacobs, Frances Harper, Anita Hill." *American Literature* 65(3):549–74.

———. 1998a. "Intimacy: A Special Issue." *Critical Inquiry* 24(2):281–88.

———. 1998b. "Poor Eliza." *American Literature* 70(3): 635–68.

———. 2007. "Nearly Utopian, Nearly Normal: Post-Fordist Affect in *La Promesse* and *Rosetta*." *Public Culture* 19(2):273–301.

———. 2008. *The Female Complaint: The Unfinished Business of Sentimentality in American Culture*. Durham, NC: Duke University Press.

———. 2011. *Cruel Optimism*. Durham, NC: Duke University Press.

Blumenthal, M., and Dana, J. 2011. "The Exclusive Revolution: Reflections on the Tent Protests." *Mondoweiss,* August 29. http://mondoweiss.net/2011/08/the-exclusive-revolution-reflections-on-the-tent-protests.html.

Bornstein, A. 2002. *Crossing the Green Line between the West Bank and Israel.* Philadelphia: University of Pennsylvania Press.

Boyarin, D. 1997. *Unheroic Conduct: The Rise of Heterosexuality and the Invention of the Jewish Man.* Berkeley: University of California Press.

Boyer, P. 1984. "From Activism to Apathy: The American People and Nuclear Weapons, 1963–1980." *Journal of American History* 70(4):821–44.

Brah, A. 1996. "Diaspora, Border and Transnational Identities." In *Cartographies of Diaspora: Contesting Identities,* ed. A. Brah. London: Routledge.

———. 2012 [1999]. "The Scent of Memory: Strangers, Our Own and Others." *Feminist Review* no. 100 (Special Issue: Recalling Scent of Memory), 6–26.

Brah, A., and Phoenix, A. 2004. "Ain't I a Woman? Revisiting Intersectionality." *Journal of International Women's Studies* 5(3):75–86.

Bryant, N. 2015. "US Raises Prospect of Israel UN Isolation," *BBC News,* April 1, 2015. www.bbc.co.uk/news/world-middle-east-32117501

Burston, B. 2011. "The Middle-Class Anarchists of the Tent City Revolution." *Ha'aretz,* July 25. www.haaretz.com/blogs/a-special-place-in-hell/the-middle-class-anarchists-of-the-tent-city-revolution-1.375160.

Burton, F. 1979. "Ideological Social Relations in Northern Ireland." *British Journal of Sociology* 30 (1): 61–80.

Butler, J. 1993. *Bodies That Matter: On the Discursive Limits of "Sex."* New York: Routledge.

———. 1997a. *Excitable Speech: A Politics of the Performative.* New York: Routledge.

———. 1997b. *The Psychic Life of Power: Theories in Subjection.* Stanford, CA: Stanford University Press.

———. 2004. *Precarious Life: The Powers of Mourning and Violence.* London: Verso.

Chalfin, B. 2008. "Sovereigns and Citizens in Close Encounter: Airport Anthropology and Customs Regimes in Neoliberal Ghana." *American Ethnologist* 35(4):519–38.

Cockburn, C. 1998. *The Space between Us: Negotiating Gender and National Identities in Conflict.* London: Zed.

———. 2007. *From Where We Stand: War, Women's Activism, and Feminist Analysis.* London: Zed.

Cohen, G. 2011. "As Gilad Shalit Goes Free, A 5-Year-Long Media Campaign Comes to a Close." *Ha'aretz,* October 18. www.haaretz.com/print-edition/news/as-gilad-shalit-goes-free-a-5-year-long-media-campaign-comes-to-a-close-1.390523.

———. 2014. "IDF to send 'voluntary draft notices' to Christian Arabs." *Ha'aretz,* 22 April. www.haaretz.com/israel-news/.premium-1.586678.

Cohen, S. 2001. *States of Denial: Knowing about Atrocities and Suffering.* Cambridge: Polity Press.

Cohen, S., & Taylor, L. 1992. *Escape Attempts: The Theory and Practice of Resistance to Everyday Life,* 2nd ed. London: Routledge.

Cohn, C. 1987. "Sex and Death in the Rational World of Defense Intellectuals." *Signs: Journal of Women in Culture and Society* 12(4):687–718.

Connell, R. W. 1987. *Gender and Power: Society, the Person and Sexual Politics.* Cambridge: Polity.

———. 2002. *Gender.* Cambridge: Polity.

Connolly, K. 2011. "Israel Suffers Summer of Economic Discontent." *BBC News,* August 2. www.bbc.co.uk/news/world-middle-east-14344515.

Crenshaw, K. 1989. "Demarginalizing the Intersection of Race and Sex: A Black Feminist Critique of Antidiscrimination Doctrine, Feminist Theory and Antiracist Politics." *University of Chicago Legal Forum* 140:139–69.

Dallasheh, L. 2010. "Political Mobilization of Palestinians in Israel: The Movement al-'Ard." In *Displaced at Home: Ethnicity and Gender among Palestinians in Israel,* ed. R. A. Kanaaneh and I. Nusair, 21–38. Albany: State University of New York Press.

———. 2013. "Making Citizenship Count: Nazareth in the Transition between the Mandate and Israel." In *Nazareth: Archaeology, History and Cultural Heritage,* ed. M. Yazbak and S. Sharif. Jerusalem: Ludwig Mayer.

Dana, J. 2011. "Racist Protest in Tel Aviv Targets Refugees and Migrants." *+972 Magazine,* April 11. http://972mag.com/israeli-racism-turns-its-ugly-head-in-south-tel-aviv/13121.

Daniel, E. V. 2000. "Mood, Moment, and Mind." In *Violence and Subjectivity,* ed. V. Das, A. Kleinman, M. Ramphele, and P. Reynolds, 333–36. New York: Oxford University Press.

Das, V. 2007. *Life and Words: Violence and the Descent into the Ordinary.* Berkeley: University of California Press.

Davidi, E. 2000. "Protest amid Confusion: Israel's Peace Camp in the Uprising's First Month." In *Beyond Oslo: The New Uprising* (MER217), ed. Middle East Research and Information Project. www.merip.org/mer/mer217/protest-amid-confusion.

Davies, B. 2006. "Subjectification: The Relevance of Butler's Analysis for Education." *British Journal of Sociology of Education* 27(4):425–38.

Dean, S. 2013. "Yotam Ottolenghi and the Authors of *The Gaza Kitchen* Discuss Food, Conflict, Culture." *Bon Appétit,* March 27. www.bonappetit.com/entertaining-style/gift-guides/article/israeli-chef-yotam-ottolenghi-talks-with-the-gaza-kitchen-authors.

De Certeau, M. 1984. *The Practice of Everyday Life,* trans. S. F. Randall. Berkeley: University of California Press.

De Jong, A. 2011. *The Silent Voice: Palestinian and Israeli Non-violent Activism and Resistance.* PhD thesis, School of Oriental and African Studies, University of London.

Deger, A. 2012. "Tel Aviv and the Failure of the Zionist Dream." *Mondoweiss,* October 2, 2012. www.mondoweiss.net/2012/10/tel-aviv-and-the-failure-of-the-zionist-dream.html.

———. 2014. Apathy in Ramallah as Negotiations with Israel Dive." *Mondoweiss,* April 6. http://mondoweiss.net/2014/04/ramallah-negotiations-israel.

Derfner, L. 2010. "Backlash in South Tel Aviv." *Jerusalem Post,* July 23, 2010. www.jpost.com/Magazine/Features/Article.aspx?id=182223.

Dolan, K. A., and Holbrook, T. M. 2001. "Knowing versus Caring: The Role of Affect and Cognition in Political Perceptions." *Political Psychology* 22(1): 27–44.

Einhorn, B. (2010). *Citiznehip in an Enlarging Europe: From Dream to Awakening.* Basingstoke: Palgrave MacMillan.

Eliasoph, N. 1997. "'Close to Home': The Work of Avoiding Politics." *Theory and Society* 26(5):605–47.

———. 1998. *Avoiding Politics: How Americans Produce Apathy in Everyday Life.* Cambridge: Cambridge University Press.

Ellis, C., and Bochner, A. P. 2000. "Autoethnography, Personal Narrative, Reflexivity." In *Handbook of Qualitative Research,* 2nd ed., ed. N. K. Denzin and Y. S. Lincoln, 733–68. Thousand Oaks, CA: Sage.

Enloe, C. 1989. *Bananas, Beaches, and Bases: Making Feminist Sense of International Politics.* Berkeley: University of California Press.

———. 2010. *Nimo's War, Emma's War: Making Feminist Sense of the Iraq War.* Berkeley: University of California Press.

Ettinger, Y., Hasson, N., and Lior, I. 2010. "Upsurge in Racism as Protestors Take to the Streets against Arabs, Migrant Workers." *Ha'aretz,* December 22. www.haaretz.com/print-edition/news/upsurge-in-racism-as-protesters-take-to-the-streets-against-arabs-migrant-workers-1.331899.

Fadil, N. 2009. "Managing Affects and Sensibilities: The Case of Not-Handshaking and Not-Fasting." *Social Anthropology* 17:439–54.

Feldman, A. 1991. *Formations of Violence: The Narrative of the Body and Political Terror in Northern Ireland.* Chicago, IL: Chicago University Press.

Foucault, M. 1988. "An Aesthetics of Existence." In *Michel Foucault—Politics, Philosophy, Culture: Interviews and Other Writings 1977–1984,* ed. L. Kritzman, 41–53. London: Routledge.

———. 1997. *Society Must Be Defended: Lectures at the College de France 1975–1976,* trans. D. Macy. London: Allen Lane.

———. 1998 [1978]. *The Will to Knowledge: History of Sexuality, Volume 1,* trans. R. Hurley. London: Penguin.

———. 2003 [1963]. "A Preface to Transgression." In *The Essential Foucault: Selections from the Essential Works of Foucault, 1954–1984,* ed. P. Rabinow and N. Rose, 442–57. New York: New Press.

Freedman, M. 2002. "Theorizing Israeli Feminism, 1970–2000." In *Jewish Feminism in Israel: Some Contemporary Perspectives,* ed. K. Misra and M. S. Rich, 1–16. Hanover, MA: Brandeis University Press.

Frenkel, S. 2011. "Protestors Collide in Tel Aviv." *National Public Radio,* August 5. www.npr.org/2011/08/05/139032549/protesters-collide-in-tel-aviv.

Fuchs, E., ed. 2005. *Israeli Women's Studies: A Reader.* New Brunswick, NJ: Rutgers University Press.

Gelbfish, R. 2011. "Tent Protest: Why We March Tonight," trans. D. Reider. *+972 Magazine,* July 23. http://972mag.com/tents4/19248.

Ghanem, A. 2001. *The Palestinian-Arab Minority in Israel, 1948–2000.* Albany, NY: SUNY Press.

———. 2010. *Palestinian Politics after Arafat: A Failed National Movement.* Bloomington: Indiana University Press.

Ghanim, H. 2008. "Thanatopolitics: The Case of the Colonial Occupation in Palestine," in *Thinking Palestine,* ed. R. Lentin, 65–81. London: Zed.

———. 2009a. "Poetics of Disaster: Nationalism, Gender, and Social Change among Palestinian Poets in Israel after Nakba. *International Journal of Politics, Culture, and Society* 22(1):23–39.

———. 2009b. *Reinventing the Nation: Palestinian Intellectuals in Israel.* Jerusalem: Hebrew University Magnes Press.

Glaser, U. 2012. "Face of a Nation." *Alondon.net,* March 5. www.alondon.net/index.php?action=art&id=5677&Face+of+a+Nation=1&lang=en_GB.

Goldberg, D. J. 1996. *To the Promised Land: A History of Zionist Thought.* London: Penguin.

Goldberg, D. T. 2008. "Racial Palestinianization." In *Thinking Palestine,* ed. R. Lentin, 25–45. London: Zed.

Gonzalez, V. V. 2007. "Military Bases, 'Royalty Trips,' and Imperial Modernities: Gendered and Racialized Labor in the Postcolonial Philippines." *Frontiers: A Journal of Women Studies* 28(3):28–59.

Gor, H. 2007. "Education for War: Preparing Children to Accept War as a Natural Factor of Life." *Center of Critical Feminist Pedagogy.* www.criticalpedagogy.org.il/english/critfemlibrary/articles/educationforwar/tabid/313/Default.aspx.

Gor, H., and Mazali, R. 2007. "Militarism and Education from a Feminist Perspective: The Case of Israel." *Center of Critical Feminist Pedagogy.* www.criticalpedagogy.org.il/english/critfemlibrary/articles/MilitarismandEducationFeministPerspective/tabid/303/Default.aspx.

Gordon, N. 2008. *Israel's Occupation.* Berkeley: University of California Press.

Gramsci, A. 1971. *Selections from the Prison Notebooks of Antonio Gramsci,* trans. Q. Hoare and G. Nowell Smith. London: Lawrence and Wishart.

Greenberg, J. 2010. "'There's Nothing Anyone Can Do about It': Participation, Apathy and 'Successful' Democratic Transition in Postsocialist Serbia." *Slavic Review* 69(1):41–64.

The Guardian. 2015. "Binyamin Netanyahu Closes Last-Minute Deal to Form New Israeli Government', May 7. www.theguardian.com/world/2015/may/06/binyamin-netanyahu-deal-form-israel-government.

Ha'aretz. 2010a. "Work Starts to Reroute West Bank Security Fence at Bil'in," February 11. www.haaretz.com/news/work-starts-to-reroute-west-bank-security-fence-at-bil-in-1.263146.

———. 2010b. "3 Hurt in Second IAF Strike on Gaza in 24 Hours, Palestinians Say," October 7. www.haaretz.com/news/diplomacy-defense/3-hurt-in-second-iaf-strike-on-gaza-in-24-hours-palestinians-say-1.317741.

———. 2011. "Haaretz Poll: Netanyahu Losing Public Support over Handling of Israeli Housing Protest," July 26. www.haaretz.com/print-edition/news/haaretz-poll-netanyahu-losing-public-support-over-handling-of-israeli-housing-protest-1.375244.

———. 2015. "LIVE BLOG: Herzog Congratulates Netanyahu, Refuses to Say Whether He'll Join Coalition," March 18. www.haaretz.com/news/israel-election-2015/1.647304.

Haraway, D. 1992. "The Promises of Monsters: A Regenerative Politics for Inappropriate/d Others." In *Cultural Studies,* ed. L. Grossberg, C. Nelson, and P. Treichler, 295–337. London: Routledge.

Harel, A. 2012. "Haredim Decry New Military Draft Bill That Does Not Include Arabs." *Ha'aretz,* June 17. www.haaretz.com/news/national/haredim-decry-new-military-draft-bill-that-does-not-include-arabs.premium-1.436798.

Hass, A. 2012. "Shin Bet Questions Israeli Activists Linked to Upcoming 'Fly-In' Protest." *Ha'aretz,* April 12. www.haaretz.com/news/diplomacy-defense/shin-bet-questions-israeli-activists-linked-to-upcoming-fly-in-protest-1.423871.

Hay, C. 2007. *Why We Hate Politics.* Cambridge: Polity Press.

Halperin-Kaddari, R. 2004. *Women in Israel: A State of Their Own.* Philadelphia: University of Pennsylvania Press.

Helman, S. 1999a. "From Soldiering and Motherhood to Citizenship: A Study of Four Israeli Peace Protest Movements." *Social Politics* 6(3):292–313.

———. 1999b. "Negotiating Obligations, Creating Rights: Conscientious Objection and the Redefinition of Citizenship in Israel." *Citizenship Studies* 3(1):45–70.

Helman, S., and Rapoport, T. 1997. "Women in Black: Challenging Israel's Gender and Sociopolitical Orders." *British Journal of Sociology* 48(4):681–700.

Hemmings, C. 2005. "Invoking Affect: Cultural Theory and the Ontological Turn." *Cultural Studies* 19(5):548–67.

———. 2011. *Why Stories Matter: The Political Grammar of Feminist Theory.* Durham, NC: Duke University Press.

Herzfeld, M. 1992. *The Social Production of Indifference: Exploring the Symbolic Roots of Western Bureaucracy.* Chicago, IL: University of Chicago Press.

Herzl, T. 1988 [1896]. *The Jewish State.* New York: Dover.

Herzog, H. 2005 [1998]. "Homefront and Battlefront: The Status of Jewish and Palestinian Women in Israel." In *Israeli Women's Studies: A Reader,* ed. E. Fuchs, 208–28. New Brunswick, NJ: Rutgers University Press.

———. 2013. "A Generational and Gender Perspective on the Tent Protests." *Theory and Criticism* 41:69–96. In Hebrew.

Hever, S. 2010. *The Political Economy of Israel's Occupation: Repression beyond Exploitation.* New York: Pluto.

———. 2012. "Exploitation of Palestinian Labour in Contemporary Zionist Colonialism." *Settler Colonial Studies* 2(1):124–32.

Highmore, B. 2002. "Introduction: Questioning Everyday Life." In *The Everyday Life Reader,* ed. B. Highmore, 1–34. London: Routledge.

Hoffmann, S. 2011. *Disciplining Movement: Sovereignty in the Context of Iraqi Migration to Syria.* PhD thesis, SOAS, University of London.

Hopkins, N. 2012. "The Israeli Defence Forces: First for Women." *The Guardian,* July 9. www.guardian.co.uk/lifeandstyle/2012/jul/09/israeli-defence-forces-women-equality.

Hovel, R., and Khoury, J. 2014. "High Court Upholds Residential Screening Law, Enabling Jewish Villages to Keep Arabs Out." *Ha'aretz,* September 18. www.haaretz.com/news/israel/.premium-1.616391.

Ilan, S. 2007. "Thou Shalt Not Be a Freier." *Ha'aretz,* January 28. www.haaretz.com/print-edition/opinion/thou-shalt-not-be-a-freier-1.211247.

Issacharoff, A. 2012. "Israeli Leftist Activists: We Are Being Sexually Harassed in the West Bank." *Ha'aretz,* March 17. www.haaretz.com/news/national/israeli-leftist-activists-we-are-being-sexually-harassed-in-the-west-bank-1.419167.

Izikovitch, G. 2011. "Top Israeli Singer Margalit Tzan'ani Allegedly Sought to Harm Journalist for Critical Remarks." *Ha'aretz,* August 18. www.haaretz.com/print-edition/news/top-israeli-singer-margalit-tzan-ani-allegedly-sought-to-harm-journalist-for-critical-remarks-1.379217.

Jacoby, T. A. 2005. *Women in Zones of Conflict: Power and Resistance in Israel.* Montreal: McGill-Queen's University Press.

Jad, I. 2009. "The Politics of Group Weddings in Palestine: Political and Gender Tensions." *Journal of Middle East Women's Studies* 5(3):36–53.

Jamal, A. 2011. *Arab Minority Nationalism in Israel: The Politics of Indigeneity.* Abingdon: Routledge.

Johnson, P., Abu Nahleh, L., and Moors, A. 2009. "Weddings and War: Marriage Arrangements and Celebrations in Two Palestinian Intifadas." *Journal of Middle East Women's Studies* 5(3):11–35.

Johnson, P., and Kuttab, E. 2001. "Where Have All the Women (and Men) Gone? Reflections on Gender and the Second Intifada." *Feminist Review* no. 69, 21–43.

Kamin, D. 2013. "Why an Article about a Middle Eastern Spice Prompted an Internet War." *The Atlantic,* June 4. www.theatlantic.com/international/archive/2013/06/why-an-article-about-a-middle-eastern-spice-prompted-an-internet-war/276529.

Kanaaneh, R. 2002. *Birthing the Nation: Strategies of Palestinian Women in Israel.* London: University of California Press.

———. 2008. *Surrounded: Palestinian Soldiers in the Israeli Military.* Stanford, CA: Stanford University Press.

Kanaaneh, R., and Nusair, I. 2010. *Displaced at Home: Ethnicity and Gender among Palestinians in Israel.* New York: SUNY Press.

Kandiyoti, D. 1991. "Identity and its Discontents: Women and the Nation." *Millennium: Journal of International Studies* 20(3):429–43.

Kashua, S. 2011a. "Middle-Class Heroes with a Shameful Secret." *Ha'aretz*, August 5. www.haaretz.com/weekend/magazine/middle-class-heroes-with-a-shameful-secret-1.377168.

———. 2011b. Moment of Glory." *Ha'aretz*, August 12. www.haaretz.com/weekend/magazine/moment-of-glory-1.378345.

Kassem, F. 2011. *Palestinian Women: Narrative Histories and Gendered Memory.* London: Zed.

Katz, S. H. 2003. *Women and Gender in Early Jewish and Palestinian Nationalism.* Gainesville: University Press of Florida.

Kaye-Kantrowitz, M. 2008. "Feminist Organizing in Israel." In *Feminism and War: Confronting US Imperialism*, ed. R. Riley, C. T. Mohanty, and M. B. Pratt, 243–49. London: Zed.

Kelly, T. 2006. *Law, Violence and Sovereignty among West Bank Palestinians.* Cambridge: Cambridge University Press.

———. 2008. "The Attractions of Accountancy: Living an Ordinary Life during the Second Palestinian Intifada." *Ethnography* 9(3):351–76.

Khalidi, R. 2006. *The Iron Cage: The Story of the Palestinian Struggle for Statehood.* Oxford: Oneworld.

Khalili, L. 2007. *Heroes and Martyrs of Palestine: The Politics of National Commemoration.* Cambridge: Cambridge University Press.

———. 2011. "Gendered Practices of Counterinsurgency." *Review of International Studies* 37(4):1471–91.

Khan, A. 2008. "The Ghettoization of the Palestinians." In *Thinking Palestine*, ed. R. Lentin, 116–30. London: Zed.

Khoury, J., Ashkenazi, E., and Harel, A. 2011. "Report: Up to 20 Protestors Killed as Hundreds of Syrians Storm Israeli Border." *Ha'aretz*, June 5. www.haaretz.com/news/diplomacy-defense/report-up-to-20-protesters-killed-as-hundreds-of-syrians-storm-israel-border-1.366068.

Khoury, J., Pfeffer, J., and Ha'aretz Service. 2011. "Eight Said Killed as IDF Fires on Infiltrators from Syria and Lebanon." *Ha'aretz*, May 15. www.haaretz.com/news/diplomacy-defense/eight-said-killed-as-idf-fires-on-infiltrators-from-syria-and-lebanon-1.361841.

Kidron, P. 2004. *Refusenik! Israel's Soldiers of Conscience.* London: Zed.

Kimmerling, B. 2001. *The Invention and Decline of Israeliness: State, Society, and the Military.* Berkeley: University of California Press.

Konopinski, N. 2009. *Ordinary Security: An Ethnography of Security Practices and Perspectives in Tel Aviv.* PhD thesis, University of Edinburgh.

Kopty, A. 2011. "Tent 1948." *Mondoweiss,* August 6. http://mondoweiss.net/2011/08/tent-1948.html.

Kotef, H., and Amir, M. 2007. "(En)gendering Checkpoints: Checkpoint Watch and the Repercussions of Intervention." *Signs* 23, no. 4 (Special Issue on War and Terror I: Raced-Gendered Logics and Effects in Conflict Zones): 973–96.

Last, M. 2000. "Reconciliation and Memory in Postwar Nigeria." In *Violence and Subjectivity,* ed. V. Das, A. Kleinman, M. Ramphele, and P. Reynolds, 315–22. New York: Oxford University Press.

Lavie, S. 2011. "Mizrahi Feminism and the Question of Palestine." *Journal of Middle East Women's Studies* 7(2):56–88.

———. 2014. *Wrapped in the Flag of Israel: Mizrahi Single Mothers and Bureaucratic Torture.* New York: Berghahn.

Lawrence, P. 2000. "Violence, Suffering, Amman: The Work of Oracles in Sri Lanka's Eastern War Zone." In *Violence and Subjectivity,* ed. V. Das, A. Kleinman, M. Ramphele, and P. Reynolds, 171–204. New York: Oxford University Press.

Lentin, R. 2000. *Israel and the Daughters of the Shoah: Reoccupying the Territories of Silence.* New York: Berghan.

———. 2004. "'No Woman's Law Will Rot This State': The Israeli Racial State and Feminist Resistance." *Sociological Research Online* 9(3). www.socresonline.org.uk/9/3/lentin.html.

———, ed. 2008. *Thinking Palestine.* London: Zed.

———. 2010. *Co-memory and Melancholia: Israelis Memorialising the Palestinian Nakba.* Manchester: Manchester University Press.

Lerner, T. 2010. "On Women's Refusal in Israel." In *Women and Conscientious Objection,* 56–62. War Resisters' International, www.wri-irg.org/system/files/WomenAndConscientiousObjection-AnAnthology.pdf.

Lev, D. 2011. "Artist Who Criticised Tent Protests May Be Fired." *Israel National News,* August 4. www.israelnationalnews.com/News/News.aspx/146389#.UhzBsLyh9RE.

Levinson, C. 2010. "Top Rabbis Move to Prevent Renting Homes to Arabs, Say 'Racism Originated in the Torah.'" *Ha'aretz,* December 7, 2010. www.haaretz.com/news/national/top-rabbis-move-to-forbid-renting-homes-to-arabs-say-racism-originated-in-the-torah-1.329327.

———. 2011. "Dozens of Hilltop Youth Set Up Camp in Israel's Biggest Tent City." *Ha'aretz,* August 3. www.haaretz.com/news/national/dozens-of-hilltop-youth-set-up-camp-in-israel-s-biggest-tent-city-1.376815

Levinson, C., and Associated Press. 2011. "Israel Approves 227 New Homes in West Bank Settlement of Ariel." *Ha'aretz,* August 15. www.haaretz.com/news/diplomacy-defense/israel-approves-227-new-homes-in-west-bank-settlement-of-ariel-1.378725.

Levinson, C., and Lior, I. 2011. "Dairy Farmers, Right-Wing Activists Join Israel Housing Protest." *Ha'aretz,* August 3. www.haaretz.com/news/national/dairy-farmers-right-wing-activists-join-israel-housing-protest-1.376803.

Levy, G. 2010. "Im Tirtzu Hides behind Respectable Mask of 'Zionism.'" *Ha'aretz*, February 7, 2010. www.haaretz.com/print-edition/opinion/im-tirtzu-hides-behind-respectable-mask-of-zionism-1.262891.
———. 2011a. "A Tale of Tent Cities." *Ha'aretz*, July 29. www.haaretz.com/weekend/week-s-end/a-tale-of-tent-cities-1.375910.
———. 2011b. "What's Missing in the Battle against Excluding Women." *Ha'aretz*, December 22. www.haaretz.com/print-edition/opinion/what-s-missing-in-the-battle-against-excluding-women-1.402843.
———. 2012. "Survey: Most Israeli Jews Wouldn't Give Palestinians Vote If West Bank Was Annexed." *Ha'aretz*, October 23. www.haaretz.com/news/national/survey-most-israeli-jews-wouldn-t-give-palestinians-vote-if-west-bank-was-annexed.premium-1.471644.
Levy, G., and Sasson-Levy, O. 2008. "Militarized Socialization, Military Service, and Class Reproduction: The Experiences of Israeli Soldiers." *Sociological Perspectives* 51(2):349–74.
Levy, Y. 2011. "Israeli NGOs Are Entrenching the Occupation." *Ha'aretz*, January 11. www.haaretz.com/print-edition/opinion/israeli-ngos-are-entrenching-the-occupation-1.336331.
Lior, I. 2010. "Thousands in Tel Aviv Protest Plans for Refugee Detention Facility." *Ha'aretz*, December 24. www.haaretz.com/news/national/thousands-in-tel-aviv-protest-plan-for- refugee-detention-facility-1.332737.
———. 2011. "Tens of Thousands March in Tel Aviv to Protest Housing Shortage, High Rent Prices." *Ha'aretz*, July 23. www.haaretz.com/news/national/tens-of-thousands-march-in-tel-aviv-to-protest-housing-shortage-high-rent-prices-1.374871.
———. 2014. "High Court Orders Closure of Detention Facility for African Asylum Seekers." *Ha'aretz*, September 22. http://www.haaretz.com/news/israel/.premium-1.617143.
Lis, J. 2011. "Knesset Meeting on Refugee Law Goes Ahead Despite Only One MK Showing." *Ha'aretz*, August 15. www.haaretz.com/print-edition/news/knesset-meeting-on-refugee-law-goes-ahead-despite-only-one-mk-showing-1.378644.
———. 2013a. "New Labour MK Stav Shaffir Creates 'Social Lobby' to Heed the People." *Ha'aretz*, February 13. www.haaretz.com/news/israeli-elections-2013/new-labor-mk-stav-shaffir-creates-social-lobby-to-heed-the-people-1.503339.
———. 2013b. "Ministers Approve 'Unconstitutional' Bill Penalizing Left-Wing NGOs." *Ha'aretz*, December 15. www.haaretz.com/news/israel/.premium-1.563674.
Lis, J., and Bassock, M. 2011. "Netanyahu Announces Plan to Negotiate with Israeli Housing Activists." *Ha'aretz*, July 31. www.haaretz.com/news/national/netanyahu-announces-plan-to-negotiate-with-israeli-housing-activists-1.376195.
Livio, O., and Katriel, T. 2014. "A Fractured Solidarity: Communitas and Structure in the Israeli 2011 Social Protest." In *The Political Aesthetics of Global Protest: The Arab Spring and Beyond*, ed. P. Werbner, M. Webb, and K. Spellman-Poots, 147–76. Edinburgh: Edinburgh University Press.

Lowrance, S. 2004. "Deconstructing Democracy: The Arab-Jewish Divide in the Jewish State." *Critical Middle Eastern Studies* 13(2):175–94.

Mandel, R. 2011. "Protestors Blast Marching Rightists." *YNet News,* August 3. www.ynetnews.com/articles/0,7340,L-4104143,00.html

Mann, B. 2001. "Tel Aviv's Rothschild: When a Boulevard Becomes a Monument." *Jewish Social Studies* (new series) 7(2):1–38.

Masalha, N. 2003. *The Politics of Denial: Israel and the Palestinian Refugee Problem.* London: Pluto.

Massad, J. 1996. "Zionism's Internal Others: Israel and the Oriental Jews." *Journal of Palestine Studies* 25(4):53–68.

———. 2006. "The 'Post-Colonial' Colony: Time, Space, and Bodies in Palestine/Israel." In his *The Persistence of the Palestinian Question: Essays on Zionism and the Palestinians,* 13–40. New York: Routledge.

Massey, D. 1994. *Space, Place and Gender.* Minneapolis: University of Minnesota Press.

Mayer, T., ed. 1994. *Women and the Israeli Occupation: The Politics of Change.* London: Routledge.

Mazali, R. 2003. "'And What About the Girls?' What a Culture of War Genders out of View." *Nashim: A Journal of Jewish Women's Studies and Gender Issues* 6:39–50.

McClintock, A. 1995. *Imperial Leather: Race, Gender and Sexuality in the Colonial Conquest.* New York: Routledge.

McNay, L. 1992. *Foucault and Feminism.* Cambridge: Polity.

Mendel, Y. 2009. "Fantasising Israel." *London Review of Books* 31(12):28–29. www.lrb.co.uk/v31/n12/yonatan-mendel/fantasising-israel.

———. 2013. "Diary: Israel's Election." *London Review of Books* 35(4). www.lrb.co.uk/v35/n04/yonatan-mendel/diary.

Mikdashi, M. 2009. "What's Music Got to Do with It?" July 4. http://sawtalniswa.com/article/328.

Misgav, C. 2013. "'Shedding Light on Israel's Backyard': The Tent Protest and the Urban Periphery." *Theory and Criticism* 41:97–120. In Hebrew.

Misra, K., and Rich, M. S., eds. 2002. *Jewish Feminism in Israel: Some Contemporary Perspectives.* Hanover, MA: Brandeis University Press.

Mitchell, T. 1990. "Everyday Metaphors of Power." *Theory and Society* 19(5):545–77.

———. 1991. "The Limits of the State: Beyond Statist Approaches and their Critics." *American Political Science Review* 85(1):77–96.

Mohanty, C. T. 1988. "Under Western Eyes: Feminist Scholarship and Colonial Discourses." *Feminist Review* no. 30 (Autumn): 61–98.

Mohanty, C. T. 2003. "'Under Western Eyes' Revisited: Feminist Solidarity through Anticapitalist Struggle." In *Feminism without Borders: Decolonizing Theory, Practicing Solidarity,* ed. C. T. Mohanty, 221–51. Durham, NC: Duke University Press.

Mohanty, C. T., Pratt, M. B., and Riley, R. L. 2008. "Introduction: Feminism and US Wars—Mapping the Ground." In *Feminism and War: Confronting U.S. Imperialism,* ed. R. L. Riley, C. T. Mohanty, and M. B. Pratt, 1–18. London: Zed.

Natanel, K. 2012. "Resistance at the Limits: Feminist Activism and Conscientious Objection in Israel." *Feminist Review*, no. 101 (Special Issue on Conflict), 78–96.

———. 2013. "This American Life in Israel-Palestine." *OpenDemocracy 50.50*, June 10. www.opendemocracy.net/5050/katherine-natanel/this-american-life-in-israel-palestine.

Navaro-Yashin, Y. 2002. *Faces of the State: Secularism and Public Life in Turkey*. Princeton, NJ: Princeton University Press.

———. 2003. "'Life is Dead Here': Sensing the Political in 'No Man's Land.'" *Anthropological Theory* 3(1):107–25.

Nevo, N. 1991. "Ideology and Practice in the Cooperative Farm Village." In *Calling the Equality Bluff: Women in Israel*, ed. B. Swirski and M. Safir, 276–81. New York: Pergamon.

Nusair, I. 2010. "Gendering the Narratives of Three Generations of Palestinian Women in Israel." In *Displaced at Home: Ethnicity and Gender among Palestinians in Israel*, ed. R. Kanaaneh and I. Nusair, 75–92. New York: SUNY Press.

Ochs, J. 2011. *Security and Suspicion: An Ethnography of Everyday Life in Israel*. Philadelphia: University of Pennsylvania Press.

Ortner, S. 1973. "On Key Symbols." *American Anthropologist* (new series) 75(5):1338–46.

Pappe, I. 2006. *The Ethnic Cleansing of Palestine*. Oxford: Oneworld.

———. 2010. "Fear, Victimhood, Self and Other: On the Road to Reconciliation." In *Across the Wall: Narratives of Israeli-Palestinian History*, ed. I. Pappe and J. Hilal, 155–76. London: I. B. Tauris.

———. 2012. "Shtetl Colonialism: First and Last Impressions of Indigeneity by Colonised Colonisers." *Settler Colonial Studies* 2(1):39–58.

Pappe, I., and Hilal, J., eds. 2010. *Across the Wall: Narratives of Israeli-Palestinian History*. London: I. B. Tauris.

Peled-Elhanan, N. 2012. *Palestine in Israeli School Books: Ideology and Propaganda in Education*. London: I. B. Tauris.

Peteet, J. 1994. "Male Gender and Rituals of Resistance in the Palestinian Intifada: A Cultural Politics of Violence." *American Ethnologist* 21(1):31–49.

Peterson, V. S. 1992. "Security and Sovereign States: What is at Stake in Taking Feminism Seriously?" In *Gendered States: Feminist (Re)Visions of International Relations Theory*, ed. V. S. Peterson, 31–64. Boulder: Lynne Rienner.

Piterberg, G. 2008. *The Returns of Zionism: Myths, Politics and Scholarship in Israel*. London: Verso.

Plonski, S. 2014. *Ordinary and Extraordinary Resistance: The Struggle for Land, Space and Place by the Palestinian Citizens of Israel*. PhD thesis, School of Oriental and African Studies, University of London.

Portugali, J. 1993. *Implicate Relations: Society and Space in the Israeli-Palestinian Conflict*. Dordrecht: Kluwer Academic.

Powers, J. 2006. *Blossoms on the Olive Tree: Israeli and Palestinian Women Working for Peace*. London: Praeger.

Puar, J. 2008. "Feminists and Queers in the Service of Empire." In *Feminism and War: Confronting U.S. Imperialism,* ed. R. L. Riley, C. T. Mohanty, and M. B. Pratt, 47–55. London: Zed.

———. 2013. "Rethinking Homonationalism." *International Journal of Middle East Studies* 45, no. 2 (special issue: Queer Affects): 336–39.

Raday, F. 1991. "The Concept of Gender Equality in a Jewish State." In *Calling the Equality Bluff: Women in Israel,* ed. B. Swirski and M. P. Safir, 18–28. New York: Pergamon.

Ram, U. 2003. "Historiosophical Foundations of the Historical Strife in Israel." In *Israeli Historical Revisionism: From Left to Right,* ed. A. Shapira and D. J. Penslar, 43–61. London: Frank Cass.

———. 2008. *The Globalization of Israel: McWorld in Tel Aviv, Jihad in Jerusalem.* New York: Routledge.

Ram, U., and Filc, D. 2013. "The 14th of July of Daphni Leef: The Rise and Fall of the Social Protest." *Theory and Criticism* 41:17–43. In Hebrew.

Ravid, B. 2010. "OECD Entrance is 'Seal of Approval,' Netanyahu Says." *Ha'aretz,* May 10. www.haaretz.com/news/diplomacy-defense/oecd-entrance-is-seal-of-approval-netanyahu-says-1.289422.

———. 2011. "The Arab Spring and Israel's Winter Hibernation." *Ha'aretz,* December 8. www.haaretz.com/opinion/the-arab-spring-and-israel-s-winter-hibernation-1.400345.

Reider, D. 2010. "The Refugees March: Notes from the Human Rights Rally." *+972 Magazine,* December 11. http://972mag.com/the-refugees-march-notes-from-the-human-rights-rally/6100.

———. 2011. "Protestors Block Streets after Landmark Rally in Tel Aviv." *+972 Magazine,* July 24. http://972mag.com/breaking-protesters-block-streets-in-central-tel-aviv/19281.

Reuters. 2013. "Israel Said Planning to Deport African Migrants to Uganda." *The Guardian,* August 29. http://uk.reuters.com/article/2013/08/29/uk-israel-migrants-africa-idUKBRE97S19120130829.

Richter-Devroe, S. 2011. "Palestinian Women's Everyday Resistance: Between Normality and Normalisation." *Journal of International Women's Studies* 12(2):32–46.

———. 2012. "Defending their Land, Protecting their Men: Palestinian Women's Popular Resistance after the Second Intifada." *International Feminist Journal of Politics* 14(2):181–201.

Rimalt, N. 2007. "Equality with a Vengeance: Female Conscientious Objectors in Pursuit of a Voice and Substantive Gender Equality." *Columbia Journal of Gender and Law* 16(1): 97–145.

Rodinson, M. 1973. *Israel: A Colonial Settler State?* Trans. D. Thorstad. New York: Monad Press for the Anchor Foundation.

Ron, J. 2003. *Frontiers and Ghettos: State Violence in Serbia and Israel.* Berkeley: University of California Press.

Rosenberg, M. 1954. "Some Determinants of Political Apathy." *Public Opinion Quarterly* 18(4):349–66.

Rosenheck, Z., and Shalev, M. 2013. "The Political Economy of the 2011 Protests: A Class and Generational Analysis." *Theory and Criticism* 41:44–68. In Hebrew.

Rouhana, N. 1998. "Israel and Its Arab Citizens: Predicaments in the Relationship between Ethnic States and Ethnonational Minorities." *Third World Quarterly* 19(2):277–96.

Roy, S. 1995. *The Gaza Strip: The Political Economy of De-development*. Washington, DC: Institute for Palestinian Studies.

———. 1999. "De-development Revisited: Palestinian Economy and Society since Oslo." *Journal of Palestine Studies* 28(3):64–82.

Sa'di, A. H. 2013. *Thorough Surveillance: The Genesis of Israeli Policies of Population Management, Surveillance and Political Control towards the Palestinian Minority*. Manchester: Manchester University Press.

Sasson-Levy, O. 2003. "Military, Masculinity, and Citizenship: Tensions and Contradictions in the Experience of Blue-Collar Soldiers." *Identities: Global Studies in Culture and Power* 10:319–45.

———. 2005 [2001]. "Gender Performance in a Changing Military: Women Soldiers in Masculine Roles." In *Israeli Women's Studies: A Reader*, ed. E. Fuchs, 265–76. New Brunswick: Rutgers University Press.

———. 2013. "A Different Kind of Whiteness: Marking and Unmarking of Social Boundaries in the Construction of Hegemonic Ethnicity." *Sociological Forum* 28(1):27–50.

Sasson-Levy, O., and Amram-Katz, S. 2007. "Gender Integration in Israeli Officer Training: Degendering and Regendering the Military." *Signs* 3, no. 1 (War and Terror II: Raced-Gendered Logics and Effects beyond Conflict Zones): 105–33.

Sasson-Levy, O., Levy, Y., and Lomsky-Feder, E. 2011. "Women Breaking the Silence: Military Service, Gender, and Anti-war Protest." *Gender and Society* 25(6):740–63.

Sasson-Levy, O., and Rapoport, T. 2003. "Body, Gender, and Knowledge in Protest Movements: The Israeli Case." *Gender and Society* 17(3):379–403.

Sayigh, R. 1998. "Palestinian Camp Women as Tellers of History." *Journal of Palestine Studies* 27(2):42–58.

Schechter, A. 2012. "A Short Guide to Israel's Social Protest." *Ha'aretz*, July 11. www.haaretz.com/news/national/a-short-guide-to-israel-s-social-protest-1.450369.

Scott, J. C. 1985. *Weapons of the Weak: Everyday Forms of Peasant Resistance*. New Haven, CT: Yale University Press.

———. 1990. *Domination and the Arts of Resistance: Hidden Transcripts*. New Haven, CT: Yale University Press.

Scott, J. W. 1988. "Deconstructing Equality-versus-Difference: Or, the Uses of Poststructuralist Theory for Feminism." *Feminist Studies* 14(1): 32–50.

Segal, L. 2008. "Gender, War, and Militarism: Making and Questioning the Links." *Feminist Review* no. 88, 21–35.

Semyonov, M., and Lewin-Epstein, N. 2004. "Introduction—Past Insights and Future Directions: Studies of Stratification in Israel." In *Stratification in Israel: Class, Ethnicity, and Gender,* ed. M. Semyonov and N. Lewin-Epstein, 1–13. New Brunswick: Transaction.

Sevy, G. 1983. "Vitality in an Age of Apathy: The Development of Spirited Human Traits in Contemporary American Culture." *Political Psychology* 4(4):745–57.

Shafir, G. 1989. *Land, Labour and the Origins of the Israeli-Palestinian Conflict, 1882–1914.* Cambridge: Cambridge University Press.

———. 1999. "Zionism as Colonialism: A Comparative Approach." In *The Israel-Palestine Question: A Reader,* ed. I. Pappe, 78–93. 2nd ed., 2007. London: Routledge.

Shafir, G., and Peled, Y. 2000. "Introduction: The Socioeconomic Liberalization of Israel." In *The New Israel: Peacemaking and Liberalization,* ed. G. Shafir and Y. Peled, 1–13. Boulder, CO: Westview.

———. 2002. *Being Israeli: The Dynamics of Multiple Citizenship.* Cambridge: Cambridge University Press.

Shalhoub-Kevorkian, N. 2009. *Militarization and Violence against Women in Conflict Zones in the Middle East: A Palestinian Case Study.* Cambridge: Cambridge University Press.

Sharoni, S. 1995. *Gender and the Israeli-Palestinian Conflict: The Politics of Women's Resistance.* New York: Syracuse University Press.

———. 1996. "Gender and the Israeli-Palestinian Accord: Feminist Approaches to International Politics." In *Gendering the Middle East: Emerging Perspectives,* ed. D. Kandiyoti, 107–26. London: IB. Tauris.

———. 2005 [1994]. "Homefront as Battlefield: Gender, Military Occupation, and Violence against Women." In *Israeli Women's Studies: A Reader,* ed. E. Fuchs, 231–46. New Brunswick: Routledge.

Sheen, D. 2011a. "South Tel Aviv Residents March to Demand Deportation of Foreigners." *Ha'aretz,* April 8. www.haaretz.com/news/national/south-tel-aviv-residents-march-to-demand-deportation-of-foreigners-1.354760.

———. 2011b. "Could Israel's Middle-Class Spearhead a National Revolution?" *Ha'aretz,* July 22. www.haaretz.com/news/national/could-israel-s-middle-class-spearhead-a-national-revolution-1.374735.

Sheizaf, N. 2011. "Tent Protest in Polls: One Big Unhappy Middle Class." *+972 Magazine,* August 3. http://972mag.com/tent-protest-in-numbers-1522720-11/20009.

Shenhav, Y. 2013. "The Carnival: Protest in a Society with no Oppositions." *Theory and Criticism* 41:121–45.

Sherwood, H. 2011. "Tel Aviv Tent City Erected in Protest against High Housing Prices." *The Guardian,* July 17. www.theguardian.com/world/2011/jul/17/tel-aviv-tent-city-house-prices.

———. 2012. "Israeli Poll Finds Majority Would Be in Favour of 'Apartheid' Policies." *The Guardian,* October 23. www.theguardian.com/world/2012/oct/23/israeli-poll-majority-apartheid-policies.

Shlaim, A. 2000. *The Iron Wall: Israel and the Arab World*. London: Penguin.
———. 2010. *Israel and Palestine*. London: Verso.
Shohat, E. 1988. "Sephardim in Israel: Zionism from the Standpoint of Its Jewish Victims." *Social Text* 19/20:1–35.
Simon, B. 2012. "From Fear to Fortune: Tel Aviv's Attitude." *60 Minutes* (CBS), May 21. www.cbsnews.com/8301-18560_162-57437327/from-fear-to-fortune-tel-avivs-attitude/.
Singerman, D. 1995. *Avenues of Participation: Family Politics and Networks in Urban Quarters of Cairo*. Princeton, NJ: Princeton University Press.
Smith, R. J. 2011. "National & Transnational Security Regimes: Israel/Palestine." *Brill Online Encyclopedia of Women in Islamic Cultures*, 6th ed.
Stein, R. 2008. *Itineraries in Conflict: Israelis, Palestinians, and the Political Lives of Tourism*. Durham, NC: Duke University Press.
Steinfeld, R. (2012). *War of the Wombs: The History and Politics of Fertility Policies in Israel, 1948–2010*. PhD thesis, University of Oxford.
Stoler, A. L. 2002. *Carnal Knowledge and Imperial Power: Race and the Intimate in Colonial Rule*. Berkeley: University of California Press.
Svirsky, G. 2002a. "Feminist Peace Activism during the al-Aqsa Intifada." In *Women and the Politics of Military Confrontation: Palestinian and Israeli Gendered Narratives of Dislocation*, ed. N. Abdo and R. Lentin, 234–48. Oxford: Berghan.
———. 2002b. "The Women's Peace Movement in Israel." In *Jewish Feminism in Israel: Some Contemporary Perspectives*, ed. K. Misra and M. S. Rich, 113–31. Hanover, MA: Brandeis University Press.
Swirski, B., and Safir, M. P., eds. 1991. *Calling the Equality Bluff: Women in Israel*. New York: Pergamon.
Tawil-Souri, H. 2012. "Uneven Borders, Coloured (Im)mobilities: ID Cards in Palestine/Israel." *Geopolitics* 17(1):153–76.
Thom. 2011. "J14: The (Dis)order of the Struggle." *+972 Blog*, August 10. http://972mag.com/the-disorder-of-the-struggle/20555.
Throsby, K. 2013. "'If I Go In Like a Cranky Sea Lion, I Come Out Like a Smiling Dolphin': Marathon Swimming and the Unexpected Pleasures of Being a Body in Water." *Feminist Review* no. 103 (Special Issue on Water): 5–22.
Tilly, C. 1982. *War Making and State Making as Organized Crime*. Working paper no. 256, Centre for Research on Social Organization, University of Michigan, Ann Arbor.
Veracini, L. 2010. *Settler Colonialism: A Theoretical Overview*. Basingstoke: Palgrave Macmillan.
———. 2011a. "Decolonising Settler Colonialisms." Presentation delivered at 7th annual SOAS Palestine Society Conference, Past is Present: Settler Colonialism in Palestine, School of Oriental and African Studies, University of London, 5–6 March 2011.
———. 2011b. "On Settlerness." *Borderlands E-Journal* 10(1):1–17. www.borderlands.net.au/vol10no1_2011/veracini_settlerness.pdf.

Verter, Y. 2011. "The Man behind the Panel." *Ha'aretz*, August 12. www.haaretz.com/weekend/week-s-end/the-man-behind-the-panel-1.378301.

———. 2014. "Poll: Breakdown of Talks Only Strengthened Right-Wing Flank." *Ha'aretz*, April 11. www.haaretz.com/news/diplomacy-defense/.premium-1.585032.

Vick, K. 2010. "Why Israel Doesn't Care about Peace." *Time*, September 2. www.time.com/time/magazine/article/0,9171,2015789,00.html.

Wedeen, L. 1999. *Ambiguities of Domination: Politics, Rhetoric and Symbols in Contemporary Syria*. Chicago, IL: University of Chicago Press.

Weichselbaumer, D. 2010. *Sex, Romance and the Carnivalesque between Female Tourists and Caribbean Men*. Lecture delivered January 28 at the Centre for Gender Studies, School of Oriental and African Studies, University of London.

Weiss, E. 2014. *Conscientious Objectors in Israel: Citizenship, Sacrifice, Trials of Fealty*. Philadelphia: University of Pennsylvania Press.

Weizman, E. 2007. *Hollow Land: Israel's Architecture of Occupation*. London: Verso.

———. 2013. *Hegemony, Law, Resistance: The Struggle against Zionist Hegemony in Israel*. PhD thesis, School of Oriental and African Studies, University of London.

Wiegman, R. 2012. "Wishful Thinking." Lecture delivered December 3 at the Gender Institute, London School of Economics and Political Science.

Williams, R. 1977. *Marxism and Literature*. Oxford: Oxford University Press.

Wolfe, P. 1991. "On Being Woken Up: The Dreamtime in Anthropology and in Australian Settler Culture." *Comparative Studies in Society and History* 33(2):197–224.

———. 2012. "Purchase by Other Means: Palestinian *Nakba* and Zionism's Conquest of Economics." *Settler Colonial Studies* 2(1):133–71.

Yiftachel, O. 2006. *Ethnocracy: Land and Identity Politics in Israel/Palestine*. Philadelphia: University of Pennsylvania Press.

Yishai, Y. (2005) [1997]. "Between the Flag and the Banner: Dilemmas in the Political Life of Israeli Women." In *Israeli Women's Studies: A Reader*, ed. E. Fuchs, 190–207. New Brunswick, NJ: Rutgers University Press.

Yuval-Davis, N. 1989. "National Reproduction and the 'Demographic Race' in Israel." In *Woman-Nation-State*, ed. N. Yuval-Davis and F. Anthias, 92–109. Basingstoke: Macmillan.

———. 1997. *Gender and Nation*. London: Sage.

———. 2005 [1980]. "Bearers of the Collective: Women and Religious Legislation in Israel." In *Israeli Women's Studies: A Reader*, ed. E. Fuchs, 121–32. New Brunswick, NJ: Rutgers University Press.

———. 2011. *The Politics of Belonging: Intersectional Contestations*. London: Sage.

Yuval-Davis, N., and Anthias, F., eds. 1989. *Woman-Nation-State*. Basingstoke: Macmillan.

Yuval-Davis, N., and Stoetzler, M. 2002. "Imagined Boundaries and Borders: A Gendered Gaze." *European Journal of Women's Studies* 9(3): 329–44.

Zertal, I. 1998. *From Catastrophe to Power: Holocaust Survivors and the Emergence of Israel.* Berkeley: University of California Press.

———. 2005. *Israel's Holocaust and the Politics of Nationhood,* trans. C. Galai. Cambridge: Cambridge University Press.

Zitun Y. 2010. "MK: African Migrant Infiltrations Like in Biblical Times." *YNet News,* November 15. www.ynetnews.com/articles/0,7340,L-3985140,00.html.

Zonszein, M. 2011. "Jewish Supremacists Visit Social Justice Protests." *+972 Magazine,* August 4. http://972mag.com/jewish-supremacy-visit-social-justice-protests.

Zrahiya, Z., Rozenberg, R., Lis, J., and Cohen, A. 2011. "Protestors Ramp Up Facebook Protest against Cottage Cheese Price Hike." *Ha'aretz,* June 17. www.haaretz.com/print-edition/news/protesters-ramp-up-facebook-protest-against-cottage-cheese-price-hike-1.368130.

ADDITIONAL WEBSITES CONSULTED

Alternative Information Centre, www.alternativenews.org/english/index.php/about-the-aic.
Anarchists Against the Wall, www.awalls.org.
Arava Institute for Environmental Studies, www.arava.org.
Association for Civil Rights in Israel, www.acri.org.il/en.
Ayalim, http://ayalim.org.il/en.
Bat Shalom, www.coalitionofwomen.org/?tag=bat-shalom&lang=en.
BDS Movement, www.bdsmovement.net.
Bil'in, A Village of Palestine, www.bilin-village.org/english.
BlueStar, www.bluestarpr.com/military-gay-rights-israel.html.
Brits for Peace Now, www.britsforpeacenow.com.
B'Tselem, Israeli Information Centre for Human Rights in the Occupied Territories, www.btselem.org.
Coalition of Women for Peace, www.coalitionofwomen.org/?lang=en.
Gisha, Legal Centre for Freedom of Movement, www.gisha.org.
Im Tirtzu, http://en.imti.org.il.
Israeli Committee Against Housing Demolitions, www.icahd.org.
Machsom Watch, www.machsomwatch.org/en.
Mahal, www.mahal-idf-volunteers.org.
Palestinian Campaign for the Academic and Cultural Boycott of Israel, www.pacbi.org.
Popular Struggle Coordination Committee, https://popularstruggle.org.
Sheikh Jarrah Solidarity, www.en.justjlm.org.
Women in Black, www.womeninblack.org/es/history.
Zochrot, http://zochrot.org/en.

INDEX

Abdo, Nahla, 40
Abu Gosh, 62–63, 74
Abu-Lughod, Lila, 122, 131, 153
active disengagement, 7–8, 15, 87, 116, 178, 196–98, 200
activism, 113–14, 118–19, 122–24, 141–45, 147–51, 155–52, 177–83, 221n6; banality of, 132–38; left-wing, 100, 132, 143, 189. *See also* protests
African migrants, 76, 88, 92, 134–36, 138, 159, 211n30, 216n15
Ahmed, Sara, 39, 60, 105, 108
alienation, 101, 168; political, x, 13, 16, 40–46, 48, 50, 178. *See also* apathy
Allen, Lori, 5, 42–43, 208n41
Alternative Information Centre (AIC), 56, 209n4
Althusser, Louis, 49–50
America/Americans. *See* United States
Amsterdam, 37, 39
Anarchists Against the Wall, 141, 147, 217n32
anger, 44–46, 92, 104, 135; masculinized, 133; of protesters, 153, 168
anti-Semitism, 28; pre-Holocaust, 41, 42
apartheid, opposition to, 136
apathy, x, 4–5, 7–17, 86, 116, 182–83, 190, 194–200, 204n9. *See also* active disengagement; alienation, political
apolitical politics, 154, 163–65, 169
Arabs, 32–33, 56, 61, 68, 72, 111, 210n30; cuisine of, 83, 212n42; othering of,

112, 115. *See also* Mizrahi Jews; Palestinians
Arafat, Yassir, 1
Arava Institute for Environmental Studies, 141, 217n29
Arba Emahot, 45, 136, 163
Argentina, 101
Ariel, 219n26
Armistice Agreement (1949), 13, 74
Ashkenazi Jews, 44, 58, 66, 84, 129, 130, 205n17; Palestinians seen as threat by, 56–58, 74, 124; in protests, 138, 139, 143, 155–57, 178–79; social status of, 10, 13, 15, 61, 67, 180–81, 192, 213n8
Asian migrants, 76, 135
Atzmaut, 44
Australia, 110, 112
autoethnographic writing, 15
Ayalim, 219–20n27

Bakhtin, Mikhail, 160, 161
banality, 4, 174, 188; of activism, 132–38; of violence, 186
Banksy, 1
Barak, Ehud, 44
Bat Shalom, 136
Bayat, Asef, 122
Bedouins, 24, 68, 70, 205n19, 220n27
Be'er Sheva, 179
Beirut, 185
belonging, 3, 26, 58–61, 79, 85, 101–6, 212n38; normative, 93, 116; class and, 112; gendered, 22–24, 26, 30, 58, 59, 113,

belonging *(continued)*
  191–93; markers of, 60, 61, 63–67, 70; military service and, 22, 101, 145, 148; politics of, 165–72; protest and, 128, 133–35, 173, 177–82, 194; sites of, 56, 59–60, 65, 174, 199, 201; Zionist, 30, 50, 102, 116–17
Ben-Gurion, David, 208n25
Bennett, Naftali, 171
Berlant, Lauren, 30–31, 34, 46–47, 105, 108, 174, 181, 191, 214n20
Bethlehem, 127
Bil'in, 139–41, 143, 144, 217nn25,26,34
Bil'in Habibti (film), 141, 217nn31,34
biopolitics, 85–86
biopower, 49
Birzeit, 3, 95, 201; University, 1, 4
blackness. *See* racialization
Black Panthers, 137–38, 156–57
BlueStar, 207n13
Blumenthal, Max, 219n24
Bohm, David, 64
Bornstein, Avram, 203n3
Brecht, Bertolt, 204n13
B'Tselem—Israeli Information Centre for Human Rights in the Occupied Territories, 198, 221n6
Burston, Bradley, 163–64
Burton, Frank, 60
Butler, Judith, 34, 36, 50, 108
bypassing, 89, 92–98, 104, 116, 157, 193

Caesaria, 51
Canada, 155
Carmeli-Pollak, Shai, 217n31
carnivalesque, 154, 160–62, 165, 172, 175, 218n11
Certeau, Michel de, 190
Christianity, 210n15
Coalition of Women for Peace, 99, 213n14
Cockburn, Cynthia, 191
Cohen, Stanley, 105
Communist Party, 28
Congo, 135
Connell, R. W., 31, 40
conscientious objection, 22, 102
corruption, 38, 41–43
cynicism, 16, 40–46, 48, 50, 208n41

Dana, Joseph, 219n24
Declaration of the Establishment of the State of Israel, 177, 208n25, 215n31
Denmark, 110, 112
despair, 6, 7, 44–46, 106, 193, 196; political, 13–15, 50, 151, 175, 184, 190, 205n23
Dharma activism, 113–14
diaspora, 21, 20, 164–65, 215n31
disengagement. *See* active disengagement
Disengagement Plan (2006), 204n8
disillusionment, 14, 15, 45–46, 50, 175, 193, 195
Doors, the, 160, 180
Druze, 13, 20, 24, 205n19

East Jerusalem, 1, 3, 5, 11, 37, 77, 106, 200, 203n1; French Hill area of, 56–57, 59, 108, 110, 124, 125; Jewish settlement in, 208n38, 219n26; military occupation of, 206n2, 216n18; protests in, 124, 207n17
Egypt, 32, 155, 157, 205n21, 208n24
Eliasoph, Nina, 204n9
elsewheres, 105–7, 193
emotions, 34, 36, 38, 56, 108, 158, 187; of alienation, 41, 44; apathy rooted in, 7, 90; collective, 20, 81; familial, 98–99; toward Palestinian laborers, 71–73, 78, 86; political, 43–48, 75, 175, 190, 193, 196, 208n41; of protesters, 132–33, 157–58, 161, 174–75; in Zionism, 30–31, 35–39, 49–50
England, 39, 136
Enloe, Cynthia, 11
entanglement, 4, 34, 42–43, 71, 99, 195, 201; awareness of, 39; of gender and racialization, 80, 193; in protests, 182; spatialized, 16, 53, 58–60, 86. *See also* Hegemonic entanglements
Eritrea, 135
estrangement, 12, 41–42, 128, 181, 190, 204n13. *See also* othering
Ethiopian Jews, 13, 173
ethnography, 4, 10, 11, 13–15, 91, 203n2
everyday life, 6, 9, 18–50, 70–71, 90, 153, 187–95; apathy and, 1, 53, 199; banality of activism in, 132–38; conflict and resistance in, 121–31; core social values central to, 21–26; education and milita-

rization in, 31–34; gender in, 30, 31, 34, 55, 61; in Jerusalem, 19–21; militarism in, 145–50; news-holiday cycle in, 34–39; in occupied territories, 4, 200, 204n3; Palestinian workers in intimate spheres of, 76–80, 85–87; politics of, 10–15, 20, 39–49, 182–83; practices of telling in, 61–62; in Tel Aviv, 18–19; Zionism in, 26–30. *See also* normalization

Facebook, 155
Fatah, 217n33
fatigue, 7, 37–39, 44, 197, 214n20; political, 39, 193, 196, 199
feeling:; structures of, 38, 208n28. *See also* emotions
Feldman, Allen, 60, 210n20
feminists, 3, 34, 44, 106, 200, 206n10, 214n21, 219n14; activism of, 94, 99, 106, 121, 143–44, 150, 176–77, 213n10; intersectional analysis by, 31, 40; in military, 25–26, 32; queer theorists and, 105, 108; right-wing denigration of, 133; on symbolic position of women, 67. *See also* gender analysis
feminization, 12, 24, 46, 73, 128, 191, 210n20, 217n24; of Holocaust, 30; of protests, 133, 136, 144, 161, 163–65
Fight Club (film), 141
First Aliya, 211n25
Foucault, Michel, 34, 49, 86, 120–22, 195, 201
Four Mothers campaign, 45, 136, 163
France, 43, 113
Frank, Pollyana, 143
fraternity, 20–31, 39, 48, 192; Zionism and, 26–30
freiers (suckers), 164–65

Gal, Irit, 212n34
Galatz, 179
Galilee, 73, 219–20n27
Gaza Strip, 11, 26, 71, 203n1, 205n21, 218n8, 221n6; de-development process in, 199; employment in Israel of workers from, 211n26; everyday life of Palestinians in, 200; Israeli pullout from, 45; Jewish settlement in, 204n8, 214n27; medical care in Tel Aviv for children from, 126, 127, 130; military occupation of, 206n2, 216n18; poverty in, 51
Geffen, Aviv, 179
gender analysis, 4, 11–12, 15, 20, 55, 154, 190, 193–94
gender roles and practices, 9, 34, 60, 61, 90, 105, 139, 172, 201, 211n30, 213n8, 218n28; in division of labor, 22, 33; in everyday life, 9, 11, 30–34, 71; in experience of Israeliness, 13; in military, 24–26, 101, 103; normative, 11, 21–26, 29–30, 34, 40, 42–43, 48, 57, 65, 82–83, 90, 99, 109, 124–25, 128–29, 146–48, 154, 162–65, 192–94; of Orthodox Jews, 66–67; of Palestinians, 75–80; politics of, 14, 20, 42–49, 121, 130, 134–35, 144, 156, 161–65, 194; privilege and, 21, 59, 64, 83, 143, 150, 192–93; racialization and, 109, 1112, 114, 209n12; spatialization and, 54–55, 57, 67–70, 86–87, 122, 191, 193; in Zionist narratives, 16, 21, 30, 39–40, 49, 50, 116, 151, 192. *See also* feminists; feminization; gender analysis; masculinization
"getting by," 5, 6, 92, 133, 190
Ghandi, Mohandas K., 148
Gilo, 127
Gisha—Legal Center for Freedom of Movement, 198, 221n6
Golan Heights, 20, 123, 205n21, 206n2, 214n27, 216n18
Goldberg, David Theo, 63–64, 71–72
"good life, the," 6, 173, 178
gradualism, 176–78, 184
Greece, 155
Greenberg, Jessica, 8, 204n9
guilt, 34, 45–46, 50, 63, 144, 189
Gush Emunim, 113, 214n27

ha'am (the people), 152, 167–72; Tower of, 159
HaDag Nachash, 164
Haganah, 212n43
Hamas, 68, 217n33
Har Adar, 14, 74–75, 78, 81, 210n19
Haraway, Donna, 105, 106, 214n23
Haredim, 66, 210n17

HaTikva (Israeli national anthem), 28, 185
Hebrew University, 22, 45, 56–57, 110, 123
Hebron, 45
hegemonic entanglements, 131–50; of banality of activism, 132–38; resistance engendered by, 138–44; of soldiering, 144–150
Hemmings, Clare, 214n21
Hendrix, Jimi, 160
Hermann, Tamar, 136
Herzfeld, Michael, 8
Herzl, Theodore, 170, 209n5
Herzog, Hanna, 219n14
Hever, Shir, 211n26
High Court of Justice, Israeli, 216n14, 217n26
Hilltop Youth, 171
Hobbes, Thomas, 105
holidays, 34–38. *See also specific holidays*
Holocaust (*Shoah*), 27–29, 36, 47–48, 65, 114–15; anti-Semitic propaganda predating, 41, 42; feminization of, 30; narratives of, 48, 208n44; survivors of, 71, 81, 207n15, 208–9n44
Holocaust Remembrance Day, 33–36, 83, 215n29
Holot detention facility, 135, 215n12, 216n14
homonationalism, 65, 210n16, 212n2

ideology, 50, 93, 111, 200, 201, 205n23; Zionist, 21, 27–28, 49, 192, 195, 197
implicate relations, 54, 80
Im Tirtzu, 57, 170, 209n5
Independence Day, Israeli, 35, 83, 114, 208n25, 214–15n29
Indignant movement, 155
infiltration, sexualized discourse of, 135
International Human Rights Day, 134–35
interpellation, 36, 49
intersectionality, 5, 12, 137, 143, 201; of everyday life with wider political realities, 93; feminist, 31, 40; of norms and hierarchies, 129
intifadas, 5, 10–11, 73, 113, 137, 139, 148, 198, 211n26, 217n34
intimacy, 10, 37, 91, 111–13, 115–16, ; of family life, 99; gender and, 90, 105; politics and, 182, 196; security and, 80; threat and, 108; of trauma, 36
intimate public, 172–79, 183
Ireland, 81; Northern, 60, 210n20
Israel Air Force, 19
Israel Defense Forces (IDF), 22, 63, 158, 205n15, 206n4, 212n43, 218n8; at checkpoints, 139, 213nn10,14; mandatory service in, 23, 206n9, 210n17; non-Jewish citizens of Israel in, 24; in Occupied Palestinian Territories, 20, 100, 142; unarmed Palestinian civilians killed by, 216n18
Israeli Committee Against House Demolitions, 136
Israeliness, 13, 58, 148, 164. *See also* Jewish Israelis

Jaffa, 14, 76–77, 93, 196
Jaffee, Martin, 27
Jameson, Frederick, 204n13
Japan, 113
Jayyus, 118
Jenkins, Henry, 105
Jerusalem, 60, 101–3, 115, 127–28, 205n21; Old City of, 3, 19, 110; protests in, 132, 138, 153, 217n34; travel between West Bank and, 97, 122, 201; Zionism in, 27–28. *See also* East Jerusalem; West Jerusalem
Jewish diaspora. *See* diaspora
Jewish Home, ix
Jewish Israelis, 4–7, 9–16, 20–43, 69–76, 96, 200–201, 203n3, 209n3, 210nn13,19, 213n12, 218n8, 221n6; activist, 113–14, 118–19, 122–24, 141–45, 147–51, 155–52, 177–83, 221n6; distinctions made between Palestinians and, 52–53, 55, 59–65, 167, 190, 210n22, 212n38; economic dominance of, 174–75; from Europe or North America; everyday life of, 10–15, 20–21, 46–49, 90–91, 188; gender norms of, 21–22, 24–26, 109, 125, 128–29, 162–65, 192–94; holidays of, 33–36, 78, 83, 114, 208n25, 212n36, 214–15n29 ; Holocaust generation of, 71, 81, 207n15, 208–9n44; of lower social status, 127–28; mandatory mili-

tary service of, 22–26, 206n4; normalization mechanisms of, 92–94, 104–7, 121–22, 127, 188–92, 204n5; Orthodox, 66, 70, 207n21, 210n17; political apathy of, 4–5, 12–15, 194–200; racism of, 66, 110, 114, 135, 168, 204–5n15, 216n15; solidarity of Palestinians and, 28, 29, 44, 45, 136, 139, 140, 143–44, 153, 156, 189, 207n17, 208n38, 217nn25,32. *See also* Ashkenazi Jews; Mizrahi Jews; Zionism
Jewish renewal, 114
Jisr az-Zarka, 51–52, 309n3
joking, 2, 89, 92–98, 104, 116, 193
Jordan, 96, 205n21
July 14th movement, 155

Kach, 219n25
Kadima, 44, 219n23
Kahlili, Laleh, 206n10
Kahane, Meir, 219n25
Kahanists, 171, 219n25
Katriel, Tamar, 219n15
Kelly, Tobias, 5, 203n3
Kfar Qasem, 82–83
Kimmerling, Baruch, 145, 146
King, Martin Luther, 148
Kiryat Arba, 137
Knesset, ix, 44, 68, 113, 164, 203n1, 218n5, 220n29
"knowingly not knowing," 86, 92, 173, 188, 190
Konopinski, Natalie, 91
Kopty, Abir, 169, 170, 219n24
Kulanu, ix

labor, 22, 33, 66, 196, 197, 205n22; Palestinian, in Israel, 72–80, 83, 86, 193, 211n27, 213n8; racialization of, 92, 159, 190, 199; resistance through, 118, 126–30, 193
Labor Party, 41, 218n5
Lapid, Yair, 220n29
Lebanon, 20, 45, 205n21; War with, 147, 184
Leef, Daphne, 155, 218n5
left wing, Israeli, 44–46, 84, 180, 204n6, 215n9; activism of, 100, 132, 143, 189; failure of mobilization efforts of, 132–33, 215n9; in protests, 163, 166, 169–71; racism and, 57, 168–69, 210n22; social and economic focus of, 127, 162, 177; in 2015 election, ix–x, 41. *See also specific parties and organizations*
Lehava, 211n30
Lentin, Ronit, 21, 27, 29–30, 65, 71, 80–81, 207n15, 208–9n44, 210n15, 215n31
Levy, Gideon, 66, 209n5
Levy, Yagil, 213–14n15, 216n23, 219n13
Liberman, Avidgor, 44, 203n1
Likud, ix, 40, 44, 203nn1,2, 205n15, 219n23
Livio, Oren, 219n15
Lomsky-Feder, Edna, 213–14n15, 219n13
Love Revolution, 159

Ma'asra, 140, 217n27
macho. *See* masculinity
Machsom Watch, 94, 99, 136, 139–40, 213nn10,14, 216n23; and Rothschild Boulevard encampment, 176, 180
Magav (border police), 19
Majdal Shams, 20
Ma la'asot? (What can we do?), 6–7, 43, 121, 151, 188, 190, 197
mapping, 55–59, 63–65, 67–70, 85, 200
marches. *See* demonstrations
March of Millions, 184
Marxian post-structuralism, 34
Marzel, Baruch, 171, 177, 219n26
masculinization, 11, 12, 30, 133, 161–65, 183, 191; hegemony of, 58–59, 82–83, 97, 125, 146; military, 21–27, 32, 46, 58, 65, 97, 115, 147–48, 164; racial, 115, 135–36; Zionist, 40
Massad, Joseph, 215n31
Massey, Doreen, 54–55, 70, 86
McCarthyism, 209n5
melancholia, 50, 151, 175
Memorial Day, Israeli, 33, 35, 36, 83, 114, 208n15, 214–15n29. *See also* Holocaust Remembrance Day
men, Israeli. *See* gender roles and practices
Mendel, Yonathan, 220n29
Mevasseret-Zion, 14, 61, 91, 108, 124, 125
Migdal Ha'Am (Tower of the People), 159
Mikdashi, Maya, 183

militarization, 109, 144–51, 166, 192, 217–18n38; in education, 32–33; of masculinity, 21–26, 32, 46, 58, 65, 97, 115, 147–48, 164; pervasive, 25, 26, 44, 112, 145, 164, 187–88. *See also* Israel Defense Forces (IDF)
Mitchell, Timothy, 49, 130–31, 150, 153
Mizrahi Jews, 44, 60, 129, 130, 179, 205n18; Black Panther organization of, 137–38, 156–57; in Israeli government, 13; racial identity of, 64–65; sexuality of, 23–24, 58–59; social status of, 159, 213n8
modernity, 20–31, 39, 48, 67, 192; Zionism and, 26–30
Modi'in, 141, 217n26
Montreal, 39
Morrison, Jim, 160, 180
motherhood, 34, 97, 125, 136, 137, 206n10

Na'alin, 139, 140, 217n25
Nabi Saleh, 139–41, 217n25
Nablus, 95, 97, 118
Naha'l Taninim nature preserve, 51–53
Nakba Day, 83, 114, 115, 208n25, 214–15n29
Naksa Day, 20, 136–37, 206n2, 216n18
National Front, 219n23
nationalism, 27, 35, 93, 168, 192, 196; patriarchal, 24, 32, 109; right-wing political, x, 40, 130, 170–72, 177, 203n1; Zionist, 21, 29. *See also* homonationalism
Negev Desert, 217n29, 219–20n27
neoliberalism, 25, 27, 123, 130, 150, 154, 192, 218n11
Netanyahu, Benjamin, ix, 41, 166, 203n2, 205n15, 219nn23,26
Neve Sha'anan, 113
Neve Shalom (Oasis of Peace), 84–85, 212n44
New Age, 114
news-holiday cycle, 34–36
New Zealand, 197
1967 War, 20, 45, 206n2, 216n18
non-participation, political, 8–9, 176, 177
normalization, 5–6, 27, 34, 88–117, 136–38, 191, 196, 213n7; of activism, 121, 132, 134, 138–40, 150, 178, 189; belonging as source of, 101–104; gendered, 11, 21–23, 30, 65, 83, 90, 99, 124, 125, 129, 146–48; repairing ruptures in, 98–101, 130; in small worlds, 104–15. *See also* bypassing; everyday life; joking; unseeing
Northern Ireland, 60, 210n20

Obama, Barack, 203n2
Occupied Palestinian Territories, 13, 42, 106, 121–22, 140, 213n8; corporate involvement in, 213n14; exposure of residents to violence in, 39; IDF in, 20, 100, 142; Green Line in, 56, 74, 78, 108, 118, 122, 125, 141; human rights violations in, 216n23, 221n6; protests in, 138–39; sexualized discourse of penetration applied to Palestinians from, 135. *See also* East Jerusalem; Gaza Strip; Golan Heights; West Bank
Occupy movements, 155, 164
Ochs, Juliana, 11
Olmert, Ehud, 219n23
Organisation for Economic Cooperation and Development, 174
Orientalism, 81, 210n22
Orthodox Jews, 66–67, 70, 207n21, 210n17
Ortner, Sherry, 157, 158, 161
Oslo Accords, 45
othering, 21, 53, 60–62, 107, 112, 209n12; of atypical Israeli men, 82–83, 181; of Palestinians, 58, 68–70, 73, 76–78; of women, 67–68, 109. *See also* racialization
Outdoor Revolution, 158

Palahniuk, Chuck, 217n30
Palestinian Israeli citizens, 70, 72, 159, 199, 203n1, 209n47; distinctions between Jewish citizens and, 53, 55, 61; Netanyahu's divisive rhetoric toward, ix, 203n2; political activism of, 134, 136, 138, 168–75; precluded from military service, 206n9, 210n17; schools for, 207n21; suspension of rights of, 211n27
Palestinian National Authority, 204n15
Palestinians, 32, 45, 68–85, 96, 149, 162–63, 215n31, 218n2, 219n25, 220nn27–29; alienation and cynicism of, 42–43, 208n41; commemoration days observed by, 20, 83, 114, 115, 136–37, 206n2,

208n25, 214–15n29, 216n18; confrontations between Israeli military and, 142; constraints on mobility of, 1, 199, 212n34; cuisine of, 81–85; distinctions between Jewish Israelis and, 52–53, 55, 59–65, 167, 190, 210n22, 212n38; employment in Israel of, 72–80, 83, 89, 92, 104, 123–24, 211n26, 212n34; everyday life of, 4, 9–12 193, 200, 204n3, n5; gender norms of, 23, 68–70, 75–76, 78, 86, 106, 143–44, 165, 193; Israeli identification categories of, 203n1, 205n19, 212n38; massacre in Beirut refugee camps of, 185; medical treatment in Israel for, 126–30; military trials of, 38; at Naha'l Taninim nature preserve, 51–53; olive harvest by, 118–20; racialization of, 65–67, 110–15, 127, 133–35, 168–69, 199, 209n12, 204–5n15, 216n15; social status of, 209n47, 213n8; solidarity of Israeli Jews and, 28, 29, 44, 45, 136, 139, 140, 143–44, 153, 156, 189, 207n17, 208n38, 217nn25,32; suicide bombings by, 26; United Nations bid for statehood by, 184; uprisings of, 5, 10–11, 20, 73, 113, 137, 139, 148, 198, 211n26, 217n34. *See also* Occupied Palestinian Territories; Palestinian Israeli Citizens

Palmach, 84, 212n43

Parliament, Israeli. *See* Knesset

Passover (Pesach), 33, 35, 78, 93–94, 208n24, 212n35

Peace Now, 94, 95, 213n9

penetration, sexualized discourse of, 135

Pentagon, 207n10

Persia, ancient, 212n36

Pesach. *See* Passover

Peteet, Julie, 10–11

political action. *See* activism

Physicians for Human Rights, 158

Polish immigrants, 15

politics, 39–50, 178; alienation from, x, 13, 16, 40–46, 48, 50, 178; emotions and, 43–48, 75, 175, 190, 193, 196, 208n41; of everyday life, 10–15, 46–49. *See also* left wing, Israeli; protests; right wing, Israeli

Pop, Iggy, 189

Popular Struggle Coordination Committee, 217n25

Portugali, Juval, 53–55, 70

privilege, 17, 39, 59, 85, 191, 209n47; of apathy, 9–10, 12, 199; in border-crossing, 1, 3; ethnicity and class-based, 10, 13, 15, 138, 159, 172, 181, 205n17; gender and, 21, 59, 64, 83, 143, 150, 192–93; resistance to, 128–29, 145–46, 156; in small worlds, 105, 113; of Zionist narrative, 29, 192

protests, 16, 99, 132–44, 152–85, 218nn2,5,11, 219nn14,24, 220nn28,29; belonging in, 165–72; in East Jerusalem, 124, 207n17, 217n25; engaging inaction in, 178–83; gender politics of, 133, 136, 144, 161–65, 194; housing, 152–53, 155–57, 161; intimate public of, 172–79, 183; in Occupied Territories, 20, 139–44, 216n18, 217nn25,26,34; right-wing, 132–33, 162–63, 166, 168–71, 177, 215n9; routinization of, 121, 132, 194; tent encampment of, 154–56, 158–62, 168–72, 180. *See also specific demonstrations and organizations*

Puar, Jasbir, 210n16

Purim, 78, 212n36

Qalandia checkpoint, 1, 3, 20, 97

Qalqilya, 118, 119

Qatane, 75

Rabbis for Human Rights, 118–19

"Rabbis' Wives Letter," 211n30

Rabin, Yitzhak, 41, 133

racialization, 55, 63–68, 70, 72, 85, 191, 192; of African migrants, 135, 159, 211n30, 216n15; of Palestinians, 65–67, 110–15, 127, 133–35, 168–69, 199, 209n12, 204–5n15, 216n15. *See also* othering

Ramallah, 3, 4, 95–97, 173

Rapoport, Tamar, 157, 163

Reading Power Station (Tel Aviv), 18

Reider, Dimi, 134

resistance, 16, 42, 80–83, 133, 138–44, 150–51, 216n23; apathy and, 5, 195–97; everyday, 120–31, 193; gender analysis of, 193–94, 217n24; impact of 2015 elections on, x; through labor, 126–29;

resistance *(continued)*
  racialized, 65; to soldiering, 145, 148–50; in Zionist normative narratives, 28–29, 36–38, 80. *See also* activism; protests
responsibility, x, 7, 43, 127, 180–81; of mothers, 34, 79, 109; political, 180, 183, 198, 213n14
Richter-Devroe, Sophie, 5
right wing, Israeli, 38, 44–46, 68, 127, 147, 204n6, 215n2; attitudes toward women of, 57; consolidation of power of, ix–x, 41, 201, 205n15, 219n23; of family members, 93–94, 113; in protests, 132–33, 162–63, 166, 168–71, 177, 215n9; two-state solution opposed by, 45, 68; Zionist, 44, 209n5. *See also specific parties and organizations*
Romans, ancient, 209n3
routinization, 91, 121–22, 150, 213n7
Russian Compound prison, 137
Russians, 13

Sabra, 21–22, 164, 165
Sabra and Shatila massacres, 184–85
Sasson-Levy, Orna, 157, 163, 205n17, 213–14n15, 219n13
Saussure, Ferdinand de, 21
Scott, James C., 122
Sde Dov Airport (Tel Aviv), 18
Sderot, 43
security, 20–31, 48, 51, 91, 144–45, 153, 192; fraternity through participation in, 23–26, 39; in intimate sites, 116, 125, 193, 201; Palestinian laborers seen as threat to, 73, 76, 79–83, 104; personal concerns about, 56–60, 91, 96, 101–3, 107–9; politics of, ix, 11, 21, 40, 99, 112, 114, 127–28, 182, 203n2, 204n6; protests and, 153, 162, 177–78; Zionism and, 26–30, 195. *See also* militarization
separation, 16, 58–60, 67, 70–71, 85, 193; degrees of, 55–58; of physical realm from behavior and consciousness, 131; political, 161, 180, 184; principle of, 53, 71. *See also* spatialization
Sephardim, Israeli. *See* Mizrahi Jews
Serbia, 8

settlements, Jewish Israeli, 102, 118–19, 136–37, 171–72, 175, 177, 186, 210n19, 214n27, 217nn25,26, 219n26; early waves of, 72, 113; expansion of, ix; fear in, 96, 108; over Green Line, 55–56, 59, 74–76, 78, 108, 110, 124–25; religiosity of, 55, 66, 70, 111. *See also names of settlements*
settler colonialism, 71, 109, 204n4
Shaffir, Stav, 155, 218n5
Shafir, Gershon, 211n25
Shalit, Gilad, 158, 218n8
Shalom Achshav (Peace Now), 94, 95, 213n9
shame, 57, 46, 50, 180–85
Sharon, Ariel, 41, 113, 208n33
Shas, ix
Sheikh Jarrah Solidarity, 28, 29, 44, 45, 136, 139, 140, 143–44, 189, 207n17, 208n38, 217n25, 208n38
Shenhav, Yehouda, 218n11
Shin Bet, 144
Shoah. See Holocaust
silencing, 98–100, 103–4, 116, 193, 219n13
Sinai Peninsula, 205n21, 206n2, 216n18
Singerman, Diana, 11, 122
Six Day War. *See* 1967 War
small worlds, 47, 104–17, 129–30, 175, 191, 193; dualism of pain and hope in, 112–15; spiritual escapes in, 110–12; systemics of, 107–9
social justice, 156–60, 186. *See also* protests
soldiering, 144–51, 166. *See also* Israel Defense Forces; militarism
solidarity, 78–80, 89, 114, 130, 138, 177–79, 215n12; international, 14; Palestinian-Egyptian, 134. *See also* Sheikh Jarrah Solidarity
Soviet Union, 28
space. *See* spatialization
Spain, 155
spatialization, 11, 51–87, 105–7, 116, 206n23, 218n4; of action and inaction, 16, 36, 46–47, 87, 113, 115, 182, 183; domestic, 97, 102, 123, 125, 126; gendered, 54, 67–70, 86–87, 122, 191, 193; mapping, 55–59; Palestinian labor's role in, 72–85; of possibility and meaning, 105–7; in protests, 154, 160–62, 166, 170, 172,

174–75, 181; racialized, 63–67, 89, 144; of social relations, 53–55; telling and, 59–63. *See also* separation; small worlds
spirituality, 110–12
subversion, 28, 48, 124–26, 129, 150–51, 161–62, 166, 183; of gender roles, 109–10, 172
Sudan, 135, 171
summarizing symbols, 157–59, 163, 165, 167–69, 174–77, 218n6
Sweden, 110, 112, 197
Syria, 20, 205n21, 216n18
systemics, theory of, 107–11, 114

Tal Law, 210n17
Tawil-Souri, Helga, 203n1
Taylor, Laurie, 105
Tel Aviv, 3, 6, 20, 62–63, 82, 122, 126, 181, 197, 198, 203n3, 213n5, 215n2; African migrants in, 136, 138, 159, 216n15; alienation from politics in, 41–43; Arab cuisine in, 83; centrality of family in, 103–4; cognitive mapping in, 55–56, ; discursive repetition of trauma in, 37–38; European modernity of, 3, 18–19, 27; everyday life in, 13, 14, 47, 49, 188, 192, 195; feminists in, 25–26, 143; former IDF soldiers in, 148–50; gendered normativity in, 146; holidays in, 83–84; mixed race children in, 32–33; political apathy in, 16–17; Pride Parade in, 88–89, 92, 106, 132, 212n2; protests in, 132–36, 152–56, 158–60, 164, 166–71, 176–77, 184; sanctioned demonstrations in, 132, 140; social status in, 10; travel between West Bank and, 1, 95–97, 141–43, 186, 201
Tel Aviv Museum of Art, 152, 155
Tel Aviv University, 155
telling, 55, 59–65, 67–70, 85, 96, 209n12, 210n20
Tibi, MK Ahmed, 218n2
Tilly, Charles, 212n4
transformation, x, 4, 9, 39, 160–62, 194, 206; economic, 167, 182; gender and, 12, 161; personal, 113; potential, 34–36, 48, 106, 157, 160, 191, 197, 199–201; social and political, x, 43, 138, 153, 166–67, 183; stasis versus, 107, 154, 199

transgression, 95, 97, 118, 120–21, 131
trauma, 36–40, 108, 174; in Zionist narrative, 27–29, 45, 102, 115
Tulkarm, Ibn, 97
Tunisia, 157
Twitter, 38, 141, 155
Tzan'ani, Margalit, 179–80

United Kingdom, 39, 139
United Nations, 184
United States, 39, 45, 204n9, 206–7n10, 214n20; Army of, 146; feminism in, 3, 25; immigrants to Israel from, 75, 189, 205n17; Independence Day in, 35; "normal life" in, 30; popular culture in, 141; protest movements in, 138, 160, 174
United Torah Judaism,
unseeing, 19, 20, 89, 92–98, 104, 116, 127, 132, 190, 193

Veracini, Lorenzo, 71
Vietnam War, opposition to, 136, 160, 161
vulnerability, 28, 57–59, 73, 79, 125, 181, 191

Wahat al-Salam. *See* Neve Shalom
Weizman, Eyal, 53
West Bank, 2–10, 122, 126, 129, 205n15, 206n2, 148; checkpoints between Israel and, 1–3, 20, 61, 94, 99, 136, 139–40, 213nn10,14, 216n23; Civil Administration in, 213n10; de-development process in, 199; everyday life of Palestinians in, 200, 204n1; Jewish settlements in, ix, 70, 75, 102, 108, 111, 118–19, 136–37, 171–72, 175, 177, 186, 210n19, 214n27, 217nn25,26, 219n26; Palestinian workers in Israel from, 79, 212n34; resistance initiatives in, 139, 141, 144, 217n25, n27; travel from Israel to, 95–96, 118
West Jerusalem, 6, 14, 37, 43, 39, 62, 68, 95, 203n3; activists in, 209n4, 215n2; apathy in, 195–96; blackness and racialization in, 64–66; bombing of, 35–36; everyday life in, 13, 20, 29, 47, 49, 188–89, 192; German Colony in, 19, 41, 110, 113, 189; leftist Jewish Israelis in, 16; Machane Yehuda market in, 56, 106; military deployment of women from, 25;

West Jerusalem *(continued)*
    normalization in, 104–5; Palestinians in, 74, 83, 104, 123; protests in, 133, 159, 180
White Night (film), 212n34
Who Profits? campaign, 213n19
Williams, Raymond, 208n28
women, Israeli. *See* gender roles and practices
Women in Black, 99, 133, 136, 157, 213n14; founding of, 139, 181; harassment of, 137; weekly protest of, 77, 132
Women Breaking the Silence (WBS), 214n15
Women's Equal Rights Law (1951), 40, 176
Woodstock, 160, 161, 180
World War I, 211n25
World War II, 164, 207n15. *See also* Holocaust

Yemenis, 23
Yesh Atid, 220n29
Yiftachel, Oren, 53, 63, 213n8
Yisrael Beitenu, 203n1, 219n23
Yisrael Goldblum Fund, 204n15
Yom Ha'Atzmaut. *See* Independence Day, Israeli
Yom HaShoah. *See* Holocaust Remembrance Day
Yom HaZikaron. *See* Memorial Day, Israeli
Yom Kippur War, 91, 137, 214n27
Yuval-Davis, Nira, 68, 102–3, 167, 210n20

Zertal, Idith, 27, 29
Zionism, 16, 26–37, 49–50, 80, 102, 130, 219n15; colonialism of, 211n25, 215n31; ethos of, 117; gender and, 26–27, 39–40, 50, 151, 192, 194; Labor, 40; normative narrative of, 21, 30–31, 35–37, 39, 49, 91–92, 115–16, 194–95, 197; right-wing, 44, 209n4

www.ingramcontent.com/pod-product-compliance
Lightning Source LLC
Chambersburg PA
CBHW021348230426
43666CB00006B/442